KUNDALINI YOGA
THE POWER IS IN YOU

KUNDALINI YOGA
THE POWER IS IN YOU

Prabhuji

KUNDALINI YOGA
THE POWER IS IN YOU

Fourteenth Edition

Printed in the United States of America

Published by Prabhuji Mission
Website: prabhuji.net

Avadhutashram
PO Box 900
Cairo, NY, 12413
USA

Painting on the cover by Prabhuji:
"Medieval Cordoba"
Acrylic on canvas, New York
Canvas size: 24" x 24"

Library of Congress Control Number: 2016915429
ISBN-13: 978-1-945894-02-2

Contents

ॐ अज्ञानतिमिरान्धस्य ज्ञानाञ्जनशलाकया ।
चक्षुरुन्मीलितं येन तस्मै श्रीगुरवे नमः ॥

om ajñāna-timirāndhasya jñānāñjana-śalākayā
chakṣur unmīlitaṁ yena tasmai śrī-gurave namaḥ

Salutations unto that holy Guru who, applying the ointment (medicine) of (spiritual) knowledge, removes the darkness of ignorance of the blinded ones (unenlightened) and opens their eyes.

This book is dedicated, with deep gratitude and eternal respect, to the holy lotus feet of my beloved masters His Divine Grace Avadhūta Śrī Brahmānanda Bābājī Mahārāja (Guru Mahārāja) and His Divine Grace Avadhūta Śrī Mastarāma Bābājī Mahārāja (Bhagwan).

Preface

The story of my life is nothing more than a long journey, from what I believed myself to be to what I truly am. It is an authentic inner and outer pilgrimage. It is a tale of transcending what is personal and universal, partial and total, illusory and real, apparent and true. My life is a flight beyond what is temporary and eternal, darkness and light, humanity and divinity. This story is not public but profoundly private and intimate.

Only what begins, ends; only what starts, finishes. One who lives in the present is neither born nor dies, because what has no beginning has no end.

I am a disciple of a seer, an enlightened being, and somebody who is nobody. I was initiated in my spiritual childhood by the moonlight. A seagull who loved flying more than anything else in life inspired me. In love with the impossible, I crossed the universe obsessed with a star. I have walked infinite paths, following the footsteps of those who could see.

Like the ocean that longs for water, I sought my home within my own house.

I am a simple intermediary who shares his experience with others. I am not a guide, coach, teacher, instructor, educator, psychologist, enlightener, pedagogue, evangelist, rabbi, *posek halacha*, healer, therapist, satsangist, psychic, leader, medium, savior, or guru. I am only a traveler whom you can ask for directions. I will gladly show you a place where everything calms upon arrival, a place beyond the sun and the stars, beyond your desires and longings, beyond time and space, beyond concepts and conclusions, and beyond everything that you believe you are or imagine that you will be.

I am just a whim or perhaps a joke from the sky and the only mistake of my beloved spiritual master.

Aware of the abyss that separates revelation and our works, we live in a frustrated attempt to faithfully express the mystery of the spirit.

I paint sighs, hopes, silences, aspirations, and melancholies, inner landscapes, and sunsets of the soul.

I am a painter of the indescribable, inexpressible, and indefinable of our depths. Or maybe I just write colors and paint words.

Since childhood, little windows of paper captivated my attention; through them, I visited places, met people, and made friends. Those tiny *maṇḍalas* were my true elementary school, high school, and college. Like skilled teachers, these *yantras* have guided me through contemplation, attention, concentration, observation, and meditation.

Like a physician studies the human body, or a lawyer studies laws, I have dedicated my entire life to the study of myself. I can say with certainty that I know what resides and lives in this heart.

It is not my intention to convince anyone of anything. I do not offer theology or philosophy, nor do I preach or teach, I simply think out loud. The echo of these words may lead you to the infinite space of peace, silence, love, existence, consciousness, and absolute bliss.

Do not search for me. Search for yourself. You do not need me or anyone else, because the only thing that really matters is you. What you yearn for lies within you, as what you are, here and now.

I am not a merchant of rehashed information, nor do I intend to do business with my spirituality. I do not teach beliefs or philosophies. I only speak about what I see and just share what I know.

Avoid fame, for true glory is not based on public opinion but on what you really are. What matters is not what others think of you, but your own appreciation of who you are. Choose bliss over success, life over reputation, and wisdom over information. If you succeed, you will know not only admiration but also true envy. However, jealousy is mediocrity's tribute to talent and an open acceptance of one's own inferiority.

I advise you to fly freely and never be afraid of making mistakes. Learn the art of transforming your mistakes into lessons. Never blame others for your faults: remember that taking complete responsibility for your life is a sign of maturity. When you fly, you learn that what matters is not touching the sky but the courage to spread your wings. The higher you rise, the smaller and less significant the world looks. As you walk, sooner or later you will understand that every search begins and ends in you.

Your unconditional well-wisher,
Prabhuji

Introduction

If we think about a large oak tree, we suppose it has well-developed roots. If it had the roots of a small plant, it would succumb to the first autumn breeze. Though concealed, the roots are vital to keeping the oak upright.

I still remember when my family emigrated from Chile, our homeland. My father used to say that when a sapling is transplanted, it adapts relatively easily, whereas for an old tree like him, it was extremely difficult to be surrounded by a new language and culture. This comparison between a person and a tree stuck with me: just as a tree's roots are proportional to its size, the depth of our internal development is proportional to our spiritual height. We flourish insofar as we are able to take root in the depths of existence. The deeper we go inward, the higher we rise. The sky is not reached by flying, but by digging into our depths.

Growing taller is nothing but an increase in size. We can grow upward, but we only mature inward. Evolution does not happen on the surface. Only as we make our way into our depths do we discover our eternity.

Kundalini yoga is a yogic path that stimulates the conscious awakening of *kuṇḍalinī-śakti*, or "coiled energy."

This energy is the transcendental consciousness; it is the creative power of God, and therefore, the creative potential in the human being.

Kundalini yoga invites us to awaken our divine potential and unveil the very secret of creation that lies hidden in the core of human nature. This involution banishes any sense of higher-lower or inside-outside.

Many spiritual paths suggest giving less attention to time and space and recommend isolation. Kundalini yoga, however, teaches that deep within every moment, lies the eternal; within all places, lies the infinite; within every human being, lies God.

Section I
Kuṇḍalinī-Śakti

Chapter 1

The astral body and prana

Humans are multidimensional structures, and their souls are enveloped in many sheaths:

1. The physical gross body, or *sthūla-śarīra,* includes the *anna-maya-kośa,* or "food sheath."
2. The subtle astral body, *liṅga-śarīra* or *sūkṣma-śarīra,* includes three layers: *prāṇa-maya-kośa* (energy sheath), *mano-maya-kośa* (mental sheath), and *vijñāna-maya-kośa* (intelectual sheath).
3. The causal body, or *kāraṇa-śarīra,* includes the blissful sheath called *ānanda-maya-kośa.*

Yoga, like most eastern medicine practices, speaks of an astral body made of prana, in which the *cakras,* or "energy centers," are found and are interconnected by *nāḍīs,* or "energy channels."

The astral and physical bodies are united by a *nāḍī* resembling a silvery thread through which vital energy flows. The physical body dies when this thread is cut, separating from the astral body forever.

The astral body

As mentioned above, we find three different layers (*kośas*) in the *liṅga-śarīra*, each with their own elements:

1. The *prāṇa-maya-kośa* is the energetic sheath composed of *nāḍīs* that connect in the chakras. Even though the form of this sheath is subtle, it is very similar to that of the physical body. It is composed of the vital airs (pranas) and the five organs of action (*karmendriyas*): mouth, hands, feet, anus, and genitals. The prana sheath is made up of 72,000 *nāḍīs*, as is indicated in the *Haṭha-yoga-pradīpikā*:

catur-aśīti-pīṭheṣu
siddham eva sadābhyaset
dvā-saptati-sahasrāṇāṁ
nāḍīnāṁ mala-śodhanam

Out of the 84 asanas, *siddhāsana* should always be practiced, because it cleanses the impurities of the 72,000 *nādīs*.

(*Haṭha-yoga-pradīpikā*, 1.41)

dvā-saptati-sahasrāṇāṁ
nāḍīnāṁ mala-śodhane
kutaḥ prakṣālanopāyaḥ
kuṇḍaly-abhyasanādṛte

Other than the practice of kundalini, there is no other way to wash away the impurities of the 72,000 *nāḍīs*.

(*Haṭha-yoga-pradīpikā*, 3.123)

dvā-saptati-sahasrāṇi
nāḍī-dvārāṇi pañjare
suṣumṇā śāmbhavī śaktiḥ
śeṣās tveva nirarthakāḥ

In the body there are 72,000 *nāḍī* openings. Of these, the *suṣumṇā*, which contains the *śāmbhavī-śakti*, is the only important one. The rest are useless. (*Haṭha-yoga-pradīpikā*, 4.18)

It is also mentioned in the Upanishads:

dvā-saptati-sahasrāṇi
pratināḍīṣu taitilam

In each of the 72,000 *nāḍīs*, there is an oil-like substance. (*Kṣurikā Upaniṣad*, 17b)

1. The *mano-maya-kośa* is the mental sheath, which consists of the instinctive mind. This mind includes both *manas* (conscious mind) and *citta* (subconscious mind, memory). It is the seat of desires and the sovereign of the organs of cognition and action. It includes the five senses of knowledge, or *jñānendriyas*: nose, tongue, eyes, skin, and ears.
2. The *vijñāna-maya-kośa* is the intellectual sheath, which includes the *ahaṅkāra* (ego) and the *buddhi* (intellect). The former is what we believe ourselves to be, that is to say, the idea of "I" that relates what happens to itself and perceives itself as the doer. The latter is the discriminating principle that evaluates and decides.

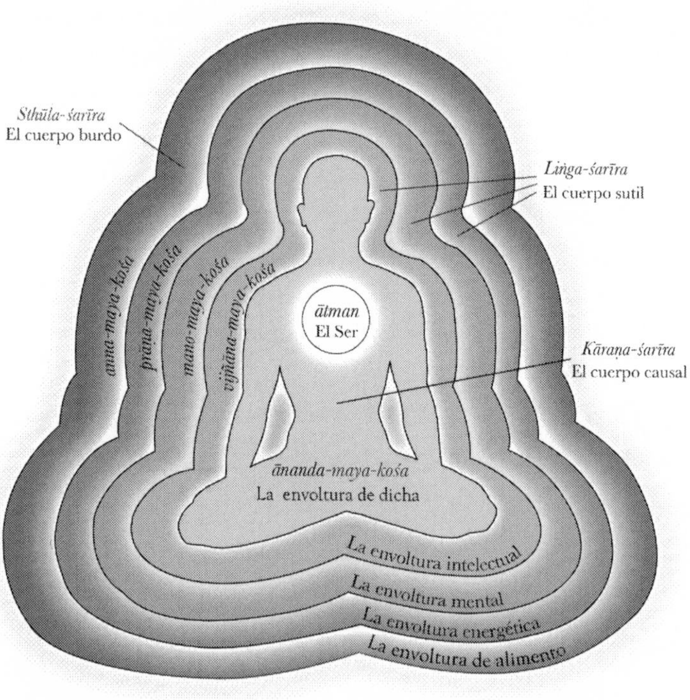

Sheaths, or *kośas*

Prana or "vital energy"

The meaning of the Sanskrit word *prāṇa* is "vital energy," but prana often refers to breathing because it is the closest expression of it in our physical experience.

Thousands of years ago, the Vedic seers (rishis) knew what our western science has only discovered in the last century: that the solid matter we perceive through our senses is nothing more than energy. The wisdom of prana forms an integral part of the Vedas. The ancient *Atharva Veda* has prayers that ask prana and *apāna* to protect life from death:

prāṇāpānau mṛtyor mā pātaṁ svāhā

> O prana and *apāna*, may my life not fall into death (the cycle of births). (*Atharva Veda*, 2.16.1)

prāṇāya namo yasya sarvam idaṁ vaśe
yo bhūtaḥ sarvasyeśvaro yasmint sarvaṁ pratiṣṭhitam

> Our respectful obeisance to prana, which, by controling the entire universe, has become paramount above all, and upon which all depend. (*Atharva Veda*, 11.4.1)

The *Chāndogya Upaniṣad* refers to the vital energy in the following way:

sa yad avocaṁ prāṇaṁ prapadya iti prāṇo vā idaṁ sarvaṁ

bhūtaṁ yad idaṁ kiñca tam eva tat prāpatsi

> I said, "I take refuge in prana," because all these beings and everything that exists are in fact prana. Therefore, I take refuge only in that.
>
> (*Chāndogya Upaniṣad*, 3.15.4)

Prana is the most subtle form of energy, the fundamental energy unit, so that we can say that the cosmos is a manifestation of prana. Everything that acts or moves in the universe is an expression of vital energy. The great master and saint of Rishikesh, His Holiness Swami Śivānanda, explains in his important book *The science of prāṇāyāma*: "Prana is the sum total of all the energy that manifests in the universe. It is the sum total of all the forces of nature." At the physical level, all capacity to perform work or produce heat is an expression of prana. Hence all potential, kinetic, mechanical, caloric, electric, and chemical energy is an expression of prana.

Prana is an expression of Brahman, the supreme sustainer of the cosmic manifestation. Life would be impossible without prana, as the pranic power makes all the functions of our body possible. It is the original energy of our mental, emotional, and biological faculties: from a thought to a yawn and all the physiological sensations, such as hunger, thirst, cold, and heat. This energy also makes the biological processes of digestion, excretion, and secretion possible. By vibrating at different wavelengths, it carries out involuntary functions, such as those of the immune and circulatory system, as well as sensory activities and bodily movements. It is prana that pumps blood from the heart through the blood vessels. Furthermore, it is the power that connects the physical body with the astral body.

Nourishment and breathing are two of the functions that renew prana in our bodies. Prana is our real food, while its conductors—water, nutrients, vitamins, oxygen, and sunshine—are the vehicles that transport it.

Types of prana

Just as electricity can generate cold, movement, light, sound, and heat, prana can manifest itself in infinite ways, such as seeing, speaking, feeling, moving, thinking, and so forth.

According to the Sankhya system, prana has five major types (*pañca-prāṇas*) and five minor ones (*pañcopa-prāṇas*). The *pañca-prāṇas* are the five main directions in which prana circulates. Each fulfills a different function:

1. Prana: Circulates in the pectoral area and regulates breathing.
2. *Apāna*: Flows between the anus and the lower abdomen. It cleans and purifies the organism by eliminating urine, semen, and feces.
3. *Samāna*: Flows around the navel and moves in the central part of the body. It governs digestion and stimulates the secretion of gastric juices. It is in charge of the appropriate distribution of nutrients in the body.

4. *Udāna*: Controls the vocal cords and the intake of food and air. It also elevates energy. For this reason, when one is sad or depressed, one must focus on the throat area, where *udāna* circulates.
5. *Vyāna*: Permeates the entire body. It is often called aura, since it is the energy that protects the whole surface of the body.

The *pañcopa-prāṇas* are:

1. *Nāga*: Alleviates pressure in the abdominal zone through burping.
2. *Kūrma*: Regulates the size of the iris based on the intensity of light, to facilitate vision. It also controls the movement of the eyelids to protect the eyes from any damage that might be caused by foreign bodies.
3. *Kṛkara*: Causes coughing, to prevent foreign substances from entering the body through the throat or nostrils.
4. *Deva-datta*: Causes yawning and induces sleep.
5. *Dhanañjaya*: Produces phlegm and remains even after the death of the body.

The evolution of prana

Brahman is the source from which everything originates, and prana is its expression and projection. Therefore, prana is not a blind force, but an intelligent energy. Brahman is the unmanifested aspect, whereas prana is its creative aspect that evolves and assumes a multiplicity of forms. It is the energy that keeps order in the movement of celestial bodies and maintains the ecological balance of our planet. It is in charge of various functions in our body that facilitate life, as described in this passage:

yad idaṁ kiñca jagat sarvaṁ
prāṇa ejati niḥsṛtam
mahad-bhayaṁ vajram udyataṁ
ya etad vidur amṛtās te bhavanti

> Everything that exists in this changing world has emerged from prana and moves within it, a great terror, like a rigid bolt of lightning. Those who know it achieve immortality.
>
> (*Kaṭha Upaniṣad*, 2.3.2)

Prana evolves and emerges first in the cosmic mind and then in grosser levels as the five basic elements, or *pañca-tattvas*: ether (*ākāśa*), air (*vāyu*), fire (*agni*), water (*āpas*), and earth (*pṛthivī*). This process can be compared to the cooling of water: as temperature drops, water becomes grosser and grosser until it turns into snow or ice. Similarly, in the dynamic process of concealment of consciousness, the universe is manifested from the subtle to the gross.

Creation occurs at both macrocosmic and microcosmic levels: what takes place in the universe also occurs in every grain of sand and in our own body. The manifestation of the body implies an evolutionary process, a transformation of prana from subtle to grosser levels, from hidden to revealed.

1. *Sahasrāra-cakra*: Brahman and its shakti lie in the causal plane in perfect union as One, prior to the manifestation of the physical body, in the seventh energy center located at the crown of the head.
2. *Ājñā-cakra*: First, the mind manifests in the sixth center.
3. *Viśuddha-cakra*: Next, ether (*ākāśa*) manifests in the laryngeal plexus.
4. *Anāhata-cakra*: Next, air (*vāyu*) manifests in the cardiac plexus.
5. *Maṇipūra-cakra*: Next, fire (*agni* or *tejas*) manifests in the solar plexus.
6. *Svādhiṣṭhāna-cakra*: Next, water (*ojas* or *āpas*) manifests in the prostatic plexus.
7. *Mūlādhāra-cakra*: Finally, earth (*pṛtvi*) manifests in the sacral plexus. After reaching the earth element, the dynamic aspect of prana remains in *mūlādhāra-cakra*, while its static aspect resides in *sahasrāra*.

Vital energy is responsible for evolution. It begins with the five elements and continues its development in the vegetable kingdom and the animal kingdom, up to human beings.

It should be noted that in the process of cosmic manifestation, Brahman and prana do not undergo any real change. Only forms and names develop or evolve. Just as the water does not change when it acquires the density of the ice, these changes are superficial changes.

The *nāḍīs* or "energy channels"

Vital energy (*prāṇa-śakti*) and mental energy (*manas-śakti*) do not flow in a disorderly way through our body, but circulate through very well-defined astral paths called *nāḍīs*. The word *nāḍī* is derived from the Sanskrit root *naḍ* meaning "to move." Vital energy flows through these delicate astral channels like blood flows through veins and arteries. Even though we cannot see the *nāḍīs*, they influence the physical body.

The structure of the *nāḍīs* is like a tube or cable with three layers: the exterior layer (*nāḍī*), the intermediate layer (*damani*), and the interior layer (*sira*). There are two types of *nāḍīs*: the conductors of prana energy (*prāṇa-vāha-nāḍīs*) and the conductors of mental energy (*mano-vāha-nāḍīs*). Astral channels emanate from the *kanda* and *meḍhra*. The word *kanda* means "root" because it is the origin of all the *nāḍīs*. The *kanda* is shaped like an egg and covered with membranes.

The *Haṭha-yoga-pradīpikā* describes its exact location:

ūrdhvaṁ vitasti-mātraṁ tu
vistāraṁ catur-aṅgulam
mṛdulaṁ dhavalaṁ proktaṁ
veṣṭitāmbara-lakṣaṇam

The *kanda* is situated above the anus, its length is one palm, and its width is four inches. It is smooth and white, as if it were wrapped in cloth.

(*Haṭha-yoga-pradīpikā*, 3.113)

The *kanda* is located above the first center, specifically in the *granthi-sthāna* (*granthi* means "knot" and *sthāna* means "platform or base"). In this area, the *kanda* connects to the *suṣumṇā-nāḍī*.

The *meḍhra* is found between the first and third chakras, as is indicated in this verse:

ūrdhvaṁ meḍhrād adho nābheḥ
kande yoniḥ khagāṇḍavat
tatra nāḍyaḥ samutpannāḥ
sahasrāṇāṁ dvi-saptatiḥ
teṣu nāḍī-sahasreṣu
dvi-saptatir udāhṛtā

> The *meḍhra* is [located] at the top of the base of the perineum and below the navel, which is the point of origin of the *nāḍīs*. It has the shape of an egg and from it 72,000 energy channels emanate. Among these thousands of channels, seventy-two are the most important.
>
> (*Yoga-cūḍāmaṇi Upaniṣad*, 14b–15)

In fact, the place where the *nāḍīs* originate is both the *kanda* and the *meḍhra*, which is the area of the *granthi-sthāna*. They are so close to each other that they are practically in the same place. Remember that we are not referring to solid matter or substance but to the astral plane.

Ten main *nāḍīs*:

There are different interpretations of the number of *nāḍīs* in the astral body. According to the *Śiva Saṁhitā* and the *Yoga-cūḍāmaṇi Upaniṣad*, there are ten main *nāḍīs*:

pradhānāḥ prāṇa-vāhinyo
bhūyas tāsu daśa smṛtāḥ
iḍā ca piṅgalā caiva
suṣumṇā ca tṛtīyagā

gāndhārī hasti-jihvā ca
pūṣā caiva yaśasvinī
alambusā kuhūś caiva
śaṅkhinī daśamī smṛtā

> Again, among these [seventy-two], there are ten main *nāḍīs* for the flow of prana. These are known as *iḍā* and *piṅgalā*, the third is *suṣumṇā*, the next ones are *gāndhārī*, *hasti-jihvā*, *pūṣā*, *yaśasvinī*, *alambusā*, *kuhū*, and the tenth is *śaṅkhinī*. In this way, they have been mentioned.
>
> (*Yoga-cūḍāmaṇi Upaniṣad*, 16–17)

The same scripture refers to the exact location of the major *nāḍīs*:

etan nāḍī mahā-cakraṁ
jñātavyaṁ yogibhiḥ sadā
iḍā vāme sthitā bhāge

dakṣiṇe piṅgalā sthitā

suṣumṇā madhya deśe tu
gāndhārī vāma-cakṣuṣi
dakṣiṇe hasti-jihvā ca
pūṣā karṇe ca dakṣiṇe

yaśasvinī vāma-karṇe
cānane cāpu alambusā
kuhūś ca liṅga-deśe tu
mūla-sthāne tu śaṅkhinī

Yogis should always be aware of this great *nāḍī* complex. *Iḍā* is on the left side and *piṅgalā* on the right. *Suṣumṇā* is in the middle. *Gāndhārī* goes to the left eye and *hasti-jihvā* to the right eye. *Pūṣā* goes to the right ear and *yaśasvinī* to the left ear. *Alambusā* goes to the face. *Kuhū* goes to the genitals and *śaṅkhinī* to the perineum.

(*Yoga-cūḍāmaṇi Upaniṣad*, 18–20)

***Suṣumṇā-nāḍī*:** *Suṣumṇā* is the main *nāḍī* because spiritual energy flows through it and, therefore, it is intimately linked to our progress on the path toward the light. *Suṣumṇā-nāḍī* extends from the first chakra toward *brahma-randhra*. Within *suṣumṇā*, there are three different *nāḍīs*: the most exterior is *vajra-nāḍī*, within that is *chitra-nāḍī*, and in the center is *brahma-nāḍī*, through which *kuṇḍalinī-śakti* ascends toward the seventh chakra.

To the left of *suṣumṇā* is *iḍā-nāḍī*, which channels

feminine and lunar energy; it regulates our psychic aspect because it carries mental energy (*manas-śakti*). To the right of *suṣumṇā* is *piṅgalā-nāḍī*, which channels masculine and solar energy; it controls our vital aspect because through it moves *prāṇa-śakti*.

***Iḍā-nāḍī* and *piṅgala-nāḍī*:** *Iḍā-nāḍī* flows from the right ovary or testicle to the left nostril. *Piṅgalā-nāḍī* flows from the left ovary or testicle to the right nostril.

Iḍā is connected to the right hemisphere of the brain and thus rules over our intuitions, understandings, and emotions. *Piṅgalā* is connected to the left hemisphere and thus influences language and logical, analytical, and rational thought.

In most human beings, the dominant brain hemisphere alternates every 90 to 180 minutes. Along with the switch, the activity of the *nāḍīs* oscillates so that sometimes *iḍā* predominates and sometimes *piṅgalā*. If *iḍā* predominates, the left nostril will be clearer. If *piṅgalā* prevails, the right nostril will be clearer. The predominant *nāḍī* will activate its nostril, and thus the activity in the nerves associated with it. *Iḍā* is connected to the parasympathetic nervous system, whereas the *piṅgalā* is connected to the sympathetic nervous system. This alternation makes us fluctuate between active and receptive states and between analytical and intuitive states.

Psychologically, the free circulation of prana through these two *nāḍīs* is closely tied to the mental activity in the two cerebral hemispheres. *Iḍā* leads to inspiration, while *piṅgalā* makes activity possible. Breathing and activity of these *nāḍīs* are interdependent, thus, by controlling our breathing, we can influence the activity of the *nāḍīs*.

Furthermore, *iḍā-nāḍī* regulates bile, lowers body temperature, and regulates blood pressure. *Piṅgalā-nāḍī* also regulates blood pressure and controls the temperature of the kidneys and the heart.

Other names for *iḍā-nāḍī* are *candra-nāḍī*, *lalanā-nāḍī*, *pitryaṇa*, śaśi, *candra-hāra*, and *śītala*. *Piṅgalā-nāḍī* is also known as *surya-nāḍī*.

***Gāndhāri-nāḍī*:** It is under the control of the *piṅgalā*. It flows on the left side of the *iḍā-nāḍī* and goes to the left eye.

***Hasti-jihvā-nāḍī*:** It is under the control of *suṣumṇā*. It flows on the reverse lateral side of *iḍā* and goes to the big toe. It provides vital energy to the nerves that surround the eyes.

***Pūṣā-nāḍī* and *yaśasvinī-nāḍī*:** *Pūṣā* flows behind the *piṅgalā* toward the right eye. *Yaśasvinī-nāḍī* flows alongside *piṅgalā*, between *pūṣā* and *sarasvatī*. *Yaśasvinī-nāḍī* controls the flow of information in the left ear, whereas *pūṣā-nāḍī* does so in the right ear. The information perceived by the ears is processed by the brain under the control of *suṣumṇā-nāḍī*.

***Alambusā-nāḍī*:** It flows from the anus, terminating in the mouth. It is related to the sense of taste.

***Kuhū-nāḍī*:** It is under the control of *iḍā*. It flows alongside *suṣumṇā-nāḍī* to the nose. It is located near the sexual organs and involved in activating them.

Śaṅkhinī-nāḍī: It is found between the *nāḍīs gāndhārī* and *sarasvatī*. It flows to the side and behind *iḍā-nāḍī* and connects to *mūlādhāra-cakra*. It is located near the kidneys and affects renal functions and urine.

Other important <u>*nāḍīs*</u>:

***Sarasvatī-nāḍī*:** It is under the control of *vajra-nāḍī*. It flows to the side of *suṣumṇā-nāḍī* and ends in the mouth.

***Payasvinī-nāḍī*:** It is under the control of *citriṇī-nāḍī*. It flows between *pūṣā* and *sarasvatī nāḍīs*. This *nāḍī* ends at the edge of the right ear and is connected to the gall bladder.

***Vāruṇī-nāḍī*:** It flows between the *yaśasvinī* and *kuhū*. Its functions include maintaining the balance of water in our body and transporting waste.

***Śūrya-nāḍī*:** It flows from the navel toward the space between the eyebrows.

***Viśvodarī-nāḍī*:** It flows between *kuhū* and *hasti-jihvā*. It is connected to *maṇipūra-cakra* and the digestive system.

Important facial *nāḍīs*: *Cakṣu-bhedna, nasikā-bhedna, karṇa-bhedna, tamas, rajas, bṛkuṭi-dhyāna, amṛta-varṣa, divya, mukhar-bindu, tejasvinī, janma-mṛtyur-ganadhākṣa, karma-phala, dikpāla, matṛkā, mūrdha, cakṣu-karṇa, apaṅg, mānya, kṛ-kaṭika, śṛṅgāṭaka, nirama, antar-daha, sam-mukha, naraka-loka,* and *svarga-loka.*

Important *nāḍīs* situated in the shoulders, chest, and stomach: *Madhyama-śayan, sthūla-kriyā, vāk-kriyā, ananta, oṁ-kāra, madhyama-vāca, uṣṭi-vitalā, prakṛti-puruṣa, pāpa-haraṇa, śipra-bhogī, karmaṇya, pañca-tatva, agni, bhūmi, āpa, ākāśa, vāyu, prāṇa, udāna, vyāna, samāna, apāna, aṅga, kṛ-kāra, kūrma, deva-dūta, dhanañjaya, mihira, rasna, deva-yāna, bhāskara, rudra-rūpa, brahma-randhra, mahā-patha, madhya-mārga, smaśāna, śāmbhavī, śakti-mārga, sūrya, agni-mārga, śasi-lalanā, pitṛ-yāna, candra-hāra, śītala, candra, śipra-gāndhārī, śipra-hasta-jihvā, muhūrartri-kuhu, pitṛ, mātṛ, bhairavī, viśāla, cāmuṇḍā,* and *śirṣa.*

Secondary *nāḍīs* in the palms of the hands and the soles of the feet: *Madhyamā, agni-śūnyā, candra-śūnyā, dhyānā, muktā, vimuktā, śila-oṁ-kārā, śalinā, śiprā, svāhā, śīnā, mādhavī, urvākā, pāvanā, vaidehī, viplakṣā, vimohī, vācā, mukta-bhedā, vaikuṇṭha, rasā-tala, mahā-tala, apratiṣṭha,* and *mahā-bhī.*

Secondary *nāḍīs* in the feet: *Mantrūḍha, dham-samudra, nava-vidyā, sūkṣma-deha, nābhī-sthāna, rakta-samudra, liṅga-sthāna, sāvitrī-candrāṇī,* and *jānu-sthala.*

List of minor *nāḍīs*: *Āṁ, agni, agni-śūnya, agni-mārga, aḥ, ākāśa, alambusā, aṁ, amṛta, ananta, aṅga, antar-daha, apa, apāna, apaṅg, apratiṣṭha, oṁ, baṁ, bhāskara, bhairavī, bhaṁ, bhūmi, brahma-randhra, bṛkuṭi-dhyāna, cakṣu-behdna, cakṣu-karṇa, caṁ, cāmuṇḍa, candra, candra-śūnya, candra-hāra, candrāṇī, chaṁ, citriṇī, daṁ, deva-datta, deva-yāna, dham, dhaṁ-samudra, dhanañ-jaya, dhyāna, divya, aiṁ, eṁ, eiṁ, phaṁ, gaṁ, gāndhāri, ghaṁ, haṁ, hasta-jihvā, iṁ, jaṁ, janma-mrityur-ganadhākṣya, jānu-sthala, jhaṁ, jihvā, kaṁ, karma-phalādi-kalpa, karmaṇya, karṇa-bhedna, khaṁ, kṛ-kaṭika, kṛ-kāra, kṣam, kuhu, kūrma, lalanā, laṁ, liṅga-sthāna, lrīṁ, lriṁ, mādhavī, madhyāna-śayana, madhyama-śūnya, madhyama-vaca, madhya-mārga, mahā-patha, mahā-tala, maṁ, mānyā, mātṛkā, mihira, mūrdha, muhuratri-kuhu, mukhar-bindu, mukta-bheda, muktā, nābhī-sthāna, naṁ, ṇaṁ, naraka-loka, nāsikā-bhedna, nava-vidyā, nir-mana, māyan, om-kāra, padavi, paṁ, pañca-tattva, pāpa-haraṇa, pāvana, payasvinī, piṅgala, pitṛ, mātṛ, pitṛ-yāṇa, prakṛti-puruṣa, prāna, pūṣa, rajas, rākā, rakta-samudra, raṁ, rasā-tala, rasna, rīṁ, ṛṣi, rudra-rūpa, saṁ, sa-mana, śāmbhavī, sammukha, śankinī, sarasvatī, śaśi, saumyā, sāvitri, śakti-mārga, śālīna, śaṁ, śīna, śītla, śila, śipra-bhogi, śiprā, śipra-gāndhārī,* *śipra-hasta-jihvā, śīrṣa, smaśāna, śṛṅgāṭaka, sthūla, sūrya, sūkṣma-deha, suṣumṇa, svāhā, svarga-loka, ṭaṁ, ṭham, tamas, tejasvinī, taṁ, thaṁ, udāna, uṁ, urvāka, ūṁ, vaca, vaidehī, vaikuṇṭha, vajra, vāk-kriya, vaṁ, vāruṇī, vāyu, vimohī, vimukta, viplakṣa, viśāla, viśvodhra, vyāna, yaṁ, yāṁ,* and *yaśasvinī.*

All the astral channels are subordinate, in one way or another, to *suṣumṇā*, because energy rises from *mūlādhāra-cakra* to the cave of Brahman (*brahma-randhra)*, which is situated in the interior of the cerebrospinal axis. We read the following:

evaṁ dvāraṁ samāśritya
tiṣṭhante nāḍayaḥ kramāt
iḍā-piṅgalā-sauṣumnāḥ
prāṇa-mārge ca saṁsthitāḥ

satataṁ prāṇa-vāhinyaḥ
soma-sūryāgni-devatāḥ
prāṇāpāna-samānākhyā
vyānodānau ca vāyavaḥ

Thus these *nāḍīs*, namely *iḍā, piṅgalā*, and *suṣumṇā*, are closely attached to the opening of the paths of prana. They are manifestations of the gods Soma (moon), Sūrya (sun), and Agni (fire), respectively, and prana moves through them [the three *nāḍīs*]. The *vāyus* (that are moved through the passages) are *prāṇa, apāna, samāna, vyāna*, and *udāna.*

(*Yoga-cūḍāmaṇi Upaniṣad*, 21–22)

The Vedic sages of antiquity explored the influence of vital energy flow through the *nāḍīs* on human health. In a healthy state, prana flows in a free and well-balanced manner throughout our body. Energetically, disease is a blockage and disharmony of prana, which can have a physical, mental, or emotional origin.

One of the innumerable purposes of hatha yoga postures is to reestablish the circulation of vital energy and overcome energetic obstructions in the *nāḍīs* that can affect our health. Asanas, *prāṇāyāma*, and relaxation allow for the expansion of prana as well as its harmonious distribution to all organs and at every level.

For a serious study of the *nāḍīs*, the following acredited books on the subject are recommended: *Jala-darśana Upaniṣad*, the *Yoga-cūḍāmaṇi Upaniṣad*, the *Yoga-śikha Upaniṣad*, the *Gorakṣāṣṭaka*, the *Siddha-siddhānta-paddhati*, the *Śāṇḍilya Upaniṣad*, and the *Ṣaṭ-cakra-nirūpaṇa*. The Upanishads also offer explanations:

tā vā asyaitā hitā nāma nāḍyo yathā keśaḥ sahasradhā bhinnas-tāvatā 'ṇimnā tiṣṭhanti śuklasya nīlasya piṅgalasya haritasya lohitasya pūrṇā

> In a person, there are nerves called *hita* that are as fine as a hair that has been divided into a thousand parts and they are filled with white, blue, brown, green, and red liquids.
>
> (*Bṛhad-āraṇyaka Upaniṣad*, 4.3.20)

atha yā etā hṛdayasya nāḍyastāḥ
piṅgalasyānimnas-tiṣṭhanti
śuklasya nīlasya pītasya lohitasyety
asau vā ādityaḥ piṅgala
eṣa śukla eṣa nīla eṣa pīta eṣa lohitaḥ

Now, [from] these arteries (channels) that belong to the heart, arise the finest essences, of the colors reddish brown, white, blue, yellow, and red. The sun is reddish brown, white, blue, yellow, and red. (*Chāndogya Upaniṣad*, 8.6.1)

tad yathā mahā-pathātata ubhau grāmau gacchatīmaṁ cāmuṁ
caivam evaitādityasya raśmaya ubhau
lokau gacchantīmaṁ cāmuṁ
cāmuṣmād ādityāt pratāyante tāsu nāḍīṣu sṛptā
ābhyo nāḍībhyaḥ pratāyante te 'muṣminn āditye sṛptāḥ

Just as a long and continuous highway passes between two villages, the rays of the sun go between both worlds (*iḍā* and *piṅgalā*) and the next (*suṣumṇā*). The rays extend from the sun and enter these channels.

They extend from these channels and permeate the sun. (*Chāndogya Upaniṣad*, 8.6.2)

tad yatraitat suptaḥ samastaḥ samprasannaḥ
svapnaṁ na vijānāty āsu
tadā nāḍīṣu sṛpto bhavati taṁ na kaścana pāpmā spṛśati
tejasā hi tadā sampanno bhavati

And when one is in complete repose in the forgiving thought of Brahman, one becomes calm and serene, in such a way that one has no dreams, then one enters into [the *ākāśa* of the heart by means of] these arteries. Then, nothing bad can happen to one who has obtained divine enlightenment.

(*Chāndogya Upaniṣad*, 8.6.3)

atha yatraitad abalimānaṁ
nīto bhavati tam abhitāsīnā
āhur jānāsi māṁ jānāsi mām iti
sa yāvad asmāc charīrād
anutkrānto bhavati tāvaj jānāti

Now when one is seriously ill, family members who are sitting around say, "Do you recognize me? Do you recognize me?" He recognizes them until abandoning the body.

(*Chāndogya Upaniṣad*, 8.6.4)

atha yatraitad asmāc charīrād utkrāmaty athaitair eva
raśmibhir ūrdhvam ākramate sa oṁ iti vāhod vā mīyate sa
yāvat kṣipyen manas tāvad ādityaṁ gacchaty etad vai khalu
loka-dvāraṁ viduṣāṁ prapadanaṁ nirodho viduṣām

But when the person leaves the body, he goes up by means of these same rays. If he is wise he rises by meditating on Om. To the extent that he transcends the mind, he reaches the sun. In fact, the door to the world of Brahman remains open for the sages and closed to the ignorant.

(*Chāndogya Upaniṣad*, 8.6.5)

tad eṣa ślokaḥ
śataṁ caikā ca hṛdayasya nāḍyas tāsāṁ
mūrdhānam abhiniḥṣṛtaikā tayordhvam āyann amṛtatvam eti
viṣvaṅṅ anyā utkramaṇe bhavanty ukramaṇe bhavanti

To confirm this, there is a verse: The heart has 101 arteries; one of these is directed toward the crown of the head. Rising toward it, one reaches immortality. The rest of the arteries are directed in other directions.

(*Chāndogya Upaniṣad*, 8.6.6)

The difference between *kuṇḍalinī-śakti* and *prāṇa-śakti*

Just as water is the common essence of both steam and ice, Brahman is the common essence of kundalini and prana. Both are expressions of the same creative female energy that originates from Brahman. Shakti is called kundalini when it descends and crosses the abstract boundaries of the causal plane (*kāraṇa-loka*). It is called prana when it arrives to the astral plane (*bhuvar-loka*).

Kuṇḍalinī-śakti is higher than *prāṇa-śakti* because it is related to the *ānanda-maya-kośa* (blissful sheath) that is subtler; when the *kuṇḍalinī-śakti* approaches the *vijñāna-maya-kośa* (intellectual sheath), it expresses itself astrally, as *prāṇa-śakti*.

The manifestation of *prāṇa-śakti* is perceived physically by the *anna-maya-kośa* (food sheath or physical body). The prana is shakti in its evolving aspect: from unity toward plurality. On the other hand, kundalini is shakti during involution: from multiplicity toward unity. Kundalini is coiled in *mūlādhāra-cakra* and when it awakens, just as a needle is drawn by a powerful magnet, it yearns to reunite with its source. In every prana phenomenon, the first energy center (*mūlādhāra-cakra*) will dominate, which is the lowest. It corresponds to the earth element. In phenomena related to kundalini, the highest center (*sahasrāra-cakra*) will predominate.

Prana descends through *suṣumṇā-nāḍī* in a similar proportion to our formation as egoic entities. The process begins in *sahasrāra-cakra* and descends during our development as human beings and culminates in *mūlādhāra*. Beginning during gestation in our mother's womb, and then as babies, kids, and adults, prana descends as we forget of our essence. Similarly, in reverse, *kuṇḍalinī-śakti* ascends as we wake up to reality.

An awakening of *kuṇḍalinī-śakti* will usually be preceded by an awakening of prana. Based on my own experience, the activation of prana is an essential and an indispensable prerequisite for awakening kundalini. Therefore, in the practice of kundalini yoga, it is recommended to start with *prāṇāyama*. Many *prāṇāyama* exercises and practices are performed in the physical body (*anna-maya-kośa*) but they influence the astral body (*liṅga-śarīra* or *sūkṣma-śarīra*). The awakening of kundalini, however, is a phenomenon that begins at the highest levels of the causal body (*kāraṇa-śarīra*) toward the bliss sheath (*ānanda-maya-kośa*).

We can see a significant difference between the ascension of prana (*prāṇotthāna*) and an awakening of kundalini. Prana rises on the astral plane from *mūlādhāra-cakra* through *piṅgalā-nāḍī* to the brain and finally disperses. The awakening of kundalini also begins in *mūlādhāra-cakra*, but at the causal level. Its ascension takes place through the *suṣumṇā-nāḍī* and reaches *sahasrāra-cakra*. While all prana awakenings occur on the astral plane and cause pleasant feelings, the ascension of kundalini is a much more powerful experience because it happens from *kāraṇa-śarīra* to *ānanda-maya-kośa*.

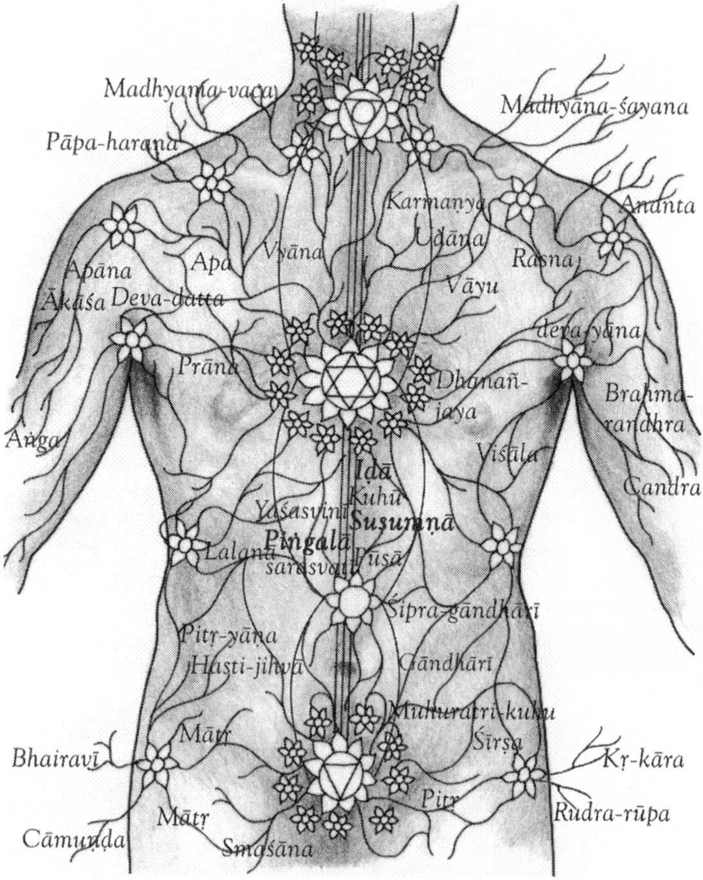

The *nāḍīs* of the body

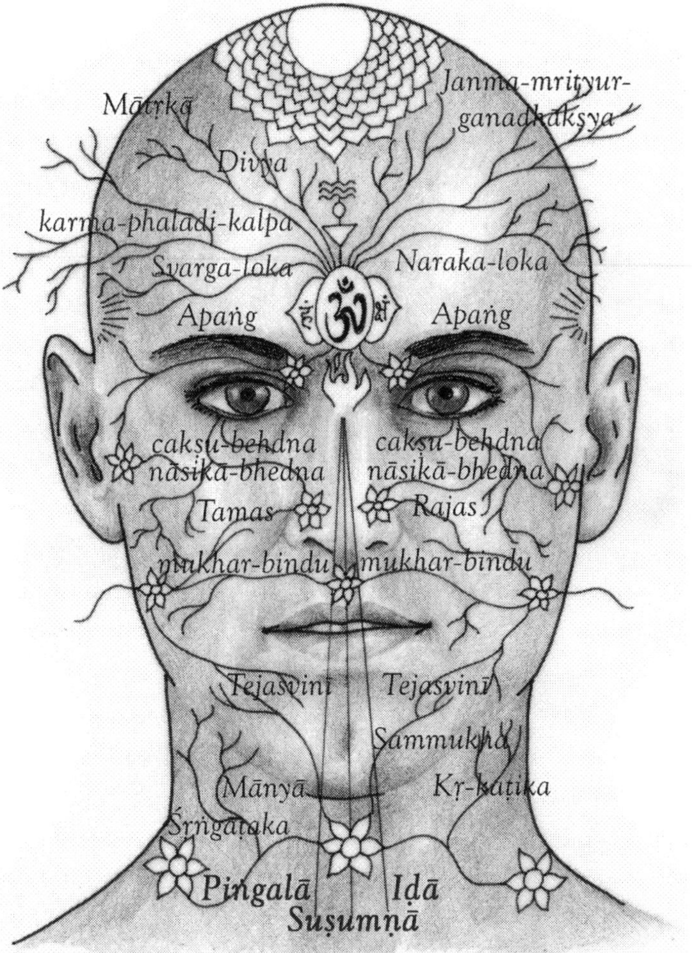

The *nāḍīs* of the face

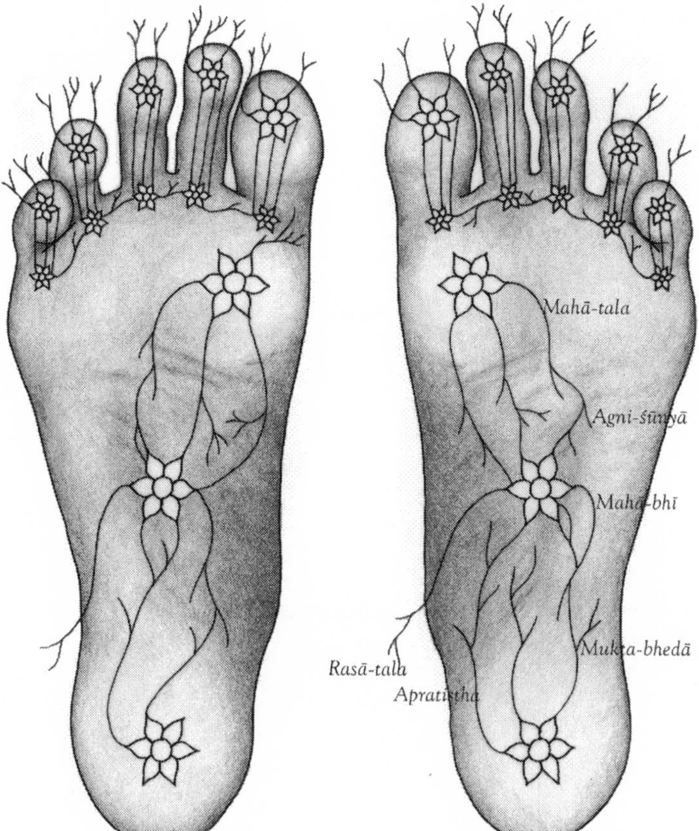

The *nāḍīs* of the feet

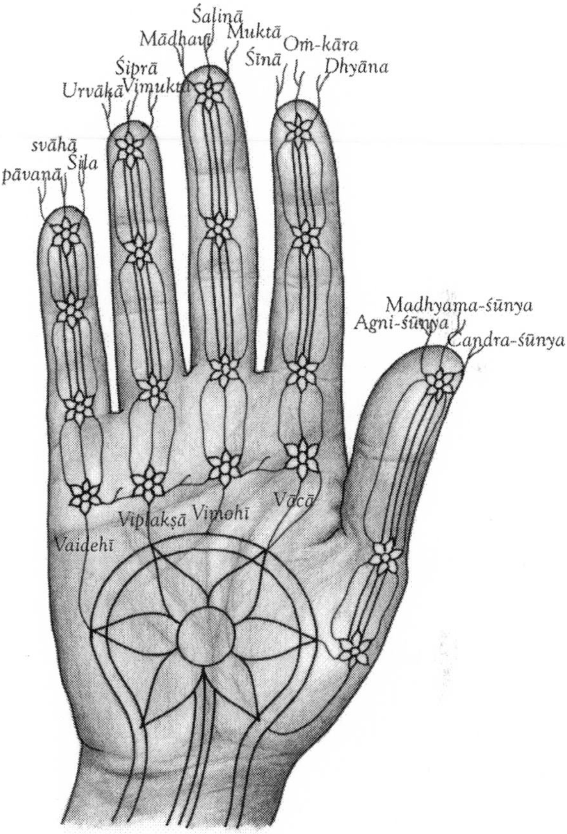

The *nāḍīs* of the hands

CHAPTER 2

CHAKRAS, *MARMAS*, AND *GRANTHIS*

In order to understand the process of kundalini yoga, it is essential to acquire at least some basic knowledge of chakras, *marmas*, and *granthis*.

Chakras or "energy centers"

catur-dalaṁ syād ādhāraṁ
svādhiṣṭhānaṁ ca ṣaḍ-dalam

nābhau daśa-dalaṁ padmaṁ
hṛdaye dvādaśārakam
ṣoḍaśāraṁ viśuddhākhyaṁ
bhrū-madhye dvi-dalaṁ tathā

sahasra-dala-saṅkhyātaṁ
brahma-randhre mahā-pathi

It has been said [of the six psychic centers] that *mūlādhāra*, the central base, has four petals. *Svādhiṣṭhāna*, one's center, has six petals. *Maṇipūra*,

> the center of the navel, has ten petals. *Anāhata*, the heart center, has twelve petals. *Viśuddha*, the center of purification, has sixteen petals, and *bhrū-madhya*, the center of the space between the eyebrows, has two petals. In the great path of the *brahma-randhra* (the opening at the crown of the head) there is a lotus of one thousand petals (*sahasrāra-cakra*).
>
> (*Yoga-cūḍāmaṇi Upaniṣad*, 4b–6a)

The meaning of the Sanskrit word *cakra* is "wheel or disc," which suggests circular movement. The chakras rotate clockwise. They are swirling metaphysical vortexes, transformers of energy both from the astral body, or *liṅga-śarīra*, and toward it. Chakras are functioning normally if they rotate clockwise at the appropriate speed to metabolize the required energy from the infinite ocean of prana. The chakras consist of a system of centers of energetic activity. They are intended to receive, assimilate, and transmit vital energies. Prana organizes its flow within them. They are the connection between two worlds or realities, the physical and the astral.

There are 88,000 chakras in the astral body. Most are minor and their importance in our energetic system is minimal. There are forty-five important energy centers and of those, only seven are the most relevant. These are *mūlādhāra*, *svādhiṣṭhāna*, *maṇipūra*, *anāhata*, *viśuddha*, *ājñā*, and *sahasrāra*, and they are located along the *suṣumṇā-nāḍī*. In regards to the chakras, the *Atharva Veda* points out:

aṣṭā-cakrā nava-dvārā
devānāṁ pūrayodhyā
tasyāṁ hiraṇyayaḥ kośaḥ
svargo jyotiṣāvṛtaḥ

The soul resides in the land of eight chakras and nine gates known as the bright land of the Lords.
(*Atharva Veda*, 10.2.39)

Learning properties and esoteric symbolism of each chakra allows us to focus our attention on each of them. This helps us become deeply aware of the essential nature of each center. The chakras cannot be seen with our physical eyes. However, we can perceive them with our senses in our physical body. They are located along the spinal cord and in the nerve plexuses.

Each one of the energy centers corresponds to a level in the cosmic process of creation and, therefore, it is related to a particular element that gives it certain characteristics and qualities. The relative material reality of names and forms is composed of five basic elements, which are called *pañca-mahā-bhūta* or *pañca-mahā-tattva*. They are the basic states of matter: ether (*ākāśa*), air (*vāyu*), fire (*tejas*), water (*āpas*), and earth (*pṛthivī*). Obviously, these states should not be understood as a mere clump of earth, a glass of water, or the flame of a candle, but in a wider sense that encompasses all their inherent qualities. For example, the heaviness and solidity of earth, the fluidity of water, the light and transforming power of fire, the lightness of air, and so on.

The chakras are a microcosm of creation. Before the cosmic manifestation, only the unified totality exists. The first expression of this unexpressed consciousness is the vibration of the universal Om. From this primordial sound, ether is manifested. When there is activity in the ether, air is formed. From the friction caused by this activity, fire is produced. Then, the liquefaction of fire leads to the manifestation of water, and finally, from solidified water, comes earth.

Each chakra is represented by a yantra (geometric diagram). The vibration of the chakra is indicated with a Sanskrit letter, or *bījākṣara*, in the center of the diagram. A lotus flower with a different number of petals symbolizes the quantity of *nāḍīs* that intersect in the chakra. In each petal, we find the Sanskrit letters that represent the specific vibration of each *nāḍī*. These flowers are open or closed according to a person's particular situation.

Furthermore, each chakra is related to a specific animal, which symbolizes the movement of prana in the center. Each center is also related to a specific plane of consciousness; there are different dimensions of existence and forms of life. According to the Vedic holy scriptures, below the earthly plane there are seven *talas*, or "lower worlds," and six *lokas*, or "worlds," above this one, which correspond to different levels of consciousness. Each *loka* has its counterpart or corresponding *tala*, similar to two electrical poles. According to the *Mahā-bhāgavata Purāṇa*, these are the following, starting from the most elevated one:

7. *Satya-loka*
6. *Tapo-loka*
5. *Jana-loka*
4. *Mahar-loka*
3. *Svar(ga)-loka*
2. *Bhuvar-loka*
1. *Bhū(r)-loka* (earthly plane)

---

1. *Atala*
2. *Vitala*
3. *Sutala*
4. *Talā-tala*
5. *Mahā-tala*
6. *Rasā-tala*
7. *Pātāla*

The chakras are linked to the nervous ganglia and the internal secretion glands of the endocrine system. The energy centers also have a great influence on our body, for example on the digestive, nervous, circulatory, and respiratory systems.

The asanas, or "postures of hatha yoga," directly influence the functioning of the chakras. Certain asanas work especially on the prana movement of specific centers. Therefore, the order in which they are practiced is of great importance. The chakras not only affect us physically, but also psychologically, sexually, and emotionally, as well as in our ability to communicate.

The techniques and practices of kundalini yoga require focusing our attention on each chakra's center of stimulation.

However, for many beginning students, it is difficult to perceive and concentrate on these internal points. Many find it easier to concentrate on the *kṣetras*, which are the corresponding locations of each chakra in the front part of the body. The *kṣetras* are not the original points of stimulation of the chakras; they are their reflections. Concentration on the *kṣetras* creates a stimulating sensation that reaches the chakras. With the exception of *mūlādhāra-cakra*, the rest of the chakras have a corresponding *kṣetra*: *svādhiṣṭhāna-kṣetra* is at the level of the pubic bone, *maṇipūra-kṣetra* is at the level of the navel, *anāhata-kṣetra* is at the level of the heart, *viśuddha-kṣetra* is at the level of the throat, *ājñā-kṣetra* is at the space between the eyebrows, and *sahasrāra-kṣetra* is on the crown of the head.

With regards to the characteristics of the centers, descriptions vary among the many scriptures and masters. Therefore, I have chosen to be faithful to two sources: the first is the opinion of my own eternal spiritual master, His Divine Grace Śrī Śrī Bābā Brahmānanda Mahārāja, and the second is my own experience, only when it is in perfect agreement with the teachings of my beloved Guru Mahārāja.

The *marmas* or "vital points"

Marmas are the 107 vital points that the *nāḍīs* cross. These are prana vortexes with great vital value, of which fifty-seven are the most important. Damage in a *marma* can be fatal because they are vital points of great sensitivity that can cut a *nāḍī* and suppress the flow of vital energy.

Ayurvedic medicine treats various diseases by applying massage, pressure, and heat to the *marma* connected to the affected organ. The asanas of hatha yoga are tremendously beneficial because they stretch the *marmas*. *Marmas* are explained in depth in the *Suśruta Saṁhitā*.

Next we will list the principal *marmas*.

***Marmas* located in the head:**

1. *Adhipati*: It is found at the crown of the head. In this *marma*, memory loss, headaches, and weakness are treated.
2. *Sīmanta*: It is found in the cranial suture. This *marma* is related to blood circulation in the head; here, migraine, epilepsy, convulsions, and amnesia are treated.
3. *Ājñā*: It is located in the space between the eyebrows. In this *marma*, loss of the sense of smell, pituitary gland problems, and colds are treated.
4. *Āvarta*: It is found above and at the ends of the eyebrows. This *marma* influences our body posture, and migraines and sinusitis are treated here.
5. *Śaṅkha*: It is located in the temples, between the eyebrows and the ears. In this *marma*, colon problems, headaches, amnesia, and dizziness are treated.
6. *Utkṣepa*: It is located above the *śaṅkha*. It is directly connected to the colon.
7. *Vidhura*: It is found below the ears. In this *marma*, the ears are stimulated.
8. *Phaṇa*: It is located on the sides of the nose. In this

marma, flu symptoms and stress release treatments take place.

9. *Śṛṅgātaka*: It is located in the palate, under the nose and in the chin. In this *marma*, the nervous system is stimulated to alleviate headaches and dizziness.

***Marmas* located in the neck:**

1. *Mantha*: It is located on the side of the neck. In this *marma*, difficulties in expression and paralysis are treated.
2. *Mānya*: It is on the side of the throat. In this *marma*, thyroid problems are treated, as it is related to the regulation and rhythm of the entire organism.
3. *Śira-mātṛkā*: It is located above the throat. This *marma* is related to blood circulation in the head.
4. *Nīla*: It is located in the throat. This *marma* influences the regulation of rhythms of the body.
5. *Kriya-kārika*: It is found at the base of the neck. In this *marma*, stress can be alleviated.

***Marmas* located on the back:**

1. *Aṁśa*: It is located above the shoulder blade, between the trapezius muscle and the clavicle. In this *marma*, *viśuddha-cakra* is stimulated.
2. *Aṁśa-phalaka*: It is located on the shoulder blades. In this *marma*, shoulder pain is treated and *anāhata-cakra* is stimulated.
3. *Pārśva-sandhi*: It is found above *nitamba-marma*. This *marma* regulates blood circulation.
4. *Nitamba*: It is located above the buttocks and

stimulates the production of red blood cells.

5. *Kukundara*: It is located to the side of the coccyx. In this *marma*, problems in the reproductive organs are alleviated and *svādhiṣṭhāna-cakra* is stimulated.
6. *Kaṭika-taruṇa*: It is located above the buttocks. In this *marma*, fatty tissues are stimulated and muscular stiffness and pain in the legs are alleviated.

Marmas located in the thorax:

1. *Āpasthambha*: It is located below the clavicle. In this *marma*, the sympathetic and parasympathetic systems are stimulated. Asthma and breathing difficulties are treated here.
2. *Apalāpa*: It is located in the middle of the armpit. In this *marma*, breast inflammation is treated.
3. *Stanārohita*: It is located on top of the breast. In this *marma*, enflamed and obstructed breasts are treated.
4. *Hṛdaya*: It is located in the center of the thorax in the solar plexus. In this *marma*, heart diseases are treated.

Marmas located in the abdomen:

1. *Nābhi*: It is located around the navel. In this *marma*, the intestines are stimulated and constipation, diarrhea, and indigestions are treated.
2. *Vasti*: It is located in the pubic area. In this *marma*, *kapha* is stimulated and prostate and problems with the reproductive organ are treated.
3. *Guda*: It is located in the perineum. In this *marma*, constipation and hemorrhoids are treated.

***Marmas* located in the lower extremities:**

1. *Tala-hṛdaya*: It is located in the center of the soles of the feet. This *marma* stimulates the lungs. Problems with blood circulation in the hands and feet are treated here.
2. *Kūrca*: It is located on the instep. This *marma* influences our sight, and foot pain is treated here.
3. *Kṣipra*: It is located in the upper part of the feet, between the big toe and the second toe. This *marma* is connected to the heart.
4. *Gulpha*: It is located below the ankle. In this *marma*, nervousness and stress are treated.
5. *Kūrca-śira*: It is located below the ankle. In this *marma*, muscular spasms are controlled.
6. *Indra-vasti*: It is located in the calf muscles. In this *marma*, digestive problems are treated.
7. *Jānu*: It is located behind the knees. This *marma* is connected to the liver.
8. *Ani*: It is located above the joints of the knees. This *marma* is related to muscular stiffness.
9. *Urvi*: It is located midway up the thigh. In this *marma*, muscular tension and circulatory disorders are treated.
10. *Viṭapa*: It is located below the groin. This *marma* is related to abdominal muscular tension and hernias.
11. *Lohitākṣa*: It is located in the center of the groin. In this *marma*, circulatory problems of the feet are treated.

***Marmas* located in the upper extremities:**

1. *Tala-hṛdaya*: It is located in the center of the palm. This *marma* is associated with lung stimulation.
2. *Kṣipra*: It is located between the index finger and the thumb. This *marma* is associated with heart stimulation.
3. *Kūrca-śira*: It is located in the lower part of the wrist. This *marma* is associated with the control of the muscular spasms.
4. *Maṇi-bandha*: It is located in the wrist area. In this *marma*, tension and stress is alleviated.
5. *Indra-vasti*: It is located midway up the arm. In this *marma*, intestinal and digestive problems are treated.
6. *Kūrpāra*: It is located on the elbow. This *marma* is connected to the liver.
7. *Ani*: It is located in the elbow joint. Tension and muscles stiffness problems are treated here.
8. *Urvi*: It is located midway up the arm. In this *marma*, muscular tension and blood circulation problems are treated.
9. *Lohitākṣa*: It is located in the middle of the armpit. This *marma* is related to circulation in the lower extremities.

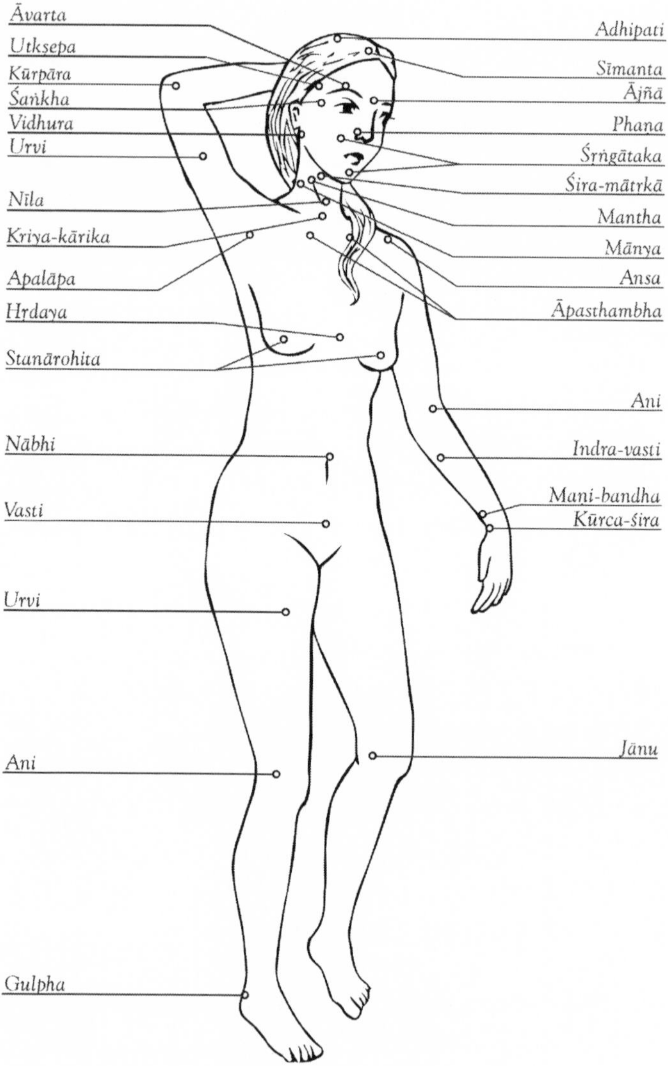
Āvarta
Utkṣepa
Kūrpāra
Śaṅkha
Vidhura
Urvi
Nīla
Kriya-kārika
Apalāpa
Hṛdaya
Stanārohita
Nābhi
Vasti
Urvi
Ani
Gulpha
Adhipati
Sīmanta
Ājñā
Phaṇa
Śṛṅgātaka
Śira-mātṛkā
Mantha
Mānya
Ansa
Āpasthambha
Ani
Indra-vasti
Maṇi-bandha
Kūrca-śira
Jānu

The frontal *marmas*

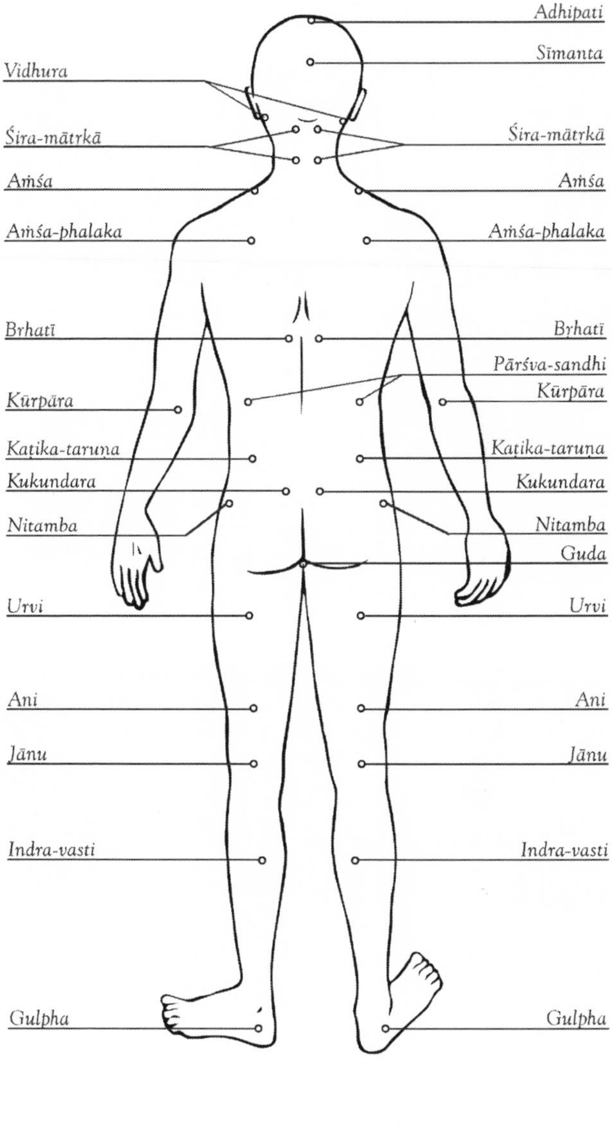

The rear *marmas*

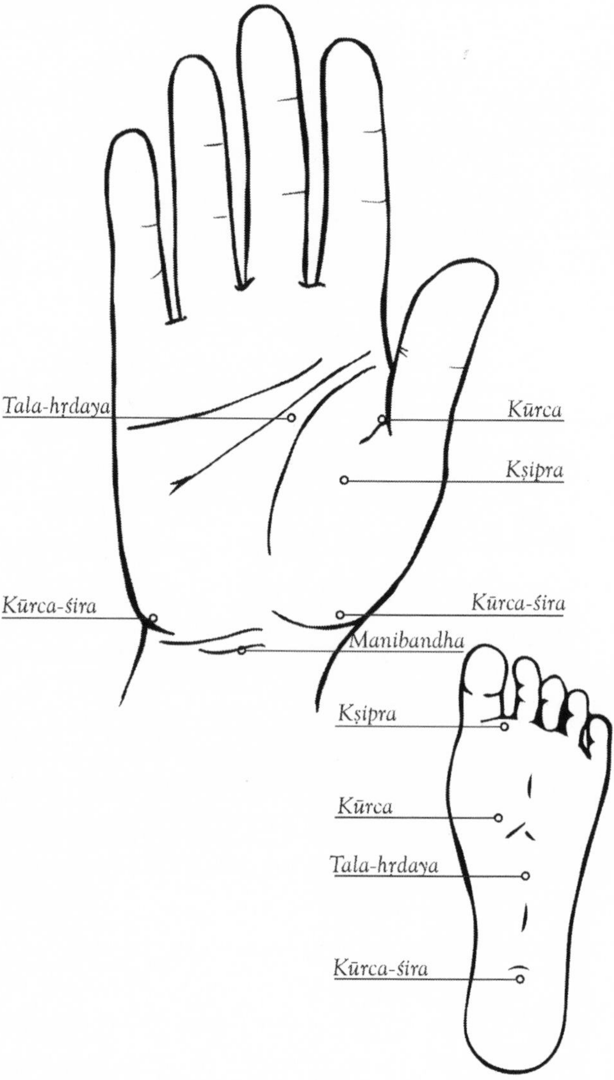

Marmas of hands and feet

The *granthis* or "knots"

The Sanskrit word *granthi* means "knot," symbolizing our earthly attachments. The *granthis* are valves whose main function is to prevent a premature elevation of kundalini. They protect us, impeding the ascension of the serpentine energy during our spiritual childhood. Until these energetic valves are transcended, elevating the divine fire is impossible.

There are those who seek to gain mystical powers and others who desire particular spiritual experiences. Only few people understand that every spiritual phenomenon is intimately linked to changes in consciousness and is nothing more than a sign of internal development. In the same way, the opening of the *granthis* is a sign of spiritual evolution which is directly related to renunciation and surrender. The three main *granthis* are called Brahmā, Vishnu, and Shiva.

***Brahma-granthi*:** It is found in *mūlādhāra-cakra* and corresponds to the tamasic qualities of ignorance and laziness. It rests upon various smaller *granthis* called *bhairavī*, *viśālā*, *cāmundā*, and *śīrṣā*, which remain closed while we continue to be submerged in illusion. This *granthi* is intimately related to our earthly or mundane attachments and is connected to enjoyment of the senses, egoism, and our affinity for storing, accumulating, and hoarding. Without transcending these obstacles, *brahma-granthi* will remain closed. *Sādhakas* must develop wisdom, devotion, and trust in a spiritual master. Only the enthusiastic and determined aspirant will manage to rise above the temptations of maya, or "illusion."

***Viṣṇu-granthi*:** It is found in the pectoral area, obstructing the rising of the serpentine power at *anāhata-cakra*. It corresponds to the qualities related to the modality of passion (*raja-guṇa*). It rests upon four smaller *granthis*: *śyāmala*, *kṛṣṇa*, *nīlāñjana*, and *ṣaṇ-mukha*. It is involved in sentimental attachments to loved ones. The obstacles to transcending *viṣṇu-granthi* are emotional. The opening of this valve is more difficult, as it is simpler to renounce our attachment to money, a car, or a house, than to relinquish our affections. To go beyond this knot, it is recommended to include bhakti yoga in our sadhana.

***Śiva-granthi* or *rudra-granthi*:** It is located in *ājñā-cakra*. It is connected to the modality of benevolence (*sattva-guṇa*). This *granthi* rests upon six lower *granthis*: *raudra*, *mukti*, *sānāthya*, *kāpāli*, *kāla-cūḍas*, and *kula-śrava*. It remains closed as long as we are attached to mystical powers, spiritual experiences, and the desire to attain enlightenment. As long as we hold on to our goals, however spiritual they may seem to us, this knot will remain closed. One of the main obstacles to transcending this valve is to perceive ourselves as "something" or "someone," with an existence independent of the Whole. The main impediment is the mistaken conception of ourselves as personalities separate from Totality. This idea, belief, or conception is what we are; therefore, the search for external solutions only exposes our ignorance that we ourselves are the problem. As long as this idea of "I" is present, it is impossible to transcend the *śiva-granthi*.

The serpentine energy will reach the higher centers only when the knots are transcended. *Granthis* are valves that, when open, allow *kuṇḍalinī-śakti* to flow. The functioning of these valves is essential to preserve our progress, because when they close in the opposite direction, they prevent regression. The sadhana recommended by the master is intended to prepare us to be an instrument in every aspect and to be appropriate receptacles for the Truth. This practice has an extremely high energetic intensity. The experience of Truth requires an instrument with the proper strength to receive such intensity without the danger of disintegration.

Chapter 3

The thirty-six *tattvas* or "categories of existence"

According to Kashmir Shaivism, God is not the external creator of the universe: he transforms himself into the creation. The manifestation of the universe is a movement of materialization of the spirit. With the elevation of kundalini, the direction is reversed and the spiritualization of matter begins. The *tattvas*, or "categories or principles of existence," correspond to the different states that consciousness adopts in the objectifying process until it expresses itself as the material universe. In the opposite direction, the *tattvas* are the steps that consciousness traverses as it returns to its original state. In order to grasp the true meaning of the awakening, ascent, and descent of *kuṇḍalinī-śakti*, it is essential to understand the thirty-six *tattvas*.

Although the early Sankhya school addressed this issue, it only postulated the twenty-five impure *tattvas*. Without a doubt, Kashmir Shaivism is the path of Hinduism that has most lucidly investigated and explained the complexity of the *tattvas*, by defining an additional five pure and six pure-impure *tattvas*.

Reality is solely consciousness. Consciousness does not create a separate universe, rather it objectifies itself. When consciousness vibrates in multiple frequencies, it manifests as diverse categories, but there is no substantial differences between them. Thus, the evolutionary process moves from the subtle to the dense, from unity toward multiplicity. When kundalini rises, consciousness involutes and is reabsorbed back into itself. Its direction reverses from solidity toward subtlety.

The human being is a tiny universe or a microcosm: the process that happens within a person also occurs macroscopically, as is noted in this verse:

citi saṅkocātmā cetano 'pi saṅkucita viśva-mayaḥ

> Even the individual, whose nature is consciousness in a contracted state, embodies the universe in a contracted form.
>
> (*Pratyabhijñā-hṛdayam*, 4)

In our embodied state, we are contractions of the universe. The descent of *kuṇḍalinī-śakti* is the universal process of manifesting the individual. The ascent of *kuṇḍalinī-śakti* begins a process or involution that leads to the dissolution (*laya*) of the individual; hence, kundalini yoga is also called *laya-yoga*, or "yoga of dissolution."

Shakti is a power that is capable of revealing or concealing the Self. Cosmic manifestation is a process that camouflages consciousness as shakti descends, whereas its ascent is the return of consciousness back into itself.

The awakening and elevation of kundalini is a process in which Shakti gradually reabsorbs the many *tattvas* until its final fusion with Shiva in *sahasrāra-cakra*.

Shiva or *Parama-śiva*, the Supreme Consciousness, is the perceiver and ultimate knower. He is the support, dwelling, home, and basis of the entire universe. He transcends time, space, and causality. He does not reside in any particular place because he lies both inside and outside everything and everyone. Since the universe is his manifestation, he cannot be categorized within the structure of the *tattvas*.

citiḥ sva-tantrā viśva siddhi hetuḥ

> Consciousness, in its freedom, brings about the attainment of the universe.
>
> (*Pratyabhijñā-hṛdayam*, 1)

The study of the *tattvas* involves learning the process of creation. As she descends, Shakti covers the indivisible consciousness and shows it as relative duality. When she ascends, Shakti gradually reveals the single consciousness. In other words, in her descent, Shakti materializes herself, concealing the Absolute, which she reveals in her ascent.

The thirty-six *tattvas* are divided into three groups: pure (*śuddha*), pure-impure (*śuddhāśuddha*), and impure (*aśuddha*).

Śuddha-tattvas or "pure categories of existence"

1. *Śiva-tattva*: This is the initial creative movement of Parama-śiva. In the subjective state of purity—from the absolute point of view of Parama-śiva—everything that exists is *aham*, or "I am." Two categories begin to differentiate within "I am": the "I" as Shiva or the Self and the "am" as Shakti, the awareness of his existence.
2. *Śakti-tattva*: While Shiva is the internal aspect of consciousness, Shakti is the external one. Both are interdependent and inseparable, like wetness to water or heat to fire. *Śakti-tattva* and *śiva-tattva* are an eternal reality of pure subjectivity that does not admit duality. Shiva and Shakti are powers that appear to be separated, but are actually two different aspects of Parama-śiva. Shakti is the creative aspect of Brahman, the dynamism of consciousness. In their union, Shiva and Shakti are the pure subjective experience of *aham*, "I am." Shakti is the mirror in which Shiva observes his own reflection, creating the subjective polarity. Therefore, from *śakti-tattva*, consciousness projects itself in a subjective polarity giving raise to *idam*, or "That." This is stated in the following verse:

sā jayati śaktir ādyā
nija-sukha-maya-nitya-nirūpam ākārā
bhāvi-carācara-bījaṁ
śiva-rūpa-vimarśa-nirmalādarśaḥ

> She, the primordial Shakti, who exceeds all and who, in her own true nature, is eternal and limitless bliss, is the seed (*bīja*) of all the moving and motionless things that are to be, and is the pure mirror in which Shiva experiences himself.
>
> (*Kāma-kalā-vilāsa*, 2)

3. *Sadā-śiva* or *sadākhya-tattva*: *Sadā-śiva* emerges from Shiva-Shakti as the first principle of the cosmic manifestation. From the pure subjectivity of "I am" (*aham*) arises "That" (*idam*), which is the root and origin of objectivity, the counterpart of subjectivity. In *Sadā-śiva*, the emphasis is more on *aham* than *idam*.
4. *Īśvara-tattva*: *Īśvara* is the Lordship principle that emerges from the pure subjectivity of *idam-aham*, "That is me," with a clear emphasis on the objectivity or *idam*. For Shiva, the cosmic manifestation is unreal as a dual-objective phenomenon, but it is real as his own expansion or continuation. The difference between the experiences of *Sadā-śiva* and *Īśvara* are remarkably subtle: the realization in both *tattvas* is practically the same, although less refined in *Īśvara*. The experience of "I am that" or "I am this universe" is that of *Sadā-śiva*, while in *īśvara-tattva*, the realization is that "this universe is my own expansion." The great saint and philosopher Utpala-deva refers to *īśvara-tattva* in the following way:

sarvo mamāyaṁ vibhava
ity evaṁ parijānataḥ
viśvātmano vikalpānāṁ
prasare 'pi maheśatā

> One who knows that all this glory of manifestation is mine [belongs to the spirit], one who realizes that the entire cosmos is the Self, possesses Lordship even when the *vikalpas* (thought constructs) have their play.
> (*Īśvara-pratyabhijñā-kārikā*, 4.1.12)

5. *Śuddha-vidyā-tattva*, or "pure wisdom": In this state, both the subjective and objective aspects of consciousness acquire the same clarity. There is instability and imbalance because sometimes *aham-idam* predominates and at other times it is reversed, *idam-aham*. In *śuddha-vidyā*, unity and multiplicity are shown as identical expressions of transcendental consciousness. This *tattva* is the last of the pure categories without differentiation. In *śuddha-vidyā*, it is the power of action (*kriyā-śakti*) that prevails, since it is from here that the categories carry impurities that allow the manifestation of consciousness.

Śuddhāśuddha-tattvas or "pure-impure categories of existence"

6. *Maya*, or "illusion": Contraction, relativity, duality,

and limitation begin here. The experience of the Divine is hidden behind the veil of forgetfulness that maya covers the Self with. While experience of the *śuddha-tattvas* is inclusive, maya separates *idam* from *aham*. Maya excludes one from the other, creating the dual cognitive state of subject and object. From maya, the *pañca-kañcukas*, or "five limiting powers," are born. These are five subtle, limiting powers through which consciousness voluntarily restricts its attributes and creates the conditions for a limited existence. The *kañcukas* are the following five *tattvas*: *kalā*, *vidyā*, *rāga*, *kāla*, and *niyati* (power, knowledge, desire, time, and space). Each *kañcuka* restricts one of Shiva's divine powers: *cit*, *ānanda*, *icchā*, *jñāna*, and *kriyā* (consciousness, bliss, will, knowledge, and action).

7. *Kalā-kañcuka*, or "limitation of power": This *tattva* reduces divine omnipotence, or the divine power of action (*kriyā-śakti*), to limited action.
8. *Vidyā-kañcuka*, or "limitation of knowledge": This *tattva* reduces divine omniscience, or the power of wisdom (*jñāna-śakti*), to limited knowledge about a particular topic or field.
9. *Rāga-kañcuka*, or "limitation of desire": This *tattva* reduces divine plenitude, or divine willpower (*iccha-śakti*), through the false impression of deficiency, which induces desires and a constant search for something or someone in order to regain plenitude.
10. *Kāla-kañcuka*, or "limitation of time": This *tattva* reduces the divine power of eternal bliss

(*ānanda-śakti*) to an internal perception of time. It refers to psychological or internal time, rather than that of clocks or calendars, which is measured in minutes, hours, or years.

11. *Niyati-kañcuka*, or "limitation of space": This *tattva* reduces divine omnipresence, or the power of consciousness (*cic-chakti*), to an illusory impression of residing in a specific place.

Aśuddha-tattvas or "impure categories"

12. *Purusha*: Maya limits universal consciousness and reduces it to individual subjects. According to Kashmir Shaivism, just as Shakti becomes prakriti, Shiva becomes the individual principle, that is to say, the soul (jiva). *Ahaṅkāra* is the subjective aspect of the ego; its experience when facing the universe is "I am not that."
13. *Prakriti*: It is nature, from which the three modes known as gunas flow: sattva (goodness), *rajas* (passion), and tamas (ignorance). Just as Purusha comes from Shiva, the origin of prakriti is Shakti. Prakriti refers to our external or superficial reality, while Purusha is our subjective internal world.

The three *antaḥ-karaṇa*s or "internal organs"

Here, thought is born and developed.

14. *Buddhi*, or "the intellect": Its function is to evaluate,

rationalize, accept, or reject what the *manas* (mind) perceives through the senses. Buddhi analyzes, reflects, determines, discriminates, and decides the nature of what is perceived.

15. *Ahaṅkāra*, or "the ego": This is the limiting "I" in its objective aspect. This phenomenon leads to take what is being experienced personally and to relate experiences to itself.
16. *Manas*, or "the mind": *Manas* sees, feels, hears, touches, and constantly conveys impressions to the subconscious mind. It is a product of ahankara, "the ego."

The *pañca-jñānendriyas* or "five cognitive organs"

Objective reality is perceived through the five cognitive organs.

17. Ears (*śrotra*) for hearing (*śravaṇendriya*).
18. Skin (*tvak*) for touching (*sparsendriya*).
19. Eyes (*cakṣu*) for seeing (*cakṣurindriya*).
20. Tongue (*rasanā*) for tasting (*rasanendriya*).
21. Nose (*ghrāṇa*) for smelling (*ghrāṇendriya*).

The *pañca-karmendriyas* or "five organs of action"

22. *Mouth* (*vāk*) for speech (*vāg-indriya*).
23. Hands (*pāṇi*) for handling (*hastendriya*).
24. Feet (*pāda*) for locomotion (*pādendriya*).

25. Anus (*pāyu*) for excretion (*pāyvindriya*).
26. Genitals (*upastha*) for reproduction (*upasthendriya*).

The *pañca-tanmātras* or "five subtle elements"

27. *Śabda*, or "sound": It stems from ether, or *ākāśa-mahā-bhūta*.
28. *Sparśa*, or "touch": Its origin is air, or *vāyu-mahā-bhūta*.
29. *Rūpa*, or "form or color": Its origin is fire, or *tejas-mahā-bhūta*.
30. *Rasa*, or "taste": It stems from the element of water, or *jala-mahā-bhūta*.
31. *Gandha*, or "smell": It stems from the element of earth, or *pṛthivī-mahā-bhūta*.

The *panca-tanmātras* are the dwelling places of our senses (hearing, touch, sight, taste, and smell). They are the subtle principles that precede them.

The *pañca-mahā-bhūtas* or "five great elements"

The last five *tattvas* are the most dense and solid. The entire universe of names and forms rests upon them. The five *mahā-bhūtas* are under the control of the three modes of nature. Our physical body is a combination of these *pañca-mahā-bhūtas*, therefore, each one of them has certain characteristics that affect us individually. They are responsible for various functions in the human body and for tissues and fluids. The five great elements are the following:

32. *Ākāśa*, "ether or ethereality": This provides the necessary space for the other four to exist. This element is under the control of sattva. This *tattva* dominates the area from the throat up to the elevated planes of the astral body.
33. *Vāyu*, "air or airiness": This element is under the control of sattva and *rajas*. It dominates the region that extends from the heart up to the throat. *Vāyu-tattva* is activated after *tejas-tattva*.
34. *Tejas*, or "fire": This element is under the control of *rajas* and dominates the region from the navel up to the heart, where digestion happens. Fire receives its energy from *ākāśa*.
35. *Āpas*, "water or liquidity": This element is under the control of *rajas* and tamas. It controls the region from the hips to the navel.
36. *Pṛthivī*, "earth or solidity": This element is under the control of tamas. It is the base and foundation of our dense body. Kundalini rests in solidity and density.

Śuddhādhvā-tattvas or "pure elements"

The first five categories are called *śuddhādhvā-tattvas*, or "pure categories." In order to understand this category, it is necessary to clarify that for Kashmir Shaivism, purity is related to the integrating experience of yoga, which means "union." It is a concept that has been brilliantly explained by Abhinava Gupta in his famous *Tantrāloka*:

mṛta-dehe 'tha dehotthe
yā cāśuddhiḥ prakīrtitā
anyatra neti buddhyantāṁ
aśuddhaṁ saṁvidaś cyutam
saṁvit tadātmyam āpannaṁ
sarvaṁ śuddham ataḥ sthitam

The impurity that the Veda attributes to a corpse and to the bodily secretions is well known and is not found anywhere else. According to the point of view of the faculty of reason, all that is separated from consciousness is impure. On the other hand, all that reaches identity with consciousness is pure.

śrīmad vīrāvalau coktaṁ
śuddhy aśuddhi-nirūpaṇe

Regarding the determination of pure and impure, the *Vīrāvali-tantra* says:

sarveṣāṁ vāhako jīvo
nāsti kiñcid ajīvakam
yat kiñcij jīva-rahitam
aśuddhaṁ tad vijānata

Life (*jīva*) is what animates everything. Nothing exists in the absence of life. All that is deprived of life should be considered impure.

tasmād yat saṁvido nāti
dūre tac cuddhi māvahet
avikalpena bhāvena
munayo 'pi tathā bhavan
loka-saṁrakṣaṇārthaṁ tu
tat tattvaṁ taiḥ pragopitam

> Therefore, all that is near consciousness bestows purity. This is also believed by mystics who are indifferent to the duality between pure and impure. In order to protect the world, they have kept this reality (*tattva*) secret.
>
> (*Tantrāloka*, 4.240b–244a)

Impurity is separation, difference, division, and duality. We purify ourselves to the extent that we perceive our existence as an integral part of the Whole. To perceive ourselves as disconnected from life and existence gives rise to all impurities. Impurity originates in ignorance, while purity originates in wisdom.

The *śuddhādhvā-tattvas* are the fruit of Shaiva sages' efforts to describe consciousness. Shiva stays in the purest subjectivity that transcends the subject-object duality. The *śuddhādhvā-tattvas* include five different categories, which are five aspects of the same consciousness. They are projections of the five main shakti*s* of the Absolute:

1. *Cic-chakti*, or "divine consciousness," projects *śiva-tattva*.
2. *Ānanda-śakti*, or "absolute bliss," projects *śakti-tattva*.
3. *Icchā-śakti*, or "divine will," projects *sadā-śiva-tattva*.

4. *Jñāna-śakti*, or "the divine omniscient power," projects *īśvara-tattva*.
5. *Kriyā-śakti*, or "manifesting power," projects *śuddha-vidyā-tattva*.

The state of *śuddhādhvā* is the divine experience of Shiva. It is a purely subjective perception, which transcends the subject-object duality. The ordinary experience of ego comprises a subject and an object. However, Shiva does not experience the universe as something distant and separate, but as an extension or projection of himself. Any experience of pure subjectivity of Shiva in the state of *śuddhādhvā* can be summarized in the word *aham*, or "I am." *Aham* is the *dhāma*, or "dwelling or abode," of all categories, just as "I am" is the basis and foundation of any individual life. The word *aham* refers to the sole subject that perceives the objective, while *idam*, or "that," is the subject's own projection.

Experience in the ordinary state of ego and perception in the *śuddhādhvā* state are radically different. The former is based upon the dual and relative subject-object platform, while the latter is a subjective experience. The egoic experience resembles a dream-like state that, in spite of being projected by dreamers, is objectivized by them. That is to say, dreamers perceive the world of dreams as separate and different from themselves. On the contrary, when we stand before a mirror, we have no doubt that the reflection is ours. This is like the pure subjective consciousness of *śuddhādhvā*. The reflection is not perceived as a separate object disconnected from the subject. It is a subjective perception because the figure in the reflection is me. Similarly, Shiva projects the universe from himself as *idam*, fully conscious that it is his own projection and, therefore, an integral part of himself. This consciousness of absolute unity is the experience of pure subjectivity that transcends duality, despite the presence of *idam* in each and every one of the *śuddhādhvā* categories.

The 36 *tattvas*

Śuddha Pure	1.	*Śiva-tattva*	
	2.	*Śakti-tattva*	
	3.	*Sadā-śiva*	
	4.	*Īśvara-tattva*	
	5.	*Śuddha-vidyā-tattva*	
	6.	Maya	
Śuddhāśuddha Pure-impure	7.	*Kalā-kañcuka*: limitation of power	*Pañca-kañcukas* Five limiting powers
	8.	*Vidyā-kañcuka*: limitation of knowledge	
	9.	*Rāga-kañcuka*: limitation of desire	
	10.	*Kāla-kañcuka*: limitation of time	
	11.	*Niyati-kañcuka*: limitation of space	
Aśuddha Impure	12.	Purusha	
	13.	Prakriti	
	14.	*Buddhi*: the intellect	*Antaḥ-karaṇa* Internal organ
	15.	*Ahaṅkāra*: the ego	
	16.	*Manas*: the mind	
	17.	*Śravaṇendriya*: hearing	*Pañca-jñānendriyas* Five cognitive organs
	18.	*Sparsendriya*: touching	
	19.	*Cakṣurindriya*: seeing	
	20.	*Rasanendriya*: tasting	
	21.	*Ghrāṇendriya*: smelling	
	22.	*Vāg-indriya*: speech	*Pañca-karmendriyas* Five organs of action
	23.	*Hastendriya*: handling	
	24.	*Pādendriya*: locomotion	
	25.	*Pāyvindriya*: excretion	
	26.	*Upastha*: reproduction	
	27.	*Śabda*: sound	*Pañca-tanmātras* Five subtle elements
	28.	*Sparśa*: touch.	
	29.	*Rūpa*: form or color.	
	30.	*Rasa*: taste.	
	31.	*Gandha*: smell.	
	32.	*Ākāśa*: ether or ethereality.	*Pañca-mahā-bhūtas* Five great elements
	33.	*Vāyu*: air or airiness.	
	34.	*Tejas*: fire.	
	35.	*Āpas*: water or liquidity	
	36.	*Pṛthivī*: earth or solidity	

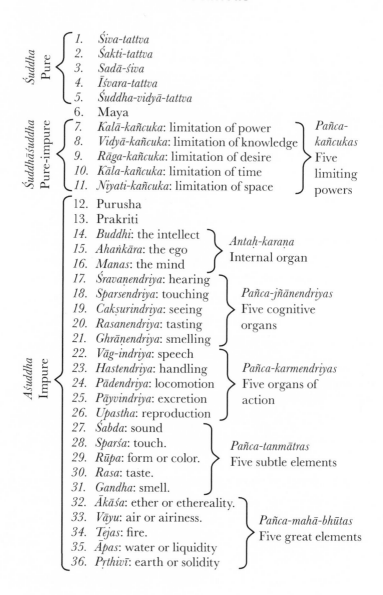

CHAPTER 4

THE DEVI OR "MOTHER OF THE UNIVERSE"

The Absolute is made up of two aspects: the transcendent, Shiva, and the immanent, Shakti. Shiva is motionless and static while Shakti is mobile and dynamic. However, Shakti is no different from Shiva. Shakti is to Shiva what liquidity is to water or what heat is to fire. She is like the sun's glare: although it originates from the sun, it hides the sun from sight.

We are all consciousness in essence. Therefore, the aspects of both Shiva and Shakti reside within each and every one of us. The dynamic aspect (*vimarśa*) lies in the first chakra, whereas the static aspect (*prakāśa*) lies in the seventh chakra.

Prakāśa and *vimarśa* are two basic principles: *prakāśa* is the divine light of consciousness and *vimarśa* is his creative cosmic power, his ability to retain a reflection of himself and of creation.

In Hinduism, *prakāśa* is tied to God the Father, whereas *vimarśa* is tied to the Divine Mother. The Devi's manifested aspect is dynamic, but her transcendental aspect is static, one with the Absolute. *Prakāśa* and *vimarśa*, identified with Shiva and Shakti respectively, constitute a couple at the supreme level.

Krishna refers to this polarity of the Self, also known as Maheśvara and Maheśvarī, with the following words:

pitāham asya jagato
mātā dhātā pitāmahaḥ
vedyaṁ pavitram oṁ-kāra
ṛk sāma yajur eva ca

> I am the father of this world, the mother, the dispenser of the fruits of actions, and the grandfather; the [one] thing to be known, the purifier, the sacred single syllable [Om], and also the *Rig*, the *Sama*, and the *Yajur* Vedas.
>
> (Bhagavad Gita, 9.17)

Kuṇḍalinī-śakti is the divine Universal Mother that resides in every human being. This is confirmed in the *Devī-bhagāvatam*:

tālu-sthā tvaṁ sadādhārā
bindu-sthā bindu-mālinī
mūle tu kuṇḍalī-śaktir
vyāpinī keśa-mūla

> [O Devi] You are *Sadādhārā* on the palate; you are the *Bindu-mālinī-śakti* in the space between the eyes. You are *kuṇḍalinī-śakti* in the *mūlādhāra*

> [chakra], and *Vyāpinī* at the roots of the hair.
>
> (*Devī-bhagāvatam*, 12.5.22)

Kuṇḍalinī-śakti, also called *citi*, is the aspect of the creative cosmic energy that lies dormant in a potential state in every human being. The word *kuṇḍalinī* comes from the Sanskrit root *kuṇḍala* (roll or spiral) and means "the coiled power" because it is coiled at the base of the spinal column, around the *svayam-bhū-liṅga*. Its name is also derived from the term *kuṇḍa*, which means "pit or cavity," indicating that this sacred force lies in the cavity of the sacrum.

Shakti is the divine creative power, and the entire universe resides in her manifestation, in her *līlā*, or "divine play." This is confirmed by Lord Brahmā, who says:

tvayaitat dhāryate viśvam
tvayaitat sṛjyate jagat
tvayaitat pālyate devī
tvam atsyante ca sarvadā

> This whole universe is supported by you, this whole universe is projected by you, this whole universe is protected by you, o Devi, and finally, you reabsorb all this into yourself forever.
>
> (*Devī-māhātmyam*, 1.75)

In the following verse, Krishna mentions two types of nature (prakritis): objective and subjective, or subtle. The first is ordinary nature (*aparā-prakriti*), which is subject to various changes. The second is the higher nature (*parā-prakriti*), which adopts the form of individual beings:

apareyam itas tvanyāṁ
prakṛtiṁ viddhi me parām
jīva-bhūtāṁ mahā-bāho
yayedaṁ dhāryate jagat

> This is my lower nature, Arjuna. Know now my superior nature, which adopts the form of individual beings and thus sustains the universe.
> (Bhagavad Gita, 7.5)

Some incorrectly think that worship of the Universal Mother, or *Viśva-mātā*, is not of Vedic origin. However, it is widely mentioned in the Vedic scriptures. The *Devī Sūkta* and the *Rātri Sūkta* in the Rig Veda's tenth *maṇḍala* are irrefutable proof that she was worshiped in the Vedic period.

We can find *Durgā Gāyatrī* in the *Yājñikā Upaniṣad* within the *Taittirīya* Āraṇyaka:

Oṁ
kātyāyanāya vidmahe
kanya-kumāri dhīmahi
tan no durgi pracodayāt

> We devote our thoughts to Durga, who was born in the hermitage of Kātyāyana. We meditate upon her, who is the princess; may this goddess inspire us to be on the right path.

We find more evidence in the *Durgā-stuti* where Arjuna, counseled by Krishna himself, dedicates the following hymn to Mother Durga and asks her to grant him victory:

sañjaya uvāca
evam ukto 'rjunaḥ saṁkhye
vāsudevena dhīmatā
avatīrya rathāt pārthāḥ
stotram āha kṛtāñjaliaḥ

Sañjaya said:

Following the advice of Vāsudeva, Arjuna, Pṛtha's son, endowed with great intelligence, and after descending from his chariot, recited the following hymn with hands joined together on the eve of battle:

namaste siddha-senāni
ārye mandara-vāsini
kumāri kāli kāpāli
kapile kṛṣṇa-piṅgale

I bow to you, O Kālī, wife of Kāpāla, you who are of a black and tawny color, leader of yogis, who are identical to Brahman, you who dwell in the forest of Mandara, you who are free of decrepitude and decay.

bhadra-kāli namas tubhyaṁ
mahā-kāli namo 'stu te
caṇḍi caṇḍe namas tubhyaṁ
tāriṇi vara-varṇini

I bow to you, Mahā-kālī, wife of the universal destroyer. O proud one, who saves people from danger, bringer of blessings to your devotees, you who are endowed with every auspicious attribute, I bow to you.

kātyāyani mahā-bhāge
karāli vijaye jaye
śikhi-picca-dhvaja-dhare
nānābharaṇa-bhūṣite

O you who sprung from the Kāta race, who deserves the most regardful worship, fierce one, giver of victory, victory itself, you who bares a banner of peacock plumes, you who are adorned with many ornaments.

aṭṭaśūla-praharaṇe
khaḍga-kheṭaka-dhāriṇi
gopendrasyānuje jyeṣṭhe
nanda-gopa-kulodbhave

O, you carry an awful spear, a sword, and shield, you are the younger sister of the head of cowherds, the eldest one, who were born in the race of the cowherd Nanda!

mahiṣā-sṛk-priye nityaṁ
kauśiki pīta-vāsini
aṭṭahāse koka-mukhe
namas te 'stu raṇa-priye

O, you who are always fond of buffalo's blood, who were born in the race of Kuśika, who were dressed in yellow robes, who had devoured demons by taking the face of a wolf, I bow to you who is fond of battle.

ume śākambhari śvete
kṛṣṇe kaiṭabha-nāśini
hiraṇyākṣi virūpākṣi
sudhūmrākṣi namo 'stu te

O Umā, Śākambharī, you who are white in color, o protector, you who has slain the demon Kaiṭabha, you who are yellow-eyed, you who are diverse-eyed and have eyes of the color of smoke, I bow to you.

veda-śruti mahā-puṇye
brahmaṇye jāta-vedasi
jambū-kaṭaka-caityeṣu
nityaṁ saṁnihitālaye

O, you who are the Vedas, the shrutis, and the highest virtue, you are propitious to the Brahmanas engaged in sacrifices, you who have knowledge of the past, who are ever-present in the sacred abodes erected to you in the cities of Jambū-dvīpa, I bow to you.

tvaṁ brahma-vidyā vidyānāṁ
mahā-nidrā ca dehinām
skanda-mātar bhagavati
durge kāntāra-vāsini

O, you are the science of Brahman among sciences, and you are the great sleep of creatures from which there is no waking. Mother of Skanda, you who possess the six (highest) attributes, O Durga (difficult to reach), you dwell in accessible regions.

svāhā-kārāḥ svadhā caiva
kalā kāṣṭhā sarasvatī
sāvitrī veda-mātā ca
tathā vedānta ucyate

You are called Svāhā, Svadhā, Kalā, Kāṣṭā, Sarasvatī, Savitrī, the mother of the Vedas, and the science of Vedanta.

kāntāra-bhaya-durgeṣu
bhaktānāṁ cālayeṣu ca
nityaṁ vasasi pātāle
yuddhe jayasi dānavān

In inaccessible regions where there is fear, in places of difficulty, in the abodes of your worshippers, and in the nether regions (*Pātāla*), you always dwell. You conquer demons in battle.

tvaṁ jambhanī mohinī ca
māyā hrīḥ śrīs tathaiva ca
sandhyā prabhāvatī caiva
sāvitrī jananī tathā

You are unconsciousness, sleep, illusion, modesty, and the beauty [of all creatures]. You are the twilight, day, Savitrī, and the mother.

tuṣṭiḥ puṣṭir dhṛtir dīptiś
candrāditya-vivardhinī
bhūtir bhūti-matāṁ saṅkhye
vīkṣyase siddha-cāraṇaiḥ

You are contentment, growth, and light. It is you who supports the sun and the moon and makes them shine. You are the prosperity of those who are prosperous. The *siddhas* (the perfected ones) and the *cāraṇas* (sadhus who wander from one place to another) behold you in contemplation.

stutāsi tvaṁ mahā-devi
viśuddhenāntar-ātmanā
jayo bhavatu me nityaṁ
tvat-prasādād raṇe raṇe

With my inner soul cleansed, I praise you. O great goddess, let victory always be with me through your grace on the battlefield.

(*Mahā-bhārata*, 6.23.3-16)

The *Devī Sūktam* refers to the Devi in the following way:

yā devī sarva bhūteṣu
viṣṇu māyeti śabditā
namas tasyai namas tasyai
namas tasyai namo namaḥ

To the divine goddess of all existence, who is addressed as the perceivable form of the consciousness that pervades everything, we bow to her, we bow to her, we bow to her, continually we bow, we bow.

yā devī sarva bhūteṣu
śakti rūpeṇa saṁsthitā
namas tasyai namas tasyai
namas tasyai namo namaḥ

To the divine goddess who resides in all existence in the form of energy, we bow to her, we bow to her, we bow to her, continually we bow, we bow.

yā devī sarva bhūteṣu
mātṛ rūpeṇa saṁsthitā
namas tasyai namas tasyai
namas tasyai namo namaḥ

To the divine goddess who resides in all existence in the form of Mother, we bow to her, we bow to her, we bow to her, continually we bow, we bow.
(*Devī Sūktam*, 6, 12, 25)

Many of the different aspects of the Devi, such as Durga or Kali, present her as a valiant, armed warrior engaged in combat with various demons. In the *Durgā-sapta-śati*, the devas praise her after she kills the demon Mahiṣāsura:

kenopamā bhavatu the 'sya parākramasya

What can stand in comparison to your courage?
(*Durgā-sapta-śati*, 4.22)

Expressions of our selfishness can be compared with demons. The battles of the Divine Mother symbolize the confrontations between kundalini and our inner demons. Different aspects of the Devi fight against them as she elevates and pierces our energy centers. *Kuṇḍalinī-śakti* does not belong to the material realm and, therefore, cannot be compared to any type of physical energy.

It is impossible to divide a person from his or her energy, and any human being devoid of power is nothing more than a corpse. Similarly, the Lord and his Shakti are inseparable. There is no real difference between worshipping God or the Divine Mother of the Universe. Moreover, shakta devotees consider devotion to her to be superior to the static paternal aspect, for Shiva is powerless without his Shakti; they see the authentic holy presence of the Lord and his infinite power in the Devi. As noted by *Śaṅkarācārya*:

śivaḥ śaktyā yukto yadi
bhavati śaktaḥ prabhavitum
na ced evaṁ devo na khalu
kuśalaḥ spanditum api

> If Shiva is united with Shakti, he becomes capable of projecting this universe; if not, he is not even capable of moving his limbs.
>
> (*Saundarya-laharī*, 1)

However, the devotee's relationship with the Absolute as a mother is quite different than as father. Maternal love is unconditional and free from judgment. The mother is ready to sacrifice everything for the well-being of her children, thus the devotee experiences unlimited acceptance. There is no sin so severe that the compassion of the Divine Mother cannot forgive. Śaṅkarācārya himself writes in this hymn:

jagad-amba vicitram-atra kim
paripūrṇa karuṇāsti cen-mayi
aparādha-paramparāvṛtam na
hi māta samupekṣate sutam

> Mother of the worlds! If your full grace is on me, what is strange about it? Even if the son has

> committed a series of mistakes, the mother does not neglect him.
>
> (*Devy-aparādha-kṣamāpaṇa Stotram*, 11)

In reference to *kuṇḍalinī-śakti*, the sage Kṣemarāja says:

citiḥ sva-tantrā viśva-siddhi-hetuḥ

> Of its own will, the universal, independent consciousness is the cause of the manifestation, maintenance, and dissolution of the universe.
>
> (*Pratyabhijñā-hṛdayam*, 1)

Transcendental consciousness does not create universes on its own, but through Shakti, which is its creative power. *Kuṇḍalinī-śakti* is a mysterious power that is *bhedābheda*, or "different and non-different." It is the universal situated in the individual, the formless that lies at the base of the form.

People who drink tap water in their own homes are in fact drinking from a shared reservoir. Similarly, the process of awakening kundalini takes place in each of us but connects us to our common source. We are like waves, and this awakening reveals to us our shared origin, which is the ocean.

The scriptures describe how *kuṇḍalinī-śakti* sleeps in the first chakra:

paścimābhimukhīḥ yonir
guda-meḍhrāntarālagā

tatra kandaṁ samākhyātaṁ
tatrāste kuṇḍalī sadā

saṁveṣṭya sakalāṁ nāḍīḥ
sārddha-tri-kuṭilākṛtiḥ
mukhe niveśya sā pucchaṁ
suṣumṇā-vivare sthitā

The yoni is in this space, facing toward the back. This space is called the root, where the goddess Kundalini dwells. It surrounds all the *nāḍīs*, and has three and a half coils. Holding its tail in its own mouth, it lies in the hole of *suṣumṇā*.

suptā nāgopamā hy eṣā
sphurantī prabhayā svayā
ahivat sandhi-saṁsthānā
vāg-devī bīja-sañjñikā

It sleeps there like a serpent and is luminous by its own light. Like a serpent, it lives between the joints; it is the goddess of speech and is called the seed (*bīja*).

jñeyā śaktir iyaṁ viṣṇor
nirjharā svarṇa-bhāsvarā
sattvaṁ rajas tamaś ceti
guṇa-traya-prasūtikā

> Full of energy and like burning gold, know this Kundalini to be Vishnu's power (shakti). It is the mother of the three qualities: sattva, *rajas*, and tamas.

Kundalini is coiled in three and a half coils that symbolize its three different manifestations:

1. *Prāṇa-kuṇḍalinī* is its vital energy aspect, which is expressed most notably on the astral and physical planes. When it is awakened, it manifests as an increase in vitality.
2. *Cit-kuṇḍalinī* is the aspect that sustains our feelings, emotions, and in general, our psychological state. When it awakens, our cognitive aptitudes expand.
3. *Parā-kuṇḍalinī* is the universal or cosmic aspect that lies in the first energy center. When it awakens, our authentic nature manifests.

Specifically, kundalini lies at the base of the spine in *mūlādhāra-cakra*. When she is awakened, she uncoils and rises in a spiral movement, producing a hissing sound like a snake. For this reason, enlightened masters and scriptures generally refer to her allegorically as a sleeping serpent or "the serpentine power." She passes through each one of the energy centers on her ascent, which culminates in *sahasrāra-cakra* at the crown of the head, where Shiva and Shakti unite.

bhitvā liṅga-trayaṁ tat parama-rasa-śive
sūkṣma-dhāmni pradīpe
sā devī śuddha-sattvā taḍid iva vilasat-tantu-rūpa-svarūpā
brahmākhyāyāḥ sirāyāḥ sakala-sarasijaṁ prāpya dedīpyate tan
mokṣākhyānanda-rūpaṁ ghaṭayati sahasā sūkṣma tāla-kṣaṇena

> The Devi, who is *śuddha-sattva* (pure goodness), pierces the three *liṅgas*, and, having reached all the lotuses that are known as the *brahma-nāḍī*, shines therein in the fullness of her luster. Thereafter, in her subtle state, as lustrous as lightning and as fine as the lotus fiber, she goes to the gleaming flame like Shiva, the supreme bliss, and suddenly produces the bliss of liberation.
> (*Ṣaṭ-cakra-nirūpaṇa* by Swami Pūrṇānanda, 51)

The awakening of kundalini is felt in the human being as a deep desire to return home, to our source, to God. This divine longing marks the beginning of a process of involution in which multiplicity is reabsorbed into the original unity.

Chapter 5

Awakening, Ascent, and Descent of *Kuṇḍalinī-Śakti*

Awakening of *kuṇḍalinī-śakti*

Kundalini yoga is an organized system intended to create the right conditions for awakening kundalini, which includes the following stages:

1. Harmonizing *iḍā-nāḍī* and *piṅgalā-nāḍī*.
2. Opening the chakras.
3. Awakening *suṣumṇā-nāḍī*.
4. Awakening *kuṇḍalinī-śakti*.

The order of these stages is crucial because the premature awakening of kundalini can cause harm. If we awaken kundalini while the chakras are still closed, it can become stuck for years. Kundalini energy can stay repressed in the first chakra if it is awakened before *suṣumṇā-nāḍī*. This leads to a series of physical and psychological problems.

1. Harmonizing *iḍā-nāḍī* and *piṅgalā-nāḍī*

Iḍā and *piṅgalā nāḍīs* are located alongside *suṣumṇā*. They are a manifestation at the individual level of the same polarity that maintains the universe at the cosmic level. *Iḍā* is refreshing and pale, while *piṅgalā* creates heat, is red in color, and is related to digestion. *Iḍā* is called *candra-nāḍī* because it channels negative feminine or lunar energy, while *piṅgalā* is called *sūrya-nāḍī* because it channels positive, masculine, or solar energy. Both prana channels meet at *suṣumṇā* in the first chakra (*mūlādhāra-cakra*). The activity of these *nāḍīs* is cyclical, but our negative habits and behaviors typical of modern society have disturbed their natural harmony and balance. However, the *nāḍīs* can be purified and their functioning can be harmonized through a sadhana that includes asanas, *prāṇāyāma*, and relaxation. Only when the balance between these two *nāḍīs* is reestablished can *suṣumṇā* be awakened.

2. Opening of the chakras

The opening of the chakras can be felt in our psychology, personality, and attitudes. In most human beings, the only open chakra is the first one, which is the highest in the animal kingdom. Thus, people mostly work to satisfy their basic and essential necessities of sleeping, eating, defending themselves, and reproducing. Kundalini yoga cannot be learned from a book or with an ordinary teacher. To advance along this path, the guidance of a realized guru is required because not every student is born at the same level of evolution. Due to spiritual efforts in past lives, some people's lower centers have already been opened and they do not need to work on these chakras. Some people are born with open chakras without even knowing it. They usually stand out in society and become important leaders. Therefore, it is essential that a spiritual master tells us, at the least, our current level of progress. The chakras can be opened through specific *prāṇāyāmas* or by repeating the appropriate mantras.

3. Awakening *suṣumṇā-nāḍī*

The awakening of the main *nāḍī* is an extremely important step in the process of kundalini yoga. If *suṣumṇā* has not awakened, it is not very helpful to awaken the chakras or even kundalini. When the serpentine power ascends, the energy that does not rise through *suṣumṇā* simply dissipates. Thus, at times, we may see practitioners that perceive a great amount of energy, and their body may writhe with that power, yet they return to their same weaknesses once the experience is over. Although the energy rises, their personalities and lives remain the same because kundalini cannot rise through the main *nāḍī* while it remains closed. Only when *suṣumṇā* awakens can kundalini freely ascend and be united with Shiva. *Suṣumṇā* can be awakened through asanas and *prāṇāyāma*, as well as by certain *kriyā-yoga* techniques. It is not advisable to attempt this without the expert guidance of an enlightened spiritual master.

4. Awakening *kuṇḍalinī-śakti*

The *Devī-gītā* refers to the awakening of *kuṇḍalinī-śakti* in the following way:

ādau pūraka-yogenāpy
ādhāre yojayen manaḥ
guda-meḍhrāntare śaktis
tām ākuñcya prabodhayet

First, inhaling in the yoga way, allow your attention to be focused on *mūlādhāra*. Between the anus and the genitals, lies [kundalini] shakti. With that key, [kundalini] should be awakened.
(*Devī-gītā* from the *Devī-bhāgavatam*, 7.35.48)

The *Yoga-kuṇḍalinī Upaniṣad* says:

kuṇḍaly eva bhavec chakti
stāṁ tu saṁcālayed budha
svasthānād ābhruvor madhyaṁ
śakti-cālanam ucyate

The shakti (mentioned above) is indeed kundalini. A wise man should take it up from its place (that is, upward from the navel) to the middle of the eyebrows. This is called *śakti-cālana*.
(*Yoga-kuṇḍalinī Upaniṣad*, 1.7)

tat sādhane dvayaṁ mukhyaṁ
sarasvaty āstu cālanam
prāṇa-rodham athābhyāsād
ṛjvī kuṇḍalinī bhavet

> In this practice, two things are necessary, *sarasvatī-cālana* (lifting of the *sarasvatī-nāḍī*) and the restraint of prana (breath). Then, through practice, kundalini (which is spiral) becomes straightened.
>
> (*Yoga-kuṇḍaliṇī Upaniṣad*, 1.8)

Spiritual evolution is not the result of a practice, technique, method, or sadhana. However, systematic practice recommended by the guru should not be neglected, because through it we can create the appropriate situation for something Divine to happen.

There are various ways in which the awakening of *kuṇḍalinī-śakti* can occur. The first is a natural awakening that occurs in people who have practiced strict sadhana in past lives. It should be remembered that many souls reincarnate repeatedly both on our planet as well as on others. Those who experience a spontaneous awakening should not be alarmed, but should approach a genuine guru who can offer them information about this phenomenon.

It is possible to awaken the divine fire through mantras. In its process of solidification, *nāda* (sound), which is the first emanation of the shakti, transforms into *bindu* (point). From *bindu* comes *bīja* (seed), which is the original name and vibration of any object. In this way, mantras are a sound structure that contains the form of *nāda*, and thus the creative power of Brahman. Vedic texts in Sanskrit emanate from the very seed of language (*bīja*). Through the practice of the mantra, it is possible to purify the *nāḍīs*, the mind, the physical body, and the astral body. This purification presents optimal conditions for the awakening of the serpentine power. In addition, repeating mantras (*japa*) directly affects the chakras and awakes kundalini from her sleep in *mūlādhāra-cakra*.

Another way of awakening the powerful force of the Mother within us is through tapasya, or "austerities." In modern society, most people live to satisfy sensual whims. From tea or coffee to drugs, television, hamburgers, and sex, everyone continually strives to please the senses. This wandering after pleasure creates mental dissipation and a loss of energy and vitality. Austerity involves allowing ourselves only what is really necessary to live, which brings inner tranquility and purifies the *nāḍīs*. The energy of tapasya disturbs the slumber of kundalini.

Associating with an enlightened master is one of the simplest ways to awaken the serpentine power. If the guru is a genuine jivanmukta (liberated in life), he or she will have the ability to channel spiritual power and transmit it to sincere aspirants who are fully open. This is called *śakti-pāta*. The master can awaken *kuṇḍalinī-śakti* through a word, a glance, physical contact, or simply by proximity and association.

The simplest practice to awaken kundalini begins with focusing the attention on *mūlādhāra-cakra*, which makes prana accumulate in this center. The pressure and heat generated by this concentration of vital energy are the agents that will awaken the serpentine power. Immediately after being awakened, kundalini uncoils from the *svayam-bhū-liṅga* and penetrates the *suṣumṇā-nāḍī* that had been previously obstructed by kundalini itself. As is stated in the *Yoga-cūḍāmaṇi Upaniṣad*:

brahma-dvāra-mukhaṁ nityaṁ
mukhenācchāya tiṣṭhati
yena dvāreṇa gantavyaṁ
brahma-dvāram anāmayam

> With her mouth, [Kundalini] is eternally closing the passage to the door of Brahman (the consciousness that permeates everything). [Passing] through that passageway, one is liberated from suffering by reaching the door of Brahman.
> (*Yoga-cūḍāmaṇi Upaniṣad*, 37)

When kundalini begins to awaken, there is mild tingling throughout the body, which expands from the feet upward. It should be noted that awaking kundalini is very different from elevating it. The latter is more difficult because it depends not only on practicing certain techniques, but on our state of purity. While many can awaken the serpentine power, only few manage to elevate it, because this requires intense practice, perseverance, patience, purity, and a deep transformation.

The ascent of *kuṇḍalinī-śakti*

Just as mercury rises in a thermometer until reaching body temperature, the elevation of *kuṇḍalinī-śakti* indicates our spiritual level. As my beloved *sannyāsa-guru*, His Holiness

Swami Jyotirmayānanda, affirms:

> The *kuṇḍalinī-śakti* works as a barometer indicating the spiritual progress and the level of consciousness in human beings. So, the more *kuṇḍalinī-śakti* ascends through *suṣumṇā*, the more integrated the personality becomes.
>
> (*Integral Yoga*, chapter 6)

The vertical ascension of the serpentine power reflects the development and evolution at the level of consciousness. Kundalini can ascend only after having transcended the desire for gratification of the senses. It only rises in those with pure hearts who are free from attachments and passions.

The *Devī-gītā* refers to the ascension of kundalini in the following way:

liṅga-bheda-krameṇaiva
bindu-cakram ca prāpayet
śambhunā tām parām śaktim-
ekī-bhūtām vicintayet

> It proceeds to pierce the mystical emblems in order until reaching *bindu-cakra*. There the supreme Shakti should be visualized in union with *Śambhu* (Shiva) as a single being.
>
> (*Devī-gītā* from the *Devī-bhāgavatam*, 7.35.49)

tatrotthitāmṛtam yat tu
druta-lākṣā-rasopamam
pāyayitvā tu tāṁ śaktiṁ
māyākhyāṁ yoga-siddhidām

In this union, the nectar of immortality is produced, from which flows a red liquid. One who manages to drink the nectar of shakti, called maya, attains perfect union.

(*Devī-gītā* from the *Devī-bhāgavatam*, 7.35.50)

The elevation of *kuṇḍalinī-śakti* is described in some scriptures as *liṅga-bheda*, or "the piercing of the mystical emblems," and in others as *ṣaṭ-cakra-bheda*, or "the piercing of the six chakras." *Kuṇḍalinī-śakti* rises to *sahasrāra-cakra* through *brahma-nāḍī*, which is located within *suṣumṇā-nāḍī*. On its way, it penetrates and pierces each chakra, embraces their lingas (mystical emblems) and unites with the devas of each chakra, absorbing their energies. During this process of involution, the serpentine power absorbs all thirty-six *tattvas*, or "categories of existence," both the gross ones and the subtle ones. As she arrives at each chakra, it dissolves the corresponding *tattvas*: *karmendriyas* (organs of action), *jñānendriyas* (cognitive organs), *mahā-bhūtas* (great elements), and *tan-mātras* (subtle elements).

It should be noted that Kashmir Shaivism has a peculiar way of assigning the five organs of action (*pañca-karmendriyas*) to each chakra. It classifies them by their subtlety and assigns them to the first five centers, from the grossest (*mūlādhāra*) to the most subtle (*viśuddha*).

The elevation process begins in *mūlādhāra-cakra* with the dissolution of the following:

1. *Mahā-bhūta*: *Pṛthivī*, or "earth."
2. *Karmendriya*: *Pāda*, or "foot."
3. *Jñānendriya*: *Ghrāṇa*, or "nose."
4. *Tan-mātra*: *Gandha*, or "smell."

The powerful current of the serpentine fire takes smell to *svādhiṣṭhāna-cakra* and proceeds to dissolve it with the following:

1. *Mahā-bhūta*: *Āpas*, or "water."
2. *Karmendriya*: *Pāṇi*, or "hands."
3. *Jñānendriya*: *Rasanā*, or "tongue."
4. *Tan-mātra*: *Rasa*, or "taste."

Taste is pulled into *maṇipūra-cakra* where it is dissolved with these:

1. *Mahā-bhūta*: *Tejas*, or "fire."
2. *Karmendriya*: *Pāyu*, or "anus."
3. *Jñānendriya*: *Cakṣu*, or "eyes."
4. *Tan-mātra*: *Rūpa*, or "shape or color."

Shape is brought to *anāhata-cakra* where it is dissolved with these:

1. *Mahā-bhūta*: *Vāyu*, or "air."
2. *Karmendriya*: *Upastha*, or "genitals."
3. *Jñānendriya*: *Tvak*, or "skin."
4. *Tan-mātra*: *Sparśa*, or "touch."

Touch is brought to *viśuddha-cakra* and there it is dissolved with:

1. *Mahā-bhūta*: *Ākāśa*, or "ether."
2. *Karmendriya*: *Vāk*, or "mouth."
3. *Jñānendriya*: *Śrotra*, or "ears."
4. *Tan-mātra*: *Śabda*, or "sound."

Sound is taken to *ājnā-cakra* and then is dissolved together with the mind (*manas*) in the universal intelligence (*mahat*). In turn, *mahat* is dissolved into *sūkṣma-prakṛti* (subtle nature), which is united with *para-bindu* (supreme point) in *sahasrāra-cakra*.

The gradual dissolution of the letters means the dissolution of the petals that sustain them, hence, the dismantling of the chakras. The first five chakras have *bījas*, consisting of the subtle seeds of the elements that they represent. During the elevation, each element emanates and is dissolved into its corresponding *bīja*.

1. When kundalini is in *mūlādhāra-cakra*, its element earth emanates and dissolves in its *bīja Laṁ*.
2. When kundalini reaches *svādhiṣṭhāna-cakra*, its element water emanates and dissolves in its *bīja Vaṁ*. Then, *Laṁ* is dissolved in *Vaṁ*.
3. When kundalini reaches *maṇipūra-cakra*, its element fire emanates and dissolves in its *bīja Raṁ*. Then, *Vaṁ* is dissolved in *Raṁ*.
4. When kundalini reaches *anāhata-cakra*, its element air emanates and dissolves in its *bīja Yaṁ*. Then, *Raṁ* is dissolved in *Yaṁ*.
5. When kundalini reaches *viśuddha-cakra*, its element ether emanates and dissolves in its *bīja Haṁ*. Then, *Yaṁ* dissolves in *Haṁ*.

As the serpentine power rises, significant changes in the character and personality of the *sādhaka* unfold, which are a result of this involutionary process of kundalini. Along with the dissolution of the earth element in the water, all influence of the first center on the mind ceases. From this moment, the mind will be influenced by the energies that interact in *svādhiṣṭhāna-cakra*. When kundalini absorbs the energetic content of the second center and reaches *maṇipūra*, *svādhiṣṭhāna* will no longer influence the mind nor the personality. At this level, *maṇipūra-cakra* will influence the mind. Likewise, when kundalini reaches the heart center and absorbs the energies of *maṇipūra*, *anāhata-cakra* will influence the mind. As it continues her ascent, kundalini will absorb the energy of the fourth center, allowing the energies of *viśuddha* to influence the mind. When it reaches the divine fire in the fifth center and consumes its energies, *ājnā-cakra* will influence the mind and personality. Finally, when *kuṇḍalinī-śakti* reaches *sahasrāra-cakra*, it leaves and merges with Shiva.

This path is also called *laya-yoga*, because the yogi experiences at an individual level the same dissolution (*laya*) that takes place in the universe at a macrocosmic scale. In this involutionary process called *laya-krama*, *sādhakas* realize that their true nature completely transcends this dissolution.

It should be noted that this yoga path does not have a monopoly on the elevation of the serpentine power, as stated in the *Haṭha-yoga-pradīpikā*:

sa-śaila-vana-dhātrīṇāṁ
yathādhāro 'hi-nāyakaḥ
sarveṣāṁ yoga-tantrāṇāṁ
tathādhāro hi kuṇḍalī

suptā guru-prasādena
yadā jāgarti kuṇḍalī
tadā sarvāṇi padmāni
bhidyante granthayo 'pi ca

Just as the serpent Śeṣa-nāga sustains the earth, mountains, and forests, kundalini is the foundation of all yoga practices. It is by the grace of the guru that the sleeping kundalini awakens. Then all the lotuses [in the six chakras] and knots (*granthis*) open.

(*Haṭha-yoga-pradīpikā*, 3.1-2)

It is a misconception that the serpent power elevates and reaches *sahasrāra-cakra* only in followers of kundalini yoga. Every *sādhaka* who realizes pure consciousness through any involutive path experiences the same phenomenon. It is like a doctor, who understands the auditory system perfectly, and an illiterate person, who has no such knowledge. Both have the same ability to hear. It is not theoretical or intellectual knowledge that awakens chakras, but purity.

Before *kuṇḍalinī-śakti* reaches the third chakra, experiences cannot be treated as authentic progress. Kundalini can climb many times to the *svādhiśṭhāna* and then descend again. Only after reaching the third center, but not before, can we be sure that the divine fire will not descend again.

The elevation of the serpentine power is not only an ascension of energy, but is also our own ascension. That is, when Shakti unites with Shiva, it is our personal aspect that fuses with the universal reality. *Amṛta*, or "the nectar of immortality," emanates from this fusion of the feminine and the masculine. Drinking this nectar will not prevent us from dying but it will awaken us to the reality that death does not exist.

Just as our vision becomes clearer at dawn, as the sun rises above the horizon, our perception gradually sharpens with the ascent of *kuṇḍalinī-śakti*. As the serpentine power rises, we can see beyond the superficial and progressively perceive greater integration. On its way to the most elevated and subtle centers, kundalini purifies various bodies and sheaths, revealing hidden spaces and dimensions to us, until the individual is dissolved in the Whole.

As the serpentine power pierces and penetrates each chakra, one has access to dimensions that usually remain hidden behind our excessive attachment to dual reality. As the divine fire reaches each chakra, we can access a new, fresh vision of life. The ascent that occurs in this process resembles climbing up the stairs of a skyscraper: the view improves as we go up.

In most human beings, the serpentine power lies dormant or moves only in the lower chakras. Their consciousness is materialistic and mundane and their lives are dominated by diverse sensory pleasures. There is a big difference between an open chakra and awakened one. Chakras can be open but not necessarily awakened. A chakra is open when it is active and works normally; its incoming and outgoing energy maintain proper levels, and it rotates clockwise. If it rotates counterclockwise, it is obstructed, blocked, or closed. An energy center is awakened only when *kuṇḍalinī-śakti* has pierced it and absorbed its *prāṇa-śakti* and the energy of its deva.

As long as kundalini is below the fifth center, we can still speak and communicate with our fellow human beings. When it ascends beyond the fifth center, the experience transcends verbalization and is therefore indescribable. In the sixth center, Bhagavān awaits, which is divinity with personal qualities. The fusion (*ekī-bhūta*) of Shiva and Shakti does not occur until the divine power of the serpent reaches the seventh center (*sahasrāra-cakra*). Only then is one blessed with a state of supra-consciousness in which the ego is transcended and universal love is realized. Death to the relative reality of names and forms is experienced, along with the complete evaporation of the difference between subject and object. To reach the crown center means completely losing a separate personality and fusing with the infinite ocean of *sac-cid-ānanda*, or "absolute existence, wisdom, and bliss."

Kundalini is compared to a serpent, a creature that does not usually attack without reason. However, it can be very dangerous if disturbed while resting. Similarly, it is not recommended to try to awaken kundalini without proper guidance and without being properly prepared. Premature attempts can cause irreparable physical and mental harm. This is the reason that the sadhana recommended by an expert master plays such an important role on this path.

The process that kundalini yoga aspires to is a shift from diversity toward the one source. Progress in this process will determine the level of consciousness of the individual. Transformation at the level of consciousness is an expansion of the contracted personality, which is the ego.

From the relative or dualistic point of view, we perceive the dichotomy of life: spirit and nature, subject and object, or Brahman and Shakti. The elevation of kundalini leads to an experience of all polarity disappearing. The one absolute nature that lies beyond multiplicity emerges.

The ascension of the divine energy leads us to a life of bliss in which we cease to perceive ourselves as something or someone separate from existence. An elevation of human nature takes place, in pursuit of a reunion and fusion with the one spirit. The awakening of kundalini is our own awakening; it is opening our eyes to reality.

The descent of *kuṇḍalinī-śakti*

In regards to the descent of kundalini, we read the following in the *Devī-gītā*:

ṣaṭ-cakra-devatās tatra
santarpyāmṛta-dhārayā
ānayet tena mārgeṇa
mūlādhāram tataḥ sudhīḥ

> Satisfying the presiding deities of the six centers by offering them the descending stream of nectar, a wise person will then lead [kundalini] back along the same path to the supporting root center [*mūlādhāra*]. For the pleasure of the gods residing in the six chakras, carry back that nectar to each on the same path until reaching *mūlādhāra*.
>
> (*Devī-gītā* from the *Devī-bhāgavatam*, 7.35.51)

When yogis drink from this nectar, they experience the ecstasy of infinite bliss. As it is stated in the *Śāradā-tilaka Tantra*:

udyantīṁ samupāsmahe nava-java-sindūra sandhyāruṇām
sāndrānanda sudhā-mayīṁ para-śivaṁ prāptāṁ parāṁ devatām

gamanāgamaneṣu lāṅghikī sā tanuyād-yoga-phalāni kuṇḍalī
muditā-kula kāma-dhenur eṣā bhajatāṁ kāṅkṣita kalpa-vallarī

> We meditate upon the divine goddess (Parā-devatā), who is ready to move, who is very quick, whose tilak is red like the dawn, who is filled with an excess of bliss because of the nectar (*suddhā*), and who has reached Lord Para-śiva.
>
> May kundalini, which is swift in her movements (transportations), which if pleased is [like] Kāma-dhenu (a mythical heavenly cow that bestows all wishes) and which is [like] *kalpa-vṛkṣa (*the wish-fulfilling tree) to those who approach it, offer [us]

all the fruits of yoga.

(*Śāradā-tilaka Tantra*, 25.67–68)

mūle bhāle hṛdi ca vilasad varṇa-rūpā savitrī
pīnottuṅga-stana-bharaṇa-man-madhya-deśā maheśī
cakre cakre galita-sudhayā sikta-gātrā prakāmaṁ
dadyādādyā śriyam avikalāṁ vāñmayī devatā vaḥ

Thoroughly moistened with oozing nectar as she passes through the chakras, may the goddess Sarasvatī (Savitrī), the great lady, the goddess in the form of words, who is in the shape of letters that shine in the base, on the forehead, and in the heart, who is a producer [of knowledge], whose middle is straining from the heaviness of a fleshy and lofty bosom, who is profusely moist from the dripping of heavenly nectar from each chakra, now bestow you with unimpaired prosperity.

(*Śāradā-tilaka Tantra*, 25.72)

In general, when kundalini is mentioned, emphasis is placed on its elevation from the first center to the seventh. However, its descent is no less important. There are those who think that after reaching the higher centers, kundalini will not descend again. One who does not understand the descent of the serpentine fire will not be able to understand an enlightened being acting in the mundane and earthly.

After the ascent of kundalini, it merges with Shiva, producing the fusion of Purusha and prakriti that eradicates the experience of duality. After the fusion of Shiva and Shakti, they remain united in the *bindu*, which later divides into two again, allowing the kundalini to descend, traveling the same path on which she ascended. The ascent is only of kundalini, from the first center toward the seventh. However, the descent is with both kundalini and Shiva. The Śāradā-tilaka *Tantra* speaks about descent of the divine fire in this way:

mūlon nidra bhujaṅga-rāja
mahiṣīṁ yāntīṁ suṣumṇāntaraṁ
bhitvādhāra samūham āsu
vilasat saudāminī sannibhām
vyomāmbhoja gatendu-maṇḍala
galad divyāmṛtaugha-plutaṁ
sambhāvya sva-gṛhaṁ gatāṁ
punar imāṁ sañcintayet kuṇḍalīm

> When Kundalini awakens and moves from the *mūlādhāra* upward like a flash of lightning along the channel of *suṣumṇā*, she pierces the six chakras as she goes upward. When she reaches *sahasrāra*, she unites with her Lord, Para-śiva. Then she returns to her home in *mūlādhāra*.
>
> (*Śāradā-tilaka Tantra*, 25.64)

Those who live life in an extroverted way, striving for money, power, sex, enjoyment, and pleasures, are considered to be materialists, whereas those who live a life of introspection, peace, and tranquility are considered to be spiritual. Materialists only move in the realm of the first three centers, which belong to the external. As long as only the first three chakras are open, we will continue to manifest a superficial personality because these three chakras function only for survival.

A person considered to be spiritual aspires to the three upper chakras, which are introspective and subjective. Their direction is toward the depths of our interior. The conflict between materialism and spirituality fractures human beings. We wish to be more spiritual, which leads us to repress or abandon materialism. We believe that the repression of the lower chakras will lead us to be saints and move only within the three upper centers. However, in enlightened beings, all the chakras function again, those considered to be low or elevated. After its union with Shiva, the serpentine power will reconstruct the entire system of chakras. This time Shakti does not descend alone, but with Shiva. Then, the chakras will function in perfect harmony and balance between spirit and matter. True religious beings are at once introverted and extroverted, materialist and spiritual, because they have realized the totality and are thus free of conflicts.

Before the ascension of the serpentine power, the ordinary mind exercises its dominion over the individuals. After its descent, transcendental consciousness will express itself through us. When kundalini elevates and fuses with Shiva, personality disappears. The return of kundalini and Shiva marks the blossoming of individuality.

A personality is a creation of society, assembled from various external elements. It is not an organic unity;

it is not integral. It is put together the same way as a clock, a radio, a car or any other mechanical device. The personality is a collection of screws with a great diversity of heads. On the other hand, individuality is a flower that stems from the depths of existence. Personality is an experience of separation, of disconnection from what surrounds us, while individuality brings with it the experience of deep communion with everyone and everything. After the descent of kundalini, one lives in a completely different state of consciousness. We live in the world without belonging to it.

Section II
The chakras: their functions and characteristics

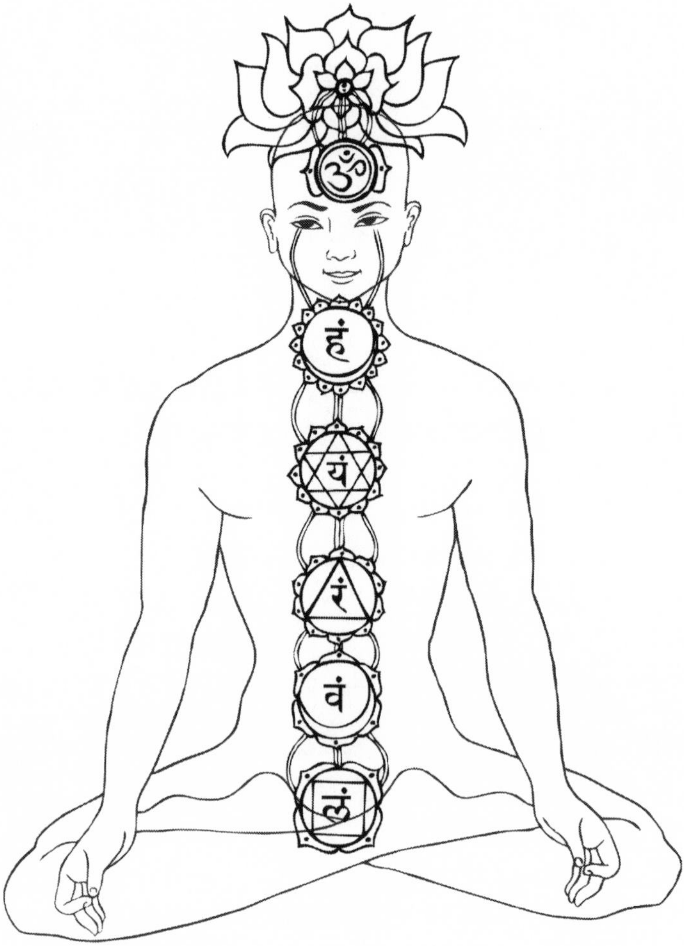

The seven chakras and their main *nāḍīs*

First Chakra

Mūlādhāra-cakra or "Root Chakra"

The *Śiva Saṁhitā* locates the first chakra in this verse:

gudād dvay-aṅgulataś cordhvaṁ
meḍhraikāṅgulatas tvadhaḥ
evaṁ cāsti samaṁ kandaṁ
samantāc catur-aṅgulam

There is a space like a bulbous root, which is four fingers wide. It is located two fingers above the rectum and two fingers below the genitals.
(*Śiva Saṁhitā*, 5.56)

paścimābhimukhīḥ yonir guda-meḍhrāntarālagā
tatra kandaṁ samākhyātaṁ tatrāste kuṇḍalī sadā
saṁveṣṭya sakalāṁ nāḍīḥ sārddha-tri-kuṭilākṛtiḥ
mukhe niveśya sā pucchaṁ suṣumṇā-vivare sthitā

The yoni is located in this space. It faces toward the back. It is called the root, where the goddess

> Kundalini dwells. It surrounds all the *nāḍīs*, has three and a half coils, and rests in the hole of *suṣumṇā*, holding its tail in its own mouth.
>
> (*Śiva Saṁhitā*, 5.57)

The first energy center in human beings is the last one in the animal kingdom. In *mūlādhāra-cakra*, the animal state culminates and the human one begins. This is where *kuṇḍalinī-śakti*, the divine potential of the individual, lies coiled.

suptā nāgopamā hy eṣā
sphurantī prabhayā svayā
ahivat sandhi-saṁsthānā
vāg-devī bīja-sañjñikā

> It sleeps there like a serpent and is luminous with its own light. Like a serpent, it lives between the joints. It is the goddess of speech and is called the seed (*bīja*).
>
> (*Śiva Saṁhitā*, 5.58)

Therefore, it is no wonder that at first, practice focuses mainly on this center. *Mūlādhāra-cakra* is associated with our corporeal survival and our relationship with physical nature. It is closely tied to sex as the means to procreate and propagate the species. Through its connection to our instincts, it brings about automatic behaviors and unconscious habits that are essential to our survival.

From this center, we obtain the vital energy that is

required to confront or avoid the dangers that threaten us. We acquire the discipline to accept limitations that are essential to maintaining a good physical state. Although it is the most basic of the chakras, it should not be underestimated as a lower or minor center. As we advance spiritually, our connection to the first chakra takes on greater importance. Here lies the *brahma-granthi*, or "knot of Brahmā." The first and seventh centers are two polarities that make up a sophisticated energy structure.

Deficiencies in the functioning of this center make us unrealistic and irresponsible. Some symptoms of a closed *mūlādhāra* are childish escapes to worlds of fairies and goblins in the name of religion and spirituality. True development brings a clearer perception of the world, life, ourselves, and reality, but never an escape or evasion.

Swami Pūrṇānanda mentions some of the benefits of meditating on this center:

dhyātvaitan mūla-cakrāntara-vivara-lasat-koṭi-sūrya-prakāśaṁ
vācām īśo narendraḥ sa bhavati sahasā sarva-vidyā-vinodī
ārogyaṁ tasya nityaṁ niravadhi ca mahānanda-yukto'ntarātmā
vākyaiḥ kāvya-prabandhaiḥ sakala-sura-gurūn sevate ṣuddha-śilaḥ

By meditating thus on kundalini who shines within *mūlā-cakra* with the brilliance of ten million suns, one becomes the lord of speech, the king of all, and an adept of all kinds of learning. One becomes eternally free of all disease, and the innermost spirits become full of great bliss. Pure of

disposition through one's deep and poetic words,
one serves all the superior gods.
(*Ṣaṭ-cakra-nirūpaṇa* by Swami Pūrṇānanda, 13)

List of properties of the *mūlādhāra-cakra*

Meaning of the name: The Sanskrit word *mūla* means "foundation, root, base, or support" and the word *ādhāra* means "substratum." Just as its name suggests, *ādhāra-cakra* (the base chakra) is the foundation of our physical existence and the whole system of chakras.

Alternative names of the chakra: This chakra has other names in Tantric terminology: *ādhāra* (the lower one), *brahma-padma* (Brahmā's lotus), *bhūmi-cakra* (the ground chakra), *catur-dala* (the four-petalled one), *catuḥ-patra* (the four-leaved one), *mūlādhāra* (the lower base), *mūla-cakra* (the root chakra), and *mūla-padma* (the foundation lotus). The Vedas and the Upanishads use the following names: *ādhāra*, *brahma*, *mūlādhāra*, *mūla-kanda* (the root-bulb), and in Puranic terminology it is called *ādhāra* or *mūlādhāra*.

Location: *Mūlādhāra-cakra* is located at the very base of the spinal cord, between the anus and the base of the genitals. As the *Śiva Saṁhitā* (5.56) indicates, it lies at the intersection of the *nāḍīs suṣumṇā*, *iḍā*, and *piṅgalā*.

***Kṣetram*:** At the base of the spinal cord.

Presiding deities or devas: Brahmā and Gaṇeśa.

Lord Brahmā is the first deity of the trimurti (Vedic triad), the creator of the universe who was born from a lotus flower that emerged from the navel of Lord Vishnu.

Brahmā, whose name literally means "evolution or development," is the deva of the four heads that face the four cardinal points or *catur-loka*. His white beards symbolize wisdom, and each mouth recites one of the sacred Vedas. Lord Brahmā has four hands, in which he holds a prayer rosary (*mālā*), the Vedas text (*pustaka*), a vessel with the water of life (*kamaṇḍalu*), and a lotus flower (*padma*). His wives are Sarasvatī, the goddess of knowledge, science, and arts, and Sāvitrī, also called Gāyatrī, who is the daughter of Vivasvan or Savitṛ, the Sun god. Lord Brahmā resides in Brahma-loka, which is located on Mount Meru in the Gandhamādana range in the Himalaya mountains. He travels through the universe on a swan (*haṁsa*).

Gaṇeśa is the sacred god with the head of an elephant. He is the son of Shiva and Pārvatī and is the god of intelligence and language. He is considered to be the great remover of obstacles, so it is auspicious to invoke him before activities or trips. He was chosen as the leader of the guards of Lord Shiva, which is the origin of his names, Gaṇeśa (Gaṇa-īśa, or "guard of the Lord") and Gaṇa-pati (Lord of the troops, or *gaṇas*). The story of Lord Gaṇeśa is narrated in chapters 13–18 of the *Śiva Purāṇa, Rudra Saṁhitā*. Skanda was born as the eldest son of the goddess Pārvatī and Lord Shiva. The ecstasy of his mother Pārvatī was so intense that her breasts produced sacred milk. Using this nectarous milk and the sandalwood paste that she used to anoint her body, she proceeded to model her second son. She called him Gaṇeśa and appointed him to be her personal bodyguard and the palace's protector. The child took the appointment so seriously that when the Lord Shiva himself arrived at the palace, he tried to prevent him from entering. Shiva was so enraged that he decapitated Gaṇeśa. Upon hearing of the tragedy, Pārvatī was in despair and threatened to destroy the entire universe. Shiva, to pacify his wife in such a difficult situation, promised to decapitate the first being that appeared and transplant its head onto her son. A fortunate elephant soon appeared and his head was removed and transplanted onto the child.

Goddess or devi: The goddess and Shakti (power) of this chakra is Ḍākinī, one of the faithful attendants of the goddess Kālī. Her eyes are brilliant and bright red, her face has the beauty of the moon, and her body is radiant. In her four hands she carries a skull (*kapāla*), a trident, a sword, and a shield.

Element or *tattva*: The element of the first chakra is earth, or *tattva-pṛthvī*, which is expressed in the way we relate to physical reality as perceived by our senses. The essential characteristics of the earth element are stability, solidity, and slowness. Every solid structure, in the universe as well as in our body, is an expression of *tattva-pṛthvī*, from the planets, mountains, and rocks to our bones, cartilage, skin, muscles, tendons, teeth, and nails. Each element has a psychological influence on its respective chakra that can be positive or negative. If the psychological influence of the earth is negative, it will be very difficult for us to accept new ideas or points of view. Our mind will acquire the solidity of a rock, making us set in our ways and ideas. If the influence is positive, we will be mature, firm, and consistent.

Color of the chakra: Red.

Color of the *tattva*: Yellow.

Power associated with this center: Concentration on this chakra awakens the knowledge of kundalini in all its various aspects, including the means to awaken it.

Esoteric symbolism of the chakra:

Number of petals: Four.

Mantras of the petals: *Vaṁ*, Śaṁ, *Ṣaṁ*, and *Saṁ*.

Mantra of the chakra: *Laṁ*.

Shape of the mandala: Square.

Animal of the chakra: The movement of the vital energy in the first center is heavy and very slow; therefore, it is symbolized by the white elephant Airāvata, which is the vehicle of Indra, the God of war, the atmosphere, the visible sky, thunderbolts, and storms. The white color represents the cloud from which the God Indra causes rain.

Plane or *loka*: *Mūlādhāra-cakra* belongs to the *bhūr-loka*, or "earthly physical plane," inhabited by human beings.

Subtle element or *tanmātras*: *Gandha*, or "smell." The information perceived by the sense of smell passes from the olfactory system to the rest of the limbic system. The system comprises a network of structures near the middle of the brain that is connected to the central nervous system. These structures work together and affect emotions, motivation, memory, and so on. For this reason, it is much easier to remember odors and fragrances than images or sounds. Although most people mistakenly believe that incense and scented oils used in Vedic ceremonies are intended to be pleasant aromas, their purpose is in fact purely spiritual. Incense is made with aromas that induce moods conducive to contemplation, introspection, concentration, and meditation. Since this Vedic art is almost forgotten these days, I have founded the company Prabhuji's Gifts to distribute incense not only because it is pleasant but because it facilitates meditation.

Gland: Physically, *mūlādhāra-cakra* controls the suprarenal glands, the circulatory system, and the excretory system. It is also closely tied to the skeleton, teeth, nails, and hair.

Cognitive organ or *jñanendriya*: Nose (*ghrāṇa*) for smelling (*ghranendriya*).

Organ of action or *karmendriya*: Anus (*pāyu*) for excretion (*pāyvindriya*). According to Kashmir Shaivism, the feet (*pāda*) for locomotion (*pādendriya*).

Energetic channel or *nāḍī*: *Alambusā.*

Bioelement or *doṣa*: *Kapha*, or "watery element."

Vital air or *vāyu*: *Apāna.*

Sheath or *kośa*: *Anna-maya*, or "physical gross body."

Gemstones: Calcite, calcopyrite, chrysoprase, amethyst quartz, diamond, garnet, red jasper, onyx, pearl, siderite, clear quartz, smokey quartz, ruby, black tourmaline, pyrite, opal, obsidian, hematite, and fire agate.

Fragrance: Sandalwood.

Aromatherapy oils: Cypress, myrrh, patchouli, musk, cedar, and lavender.

Planet or *graha*: Maṅgala, or "Mars."

Recommended postures or asanas: Triangle posture (*trikoṇāsana*) and forward fold posture (*pāda-hastāsana*).

Secondary chakras related to *mūlādhāra-cakra*: *Rudrā*, *carcikā*, *rudra-cāmuṇḍā*, *siddha-cāmuṇḍā*, *siddha-lakṣmī*, *siddha-yogeshwarī*, *rupa-vidyā*, *śyāmā*, *dhanturā*, *tārā*, *sodaśī*, *bhatravī*, *cinnamastā*, *dhūmavatī*, *bagalā*, *mātaṅgī*, and *kamalā*.

Balanced functioning of the chakra: If *mūlādhāra-cakra* is functioning normally, we experience an intense desire to live. It is closely tied to confidence and our relationship to money, home, and work. It influences our ability to nourish ourselves and stay strong. If this center is open, it allows us to clearly analyze situations we find ourselves in. We experience great strength of will, constancy, capacity for renewal, and we feel very close to nature. A proper connection with the first center keeps us appropriately situated in physical reality, with a fighting spirit and essential tools for our development in the world.

Imbalanced functioning of the chakra: The characteristic symptoms are insecurity, tension, fear, paranoia, exaggerated worrying, disconnection from reality, and even feelings that one's survival is threatened. There are various physiological symptoms that come from an imbalance, such as laziness, weakness of the legs, back problems, difficulties with the teeth, gums, bones, joints, and blood circulation. Hyperactivity of the chakra causes overeating, and if it is closed, we lose our appetite. Hyperactivity is also expressed as difficulty in accepting other points of view and in changing one's opinion, excessive material attachment, obsession with routine, and an exaggerated search for security. Generally, one who desires security makes efforts to maintain a routine life, moves within the known, and paints the present with the colors of yesterday. For one who pursues security, the present is a genuine threat. A desire for routine forces one to accept a life that revolves around eating, sleeping, mating, and self-protection. The necessity for security creates enmity and rejection of all who physically, mentally, or spiritually threaten routine.

Yantra: The yantra that represents *mūlādhāra-cakra* has four petals whose letters are *Vaṁ*, *Śaṁ*, *Ṣaṁ*, and *Saṁ*. The vibration of the very center or *bīja* of the first chakra is represented by the letter *Laṁ*. Within it lies a yellow square that symbolizes the earth element. In the lower part of the square there is a downward-pointing triangle with a yoni that symbolizes the shakti, or femininity, and a linga that symbolizes Shiva, or masculinity.

मूलाधार चक्र

Mūlādhāra-cakra yantra

Second chakra

Svādhiṣṭhāna-cakra or "Sacral chakra"

tasmin dṛṣṭe mahā-yoge
yātāyāto na vidyate
sva-śabdena bhavet prāṇaḥ
svādhiṣṭhānaṁ tad-āśrayaḥ

svādhiṣṭhānāśrayād asmān
meḍhram evābhidhīyate
tantunā maṇivat proto
yo 'tra kandaḥ suṣumnayā

Attaining the highest state of yoga, one does not remain in (there is no trace of) coming and going (the cycle of births and deaths). The word *Self* refers to prana (vital force), and *svādhiṣṭhāna* takes the place of prana. Due to its location, *svādhiṣṭhāna* is also known as *meḍhra*. This point, which is the root of *suṣumṇā*, is like a string of jewels.

(*Yoga-cūḍāmaṇi Upaniṣad*, 11-12)

atha svādhiṣṭhāna-cakra-vivaraṇam:
dvitīyan tu sarojaṁ ca liṅga-mūle vyavasthitam
bādi-lāntaṁ ca ṣaḍ-varṇaṁ paribhāsvara-ṣad-dalaṁ
svādhiṣṭhānābhidhaṁ tat tu paṅkajaṁ śoṇa-rūpakam
bālākhyo yatra siddho 'sti devī yatrāsti rākiṇī

> The second chakra is situated at the base of the genitals. It has six petals with the letters *ba*, *bha*, *ma*, *ya*, *ra*, and *la*. Its stalk is called *svādhiṣṭhāna*, the color of the lotus is blood red, its presiding adept is called Bāla, and its goddess is Rākiṇī.
>
> (*Śiva Saṁhitā*, 5.75)

The two first energy centers are closely tied to the subconscious (*citta*), which is the vessel that contains our individual and collective karmas. The difference is that the subconscious expresses itself actively in *mūlādhāra*, whereas in *svādhiṣṭhāna* it lies in a subtle or potential state. When only *mūlādhāra-cakra* is working properly, our attitude toward people around us is defensive and utilitarian. We are ready to fight and compete to ensure our basic needs. When *svādhiṣṭhāna-cakra* has also been opened, we take into account the needs of our fellow human beings. They cease to be merely "other people" and become relatives, friends, neighbors, co-workers, and compatriots.

When only the first energy center is open, we are only interested in fulfilling basic needs and maintaining our physical body. If *svādhiṣṭhāna-cakra* is also functioning, we resolve our survival problems, experience pleasure, and enjoy our possessions.

In this chakra we perceive pleasure, but since its element is water, we are at risk of degrading ourselves because liquids flow downward. *Sanātana-dharma* does not condemn feeling pleasure, but it does condemn pursuing pleasure obsessively. We can avoid grave dangers if we comprehend the slavery that comes from addiction to earthly enjoyments. Transforming the pursuit of pleasure into a lifestyle curtails our liberty and hinders bliss. Worldly pleasures leave us with the sensation that although we are pleased, we are not blissful. In this way, we fall into addiction as we constantly try to increase the dose of pleasure.

It is important to understand that enjoyment is not a synonym for bliss, but quite the opposite. An alcoholic, for example, may enjoy drinking but lives in pain. A drug addict may experience pleasure but lives in hell. Enjoyment offers only happiness, which is just the opposite of suffering. The search for pleasure is born from pain and sorrow; it is merely a reaction to misery and an effort to flee from the pain.

Addiction to worldly pleasure makes us mentally, emotionally, and spiritually nearsighted. Dependence on earthly enjoyments impels us to rationalize our weaknesses with superficial constructs. We paint a distorted version of reality and judge others against our painting: those who warn of the danger of our addictions are unpleasant people and those who justify them are our friends, even if cigarettes, alcohol, or drugs threaten our health and well-being. However, beyond the search for pleasure lies the hunger for God, which can never be satiated by increasing sensual satisfaction, but only by realizing absolute bliss, which does not belong to a dual reality and has no opposite. Without renunciation, innocence cannot flourish. Addiction to sensual enjoyment spoils our innocence and severs our moral and ethical integrity.

Rather than striving to attain pleasure, the sacred Bhagavad Gita tells us to look upward and open ourselves to bliss:

viṣayā vinivartante
nirāhārasya dehinaḥ
rasa-varjaṁ raso 'py asya
paraṁ dṛṣṭvā nivartate

> The objects of the senses leave one who abstains from them, but not the desire to enjoy them. However, even this desire is lost in one who has realized the Supreme.
>
> (Bhagavad Gita, 2.59)

The Bhagavad Gita does not argue for repressing worldly enjoyment but rather sublimating it. Pleasures bestowed by objects can be transcended quite naturally when we relish a superior taste, the taste of the Self. Renunciation is neither a fight against ourselves nor does it come from destroying our passions. It is a consequence of our spiritual elevation. We naturally pass from childhood to adolescence without needing to repress childhood. Similarly, we cease playing with worldly toys once we reach spiritual maturity. When we experience divine bliss, repression is unnecessary because what once attracted us no longer has any luster. In this state, the charm of worldly pleasures disappears and decays effortlessly.

In addition, both *svādhiṣṭhāna* and *mūlādhāra* are tied to sexuality. The former is related to procreating and the latter is related to eroticism and sensuality. *Svādhiśṭhāna* is the quintessential Tantric chakra in which we find desire, eroticism, pleasure, passion, imagination, and creativity. This is where our wish to feel attractive and desired is born.

Generally, addiction to sex is a symptom of a blocked second center. If we wish to overcome this addiction, it is more important to open the second center than to foster a repressive struggle against our sexuality. Sex becomes addictive if its only function is to provide momentary physical pleasure.

There are three different positions to take toward sexuality: puritanical repression, libertine permissiveness, and religious sublimation. Those who repress, poison the soul. They become obsessive and neurotic. Libertines develop habits that turn them into dishonorable slaves, as you cannot extinguish a fire with buckets of gasoline. Religion offers us sublimation as the only alternative to be free. Sublimation means observing without mentally interfering. Any attempt to transcend our weaknesses without observation or understanding will only be another type of blind repression. Like alchemy, authentic sublimation transforms sex into love.

It is not possible to be an authentic sannyasi merely

through blind repression. Repression without observation is aggressive; it is in conflict with the principle of ahimsa, or "non-violence." Celibacy is the pinnacle of sexuality, not by stifling it but by realizing it. Monks bloom from sublimation and love. To sublimate our sexuality does not mean to destroy it, but to overcome the need for another person to experience it. The experience of our sexuality, when it is free of relationships and dependence on others, leads us to meditation.

List of the properties of *svādhiṣṭhāna-cakra*

Meaning of the name: The word *sva* means "itself" and *adhiṣṭhāna* means "residence or abode," so *svādhiṣṭhāna* means "the place where the Self dwells or resides" or "the abode of the Self."

Other names of the chakra: Tantric terminology refers to this chakra as *adhiṣṭhāna* (the abode), *bhīma* (the terrible one), *ṣaṭ-patra* (the six-petalled one), *ṣaḍ-dala-padma* (the six-petalled lotus), and *vāri-cakra* (the water chakra). In the Vedas and Upanishads, it is called *meḍhra* or *svādhiśṭhāna*.

Location: *Svādhiṣṭhāna-cakra* is at the very base of the genitals, close to *mūlādhāra* and within *suṣumṇā-nāḍī*.

***Kṣetram*:** In the front of the body at the level of pubic bone, just above the genitals.

Presiding deity or deva: The deity that rules the *svādhiśṭhāna-cakra* is Vishnu, as described by Swami Pūrṇānanda:

tasyāṅka-deśa-kalito harir eva pāyān
nīla-prakāśa rucira-śriyam ādadhānaḥ
pītāmbaraḥ prathama-yauvana-garva-dhārī
śrī-vatsa-kaustubha-dharo dhṛta-vedabāhuḥ

> May Lord Hari protect us, who is within it (the *bindu*, in the middle of *svādhiśṭhāna-cakra*), whose body is of luminous blue and is beautiful to behold, who is dressed in yellow raiment, who is in the pride of early youth, who has four arms, who has a *śrī-vatsa* (curl of hair), and who has the *kaustubha* jewel.
>
> (*Ṣaṭ-cakra-nirūpaṇa* by Swami Pūrṇānanda, 16)

Within the trimurti (Vedic triad), Brahmā is the creator, Shiva is the destroyer, and Vishnu maintains cosmic order. Hence it is natural for Vishnu, the preserver aspect of God, to be the deity of a center related to sexuality, because without it, living beings would become extinct. The fact that Brahmā occupies the first place in the trimurti does not mean that Vishnu is secondary or inferior. According to the *Padma Purana*, Lord Vishnu is the principal deity because he divided himself into creator, preserver, and destroyer. Vaishnavism considers Vishnu to be the supreme God, while according to *Gauḍīya* Vaishnavism, Lord Krishna is the Supreme divinity and even the origin of Lord Vishnu. Lord Vishnu, also known as Mahā-viṣṇu, represents the sattva guna, or "the modality of benevolence." His name means "omnipresent," as he is both immanent and transcendent reality. Another common name for Vishnu is Nārāyaṇa, which means "he who has made the hearts of human beings his abode." His bed is the serpent Śeṣa or Ananta, which floats over the waters of the Ocean of Milk or Causal Ocean, called Kṣīra-samudra. Lakṣmī, the goddess of fortune, gently massages his sacred lotus feet. From his navel, a lotus flower grows, from which Brahmā is born, who is the creator of the universe. His skin is a dark shade of blue, like a rain cloud, so he is described as *nīla-megha-śyāma*. He carries a garland called Vaijayantī, which represents the subtle elements or *bhūta-tanmātras*. His omnipresence is represented by his four arms, which symbolize the four cardinal points. The arms hold a lotus flower (*padma*), a conch shell (*śaṅkha*), a disk (*cakra*), and a golden club (*gada*). The lotus flower symbolizes the evolution and development of the universe, the seashell symbolizes the five elements or *pañca-bhūta*, the disk represents the cosmic mind, and the club represents the cosmic intellect. His vehicle is the loyal Garuḍa, god of the birds. Six divine glories are attributed to Vishnu: knowledge (jnana), mystic powers (*aiśvarya*), potency (shakti), power (*bala*), virility (*vīrya*), and radiance (*tejas*).

Goddess or devi: The goddess of this chakra is Rākiṇī, who is seated on a double lotus. She is blue and has three red eyes. She is heavily bejeweled with beautiful ornaments. Her protruding teeth give her a ferocious appearance, and in her four hands she is holding a hatchet, a trident, a lotus flower, and a drum. She is the goddess of the vegetable world, suggesting that vegetarianism is essential to transcend this center.

atraiva bhāti satataṁ khalu rākiṇī sā
nīlāṁbujodara-sahodara-kāntiśobhā
nānāyudhodyata-karair lasitāṅga-lakṣmir
divyāṁbarābharaṇa-bhūṣita-matta-cittā

It is here, in *svādhiśṭhāna*, where Rākiṇī always dwells. She is the color of a blue lotus. The beauty of her body is enhanced by her uplifted arms holding various weapons. She is dressed in celestial garments and ornaments, and her mind is exalted by drinking ambrosia.

(*Ṣaṭ-cakra-nirūpaṇa* by Swami Pūrṇānanda, 17)

Element or *tattva*: Water, *āpa-tattva* or *āpas*. All liquidity in the universe is an expression of the water element. It can be expressed on the macrocosmic level as the seas, lakes, rivers, and so forth, as well as on the microcosmic level within the body as the bloodstream, urinary excreta, bile, lymphatic fluid, perspiration, saliva, breast milk, and the like. It is related to the tongue, appetite, reproductive organs, and absorption of nutrients. It controls the sexual hormones and influences the bladder, the kidneys, the sexual organs, the blood, the lymph nodes, and gastric juices. According to Ayurvedic medicine, water balances the *tri-doṣa*, which are the three basic principles or moods. Therefore, when this element positively influences people, they develop positive feelings toward others. On the other hand, a symptom of its negative influence is excessive emotion.

For the consumption of water to be really healthy, it is important to consider the constitution of the person and the season. Ayurvedic medicine offers the following basic advice for the healthy consumption of water:

1. If indigestion is present, drinking chilled or cold water is not advised as it will only intensify the symptoms.
2. For good digestion, drink water during meals.
3. Drinking water at the beginning of meals is good for losing weight because it diminishes the appetite.
4. Drinking water at the end of meals reduces the effectiveness of digestion and can cause weight gain.

Color of the chakra: Orange.

Color of *tattva*: White.

Power associated with this center: This center is associated with the power of communicating with the astral plane and astral beings. During the ascension from the first to third centers, certain mystic powers are awakened. They can be considered tests of our maturity.

Esoteric symbolism of this chakra:

Number of petals: Six.

Mantras of the petals: *Baṁ*, *Bhaṁ*, *Maṁ*, *Yaṁ*, *Raṁ*, and *Laṁ*.

Mantra of the chakra: *Vaṁ*.

Shape of the mandala: Half-moon.

sindūra-pūra-rucirāruṇa-padmam anyat
sauṣumṇa-madhya-ghaṭitaṁ dhvaja-mūla-deśe
aṅga-cchadaiḥ parivṛtaṁ taḍid-ābha-varṇair
bādyaiḥ sa-bindu-lasitaiś ca puraṁ-darāntaiḥ

There is another lotus placed inside *suṣumṇā* at the root of the genitals. Its color is a beautiful vermilion. On its six petals are the letters from *ba* to *puram-dara* (*la*), with the *bindu* superimposed, of the brilliant color of lightning.

(*Ṣaṭ-cakra-nirūpaṇa* by Swami Pūrṇānanda, 14)

tasyāntare pravilasad-vi-śada-prakāśam
ambhoja-maṇḍalam atho varuṇyasya tasya
ardhendu-rūpa-lasitaṁ śarad-indu-śubhraṁ
vaṅ-kāra-bījam amalaṁ makarādhirūḍham

Within it is the bright, white, watery region of Varuṇa, in the shape of a half-moon, and therein is the *bīja Vaṁ*, seated on a crocodile (*makara*), as pure and white as an autumn moon.

(*Ṣaṭ-cakra-nirūpaṇa* by Swami Pūrṇānanda, 15)

Animal of the chakra: This chakra's animal is the crocodile, which is the vehicle (*vāhana*) of Gaṅgā and Varuṇa, the Lord of the cosmic oceans who is mentioned in the Vedas as the most important god after Indra. The crocodile is one of the largest and most ferocious reptiles in the animal kingdom. It has so much strength it can dismember its prey in the water. Its skin has scales that are like armor for their durability and resistance. When submerged under water, only the crocodile's eyes and the wings of its nose protrude, so it can watch its prey without being seen and make surprise attacks. It moves in the water with ease and amazing agility. The crocodile represents the grave dangers of sexuality and of pleasure in general, as well as idleness and insensitivity. Connecting too much with this center's energy can result in an excessive attraction to pleasure and sensual enjoyment. The life of such a person is characterized by permissiveness.

Plane or *loka*: The second center corresponds to the astral plane or *bhuvar-loka*. It is a plane of existence and consciousness that parallels our physical reality. While sleeping, we expand in order to enter the astral world, which is completely unknown to most people. We penetrate it with our astral body, the *sūkṣma-śarīra* or *liṅga-śarīra*, which is similar to our physical body but much more subtle.

Subtle element or *tanmātra*: *Rasa*, or "taste." *Svādhiṣṭhāna-cakra* is connected to the sense of taste, which is perhaps the most sensitive of our senses. Human beings can detect five different basic tastes: sweet, salty, sour, bitter, and umami, which is the taste of glutamic acid, typically encountered in meats and cheeses. The ability to taste allows us to avoid poisonous substances and rotten food. In the religious and spiritual sense, taste represents the ability to identify all that can be harmful to our religious development or spiritual health. The loss of the sense of taste can be an indication of health problems such as obesity, diabetes, hypertension, malnutrition, as well as some degenerative diseases of the nervous system such as Parkinson's or Alzheimer's. In the process of *Sanātana-dharma*, the sense of taste is spiritualized. For this reason, the serious aspirant is strictly prohibited from consuming toxic chemicals, drugs, cigarettes, coffee, and even tea.

Moreover, it is recommended to fast one day a month or a week, in order to become aware of how much this sense controls our mind and dominates our life.

Gland: The gonads, or the sexual glands. In women they are the ovaries and in men they are the testicles.

Cognitive organ or *jñānendriya*: Tongue (*rasanā*) for tasting (*rasanendriya*).

Organs of action or *karmendriya*: Genitals (*upastha*) for reproduction (*upasthendriya*). According to Kashmir Shaivism, hands (*pāṇi*) for handling (*hastendriya*).

Energetic channel or *nāḍī*: *Kuhu.*

Bioelement or *doṣa*: *Kapha*, or "watery element."

Vital air or *vāyu*: *Vyāna.*

Sheath or *kośa*: *Prāṇa-maya*, or "energetic body."

Gemstones: Moss agate, fire agate, aquamarine, alexandrite, amazonite, aventurine, celestine, white quartz, amethyst quartz, jade, malachite, rhodonite, tourmaline, clear quartz, topaz, Brazilian topaz, amber, chrysocolla, and granite.

Fragrance: Vanilla.

Aromatherapy oils: Ylang-ylang, sandalwood, jasmine, rose, and petitgrain.

Planet or *graha*: Bṛhaspati, or "Jupiter."

Recommended postures or asanas: The crow posture (*kakāsana*), the peacock posture (*mayūrāsana*), and the pincers posture (*paścimottānāsana*).

Secondary chakras related to the *svādhiśṭhāna-cakra*: *Taralā*, *ramaṇī*, *taraṇī*, *bhānavī*, *nainī*, *janti*, *indrāṇī*, *astibakṣī*, *agnayī*, *māṁsa-priya*, *yamā*, *mahā-daṁaṣṭra*, *nairutti*, and *dīrgha-daṁaṣṭra*.

Balanced functioning of the chakra: When this center is open, we experience vitality, harmony in married life, physical stability, deep communication with our surroundings, security, emotional tranquility, interest, a need for physical contact and caress, a joyful appearance, a balanced liver and gallbladder, and a constant body temperature. A good functioning of this chakra manifests as creativity and enthusiasm in life and great resilience because it stimulates the nervous system. People whose *svādhiṣṭhāna* is functioning in a balanced way will be sure of themselves, have healthy feelings of friendliness and fellowship, and be aware of the futility of accumulating possessions to attain bliss.

Imbalanced functioning of the chakra: When this chakra is closed, the psychological symptoms are sentimentalism, vacillation, disinterest, difficulty in making decisions, apathy, depression, dependence on the past, excessive materialism, unhealthy appearance, sexual blocks, and a lack of energy, enthusiasm, vitality, sensitivity, and motivation to satisfy desires. Physiologically, the blockage of this center will be expressed as shallow breathing, fatigue, weakness, problems in the nervous system, nervousness, diseases of the liver and gallbladder, problems with the lower back, constipation, and migraines. Hyperactivity of this energy center provokes obsessive sexual thoughts and a perspective of the world limited to one's own sensations, pleasure, and impulses.

Yantra: The yantra that represents the second chakra is made up of six petals, which symbolize the number of *nāḍīs* that emanate from it and the negative traits that it overcomes: anger, jealousy, hatred, cruelty, desire, and pride. Within this center's mandala there is a half-moon that symbolizes its element, water. The Sanskrit letters for its petals are *Baṁ*, *Bhaṁ*, *Maṁ*, *Yaṁ*, *Raṁ*, and *Laṁ*. The pulsation of the very center of *svādhiṣṭhāna-cakra* is represented by the letter *Vaṁ*.

स्वाधिष्ठान चक्र

Svādhiṣṭhāna-cakra yantra

THIRD CHAKRA

MAṆIPŪRA-CAKRA OR "SOLAR PLEXUS CHAKRA"

nābhau tu maṇivad bimbaṁ
yo jānāti sa yogavit
tapta-cāmīkarābhāsaṁ
taḍil-lekheva visphurat
tri-koṇaṁ tat puraṁ vahner
adho meḍhrāt pratiṣṭhitam
samādhau paramaṁ jyotir
anantaṁ viśvato mukham

In the navel, it appears like a precious stone (*maṇipūra*). One who knows this knows yoga. It is lustrous like hot gold and iridescent like a bolt of lightning. Therein is the triangle, the seat of fire, below which is *meḍhra*. By meditating on samadhi (on this region) [the yogi] sees the all-pervading eternal light.

(*Yoga-cūḍāmaṇi Upaniṣad*, 9–10)

A balanced third energy center allows us to cultivate

willpower to overcome our shortcomings and to gain greater control over our lives. An open *maṇipūra* involves a significant level of maturity and development. While we find pleasure in *svādhiṣṭhāna*, the third chakra provides the energy to catch ourselves and not allow pursuits of pleasure that would create addictive habits. From the navel center, it is possible to sublimate the instinctive demands of *mūlādhāra* and the desires of *svādhiṣṭhāna*. We can recognize that *maṇipūra-cakra* is open by the absence of basic evolutionary conflicts that afflict us when the first two centers are stagnant.

The balanced activity of this center allows us to see others and reality from the perspective of power, which is expressed as energy, dynamism, and willpower. In our society, to dominate others is sign of success. Therefore, it is very easy to suffer from an imbalance of this center and want to express power to control others for our advantage. We must be careful not to use our power to manipulate our fellow human beings. All power we obtain in this relative world is limited. It is far better to put all power in the service of God and humanity, which is God's manifestation. We should not follow the example of the demon Rāvaṇa, as described in the *Rāmāyaṇa*. He wanted Sītā for himself, but without Lord Rāma; that is to say, he wanted the shakti, or "power of the Lord," without surrendering to the Lord. Strive not to gain power, but renounce all possessions for God. True power lies in our complete surrender to the supreme power.

All three first centers can be considered the gross or bodily chakras, but while the first and second are of the nature of tamas, *maṇipūra-cakra* is of *rajas*. Therefore, the third center makes us extroverted and promotes activity. Under the guidance of an authentic spiritual master, we will be capable of channeling this center's rajasic energy in the proportion and the direction necessary to live with passion but not become impassioned. That is to say, to use it and not to be used by it. When we are capable of living our lives with passion, every moment will be impregnated with the magic of our energy and acquire deep meaning.

When we live with the two first centers open but with the third closed, we are pulled by circumstances. We lack enthusiasm and motivation. We follow the herd, the masses, and the public. The third chakra gives us the necessary energy to question our actions and encourage us to pursue our dreams. Then we clearly define our aspirations, live as we chose, and feel motivated. We clearly understand what we want, why, and to what end.

List of the properties of *maṇipūra-cakra*

Meaning of the name: In Sanskrit, *maṇi* means "jewel" and *pura* means "city," so this center's name means "the city of jewels." When it is open, it reveals the jewels of self-esteem, enthusiasm, self-assurance, and many other traits.

Other names of the chakra: In the Tantric scriptures, this chakra is also called *daśa-cchada* (the one with ten leaves), *daśa-patrāmbuja* (the lotus with ten leaves), *daśa-patra* (the one with ten leaves), *maṇipūraka* (the city of jewels), *nābhi-padma* (the lotus of the navel), *daśa-dala-padma* (the lotus with ten petals), and *nābhi-paṅkaja* (the lotus of the navel). The Vedas and Upanishads refer to the *maṇipūra-cakra* (the city of the jewels' chakra) with the following names: *maṇipūraka* (the city of jewels) and *nābhi-cakra* (the navel chakra). In the Puranas it is called *nābhi-cakra*, or "the navel chakra," because of its location.

Location: The third chakra is found within *suṣumṇā-nāḍī*, in the navel area.

Kṣetram: At the navel.

Presiding deity or deva: The deity that rules over the third center is Bradhna-rudra, or the red Shiva, who is seated on a tiger hide and has a golden beard. Also called Sadyo-jāta (self-born), he is one of the five main aspects of Shiva in which he expresses his indignation at suffering and his destructive rage over the evil produced by human ignorance. It is not an egoistic anger, but is like the fury of a father who sees his son separated from dharma. It is an anger born of love that wants to destroy illusion and ignorance, which is the origin of our pain. As we read in this verse, the devotees of Lord Shiva even worship his sacred anger:

namas te rudra manyava
uto ta iṣave namaḥ
namaste astu dhanvane
bāhubhyām uta te namaḥ

> O Rudra-deva, my salutations to your anger and your arrows. My salutations to your bow and to your two hands.
>
> (*Vājasaneya Saṁhitā* of *Śukla Yajur Veda*, 16.1)

Goddess or devi: The shakti of this chakra is Lākinī, the goddess of three heads. She has a dark complexion and wears a beautiful yellow sari. Lākinī has four hands that carry a thunderbolt or *vajra*, an arrow from Kāma, the god of desire, fire, and with the fourth hand she makes the mudra that makes fear disappear.

atrāste lākinī sā sakala-śubha-karī veda-bāhūj jvalāṅgī
śyāmā pītāmbarādyair vividha-viracanālaṅkṛtā matta-cittā
dhyātvaitan nābhi-padmaṁ prabhavati nitarāṁ saṁhṛtau pālane vā
vāṇī tasyānanābje nivasati satataṁ jñāna-saṁbodha-lakṣmīḥ

> Here abides Lākinī, the benefactress of all. She is four-armed, of radiant body, dark-skinned, clothed in yellow dress, decorated with various ornaments, and exalted by drinking ambrosia. By meditating on this navel lotus, the power to destroy and create [the world] is acquired. *Vāṇī* (the divine sound), with all the wealth of knowledge, always recides in the lotus of her face.
>
> (*Ṣaṭ-cakra-nirūpaṇa* by Swami Pūrṇānanda, 21)

Element or *tattva*: The element of this chakra is *agni*, or "fire." Its fundamental qualities are light, clarity, and heat. It is expressed in the universe as the sun and the stars. *Maṇipūra-cakra* is the seat of digestive fire and is responsible for our digestive system and metabolism. An imbalance in the third center is generally linked to stomach problems and diabetes. We also find the fire present in the retina of the eye that perceives light and in the gray matter of the brain cells. Physically, fire is the element that has the power to transform and purify the body's energy. Similarly, this center is considered to be the great purifier because fire is capable of burning, evaporating, or transforming the gross into the subtle.

Color of the chakra: Yellow.

Color of the *tattva*: Red.

Power associated with this center: Perfect knowledge of one's body. Upon awakening this center, *sādhakas* are graced with the gift to heal diseases.

Esoteric symbolism of the chakra:

Number of petals: Ten.

Mantras of the petals: *Ḍaṁ*, *Ḍhaṁ*, *Ṇaṁ*, *Taṁ*, *Thaṁ*, *Daṁ*, *Dhaṁ*, *Naṁ*, *Paṁ*, and *Phaṁ*.

Mantra of the chakra: *Raṁ*.

Shape of the mandala: Triangle.

Animal of the chakra: The pranic activity of the third center is symbolized by the ram, whose wool is associated with heat. This beautiful animal is the vehicle of Agni, the god of fire, which is the element of this chakra. The ram is the vehicle that carries the *bīja* of *maṇipūra*. When *kuṇḍalinī-śakti* reaches this center, its thrust is like that of a ram.

Plane or *loka*: The dimension or level of consciousness of *maṇipūra-cakra* is *svarga*, *svar-loka*, or "the celestial plane."

Subtle element or *tanmātra*: *Rūpa*, or "form or color." The sense of *maṇipūra-cakra* is vision, which allows the brain to perceive light through the eyes. This lets us distinguish shape, appearance, color, movement, and distance. This sense determines the perception of the world that surrounds us. In the two first centers, we move only in the world of instincts, but beginning with *maṇipūra*, we come closer to humanity. It was not by chance that the great Vedic sages were called *ṛṣis*, or "seers": they saw absolute reality, their souls, and God. In this center, we reach a level of consciousness in which we begin to open our eyes.

Gland: The pancreas. The function of this chakra is to absorb and distribute, control all digestive functions, the spleen, the liver, the pancreas, the kidneys, as well as the other glands and organs tied to nutrition and excretion in our body. *Maṇipūra* is also related to menstrual flow.

Cognitive organ or *jñānendriya*: Eyes (*cakṣu*) for seeing (*cakṣur-indriya*).

Organ of action or *karmendriya*: Feet (*pāda*) for walking (*pādendriya*). According to Kashmir Shaivism, the anus (*pāyu*) for excretion (*pāyvindriya*).

Energetic channel or *nāḍī*: *Viśvodarā.*

Bioelement or *doṣa*: *Pitta*, or "fiery element."

Vital air or *vāyu*: *Samāna*. The third center is like a central distributor of prana that spreads and distributes vital energy throughout the body.

Sheath or *kośa*: *Prāṇa-maya*, or "vital body."

Gemstones: Fire agate, aquamarine, chrysoprase, diamond, fluorite, tabby jasper, ruby, tourmaline, turquoise, sapphire, Brazilian topaz, jade, amber, and peridot.

Fragrance: Lavender.

Aromatherapy oils: Bergamot, ylang-ylang, cinnamon, chamomile, lemon, thyme, and vetiver.

Planet or *graha*: Sūrya, or "Sun."

Recommended postures or asanas: The bow posture (*dhanur-āsana*), spinal stretch (*ardha-matsyendrāsana*), and the locust posture (*śalabhāsana*).

Secondary chakras related to *maṇipūra-cakra*: *Adya-cakra*, *bhīma*, *brahma-mānya-cakra*, *ajitā*, *brahma-vādinī*, *chandogrā*, *candikā*, *ambā*, *dhātrī*, *agni-hotrī*, *vidyā*, *avidyā*, *dhriti*, *jaya-vijayā*, *jayā*, *kārtikī*, *kālinī*, *kalyānī*, *jalodharī*, *kaṅkālī*, *kāpālī*, *kapilā*, *sarva-bhūta-damanī*, *sarpa-bhuṣanī*, *rudrā*, *nara-simhī*, *madonmathanī*, *maheśvarī*, *śankara-priyā*, *sarasvatī*, *sāvitrī*, *vaṅgā*, *virūpā*, *yoga-māyā*, *yoga-sad-bhāvā*, and *yoginī-cakra*.

Balanced functioning of the chakra: When this center is open, one experiences self-esteem, confidence, lightness, enthusiasm, self-confidence, and the capacity to accept and enact authority. The following qualities are manifested: dynamism, motivation, persistence, trust, the ability and power to make changes in life, to be able to rise above oneself, firmness, self-acceptance and in turn, the feeling of being valued and accepted by others. Similarly, a properly functioning third chakra allows the fire element to be expressed as a healthy digestive system, abundant energy, great vitality, a brilliant mind, a quick intellect, and an ardent aspiration for the Truth.

Imbalanced functioning of the chakra: People with closed *maṇipūras* invest tremendous efforts and sacrifices in seeking the admiration of others. They do so at the cost of causing pain and suffering to friends and relatives. They live in constant competition with others. Many suffer from lack of willpower or too much of it. Those with weak willpower become frustrated at not being able to resist. Constantly satisfying the demands of others, they are considered good husbands or wives, friends, fathers, partners, and in general, good people. The problem is that they do not consider themselves "good" but feel that they are being used. Such people lose self-confidence when they see themselves saying "yes" when they should be saying "no." On the other hand, people with excessive willpower see every situation as a threat to their position or as an opportunity to climb still further up the social ladder. This attitude transforms all situations into battles and all activities into competitions that test their courage and abilities. When the third chakra is imbalanced, relationships with peers are colored by an interest in power and self-centered ambitions. Such people are uncomfortable seeing the talents or triumphs of others and enjoy others' failures. The characteristic symptoms of a deficient functioning of this chakra are dependence and excessive attachment, insecurity, boredom, depression, unjustified sadness, indifference, stubbornness, egoism, and unbalanced emotions. The fire element can be expressed negatively as anger, irritability, hatred, jealousy, rancor, and resentment. Physically, this leads to a lack of flexibility, muscle tensions, and lower back problems.

Yantra: The diagram of this chakra has ten petals that symbolize the ten pranas, or "vital forces." The mandala has a triangle in its center, which is fire red. The Sanskrit letters of the petals are *Ḍaṁ*, *Ḍhaṁ*, *Ṇaṁ*, *Taṁ*, *Thaṁ*, *Daṁ*, *Dhaṁ*, *Naṁ*, *Paṁ*, and *Phaṁ*. The *bīja* vibrating in the heart of *maṇipūra-cakra* is *Raṁ*.

tasyordhve nābhi-mūle daśa-dala-lasite pūrṇa-megha-prakāśe
nīlāmbhoja-prakāśair upahita-jaṭhare ḍādi-phāntaiḥ sacandraiḥ
dhyāyed vaiśvānarasyāruṇa-mihira-samaṁ maṇḍalaṁ tat tri-koṇaṁ
tad bāhye svastikākhais tribhir abhilasitā tatra vahni-svabījam

> Above it (*svādhiṣṭhāna-cakra*), at the root of the navel, is the shining lotus of ten petals, which is the color of clouds filled with water. Within it are the letters *Ḍa* to *Pha*, of the color of the blue lotus, with the *nāda* and *bindu* above them. Meditate on this region of red fire, triangular in form and shining like the rising sun. Outside it there are three *svastika* marks and within, the *bīja* of *vahni* (fire) itself.
>
> (*Ṣaṭ-cakra-nirūpaṇa* by Swami Pūrṇānanda, 19)

मणिपूर चक्र

Maṇipūra-cakra yantra

Fourth Chakra

Anāhata-cakra or "Heart Chakra"

tasyordhve hṛdi paṅkajaṁ sulalitaṁ bandhūka-kanty-ujjvalaṁ
kādyair dvādaśa-varṇakair upahitaṁ sīndūra-rāgānvitaiḥ
nāṁnānāhata-saṁjñakaṁ sura-taruṁ vāñchātirikta-pradaṁ
vāyor maṇḍalam atra dhūma-sadṛśaṁ ṣaṭ-koṇa-śobhānvitaṁ

Above that (*maṇipūra-cakra*), in the heart, is the enchanting lotus, of the bright color of the Bandhūka flower, with the twelve vermillion letters beginning with *Ka* placed therein. It is known by its name of *anāhata*, and is like the celestial wishing-tree, bestowing even more than desired. The beautiful region of Vāyu is here, which has six corners and is the color of smoke.
(*Ṣaṭ-cakra-nirūpaṇa* by Swami Pūrṇānanda, 22)

tan madhye pavanākṣaraṁ ca madhuraṁ dhūmāvalī-dhūsaraṁ
dhyayet pāṇi-catuṣṭayena lasitaṁ kṛṣṇādhirūḍhaṁ paraṁ
tan madhye karuṇā-nidhānam amalaṁ haṁsābham īśābhidhaṁ
pāṇibhyām abhyaṁ varaṁ ca vidadhal loka-trayāṇām api

> Meditate in the midst of it (*anāhata-cakra*), on the sweet and excellent *pavana-bīja* (*Yaṁ*), which is gray like a trail of smoke, has four arms, and is seated on a black antelope. And within it, also [meditate] upon the Abode of Mercy and the Immaculate Lord who is lustrous like the sun, whose two hands make gestures that grant boons and dispel the fears of the three worlds.
>
> (*Ṣaṭ-cakra-nirūpaṇa* by Swami Pūrṇānanda, 23)

The heart chakra, as many call it, serves as the link between the three gross chakras (*mūlādhāra*, *svādhiṣṭhāna*, and *maṇipūra*) and the three subtle chakras (*viśuddha*, *ājñā*, and *sahasrāra*). The first three chakras represent the body and the physical reality of names and forms; the last three represent our interior world and the soul. *Anāhata-cakra* is a center of transition toward the more subtle and elevated dimensions of consciousness. The first three centers are human; the last three are divine. The fourth center transforms whatever is gross in the lower centers and makes it more subtle and refined, so that it may harmonize with higher planes of consciousness.

If we look carefully, we will see that modern humans—with their fears, preferences, desires, jealousy, and ambitions—only move within the limits of the first three chakras. In fact, they live an animal life in a human body. Today's society has unbalanced the functioning of *anāhata-cakra* and most people do not go beyond the limits of the first three centers. Their lives are restricted to eating, sleeping, mating, and fighting. They die and leave their bodies without even imagining that there might be something beyond these limits.

Love is beyond the chakras related to survival, sex, and power. Here lies the *viṣṇu-granthi*, or "the knot of Vishnu," which warns us that emotions and feelings entail the great danger of attachment and slavery. The center of love lies above the plane of needs. With only three first centers open, we still perceive ourselves as entities independent of the universe, separate and disconnected from the rest of creation. Only when *anāhata* awakens do we experience harmony and unity with other living beings and life. Existence blooms. Therefore, love is a luxury that not everyone can afford. Only when the fourth center opens can we be considered yogis; until this happens we are still *sādhakas*, or "aspirants."

The functioning of this center influences our expression of feelings toward those around us. If we only identify with our physical body, love is expressed as sex. If we climb a rung in the ladder of evolution, we identify with the mind. When perceiving ourselves as thinking entities, sexuality is manifested as romantic and sentimental attachment in the style of Romeo and Juliet. Love manifests as religion only in those who reveal their own authenticity as pure consciousness. Only then is the sacred madness called *love* experienced in all its fullness.

From the rational mind's point of view, love is lunacy. It is not that love is irrational, but that the logic of the head and the heart are very different. Their directions are diametrically opposed: the mind finds gain in receiving and accumulating, while the heart does so in giving and sharing. The mind is always looking to possess something or someone, while the heart yearns to be possessed by the Whole. The most important matters for the heart are irrelevant for the mind, such as the soul, God, or religion. The mind is interested in religion only as a business; its interest in the sacred stems from the expectation of some type of benefit or gain. The head is calculating; it is focused on aims, objectives, purposes, and goals. Unconditional love threatens its comfort, and surrender challenges its safety. The mind resists and escapes from the Truth; the heart pursues it at all costs.

The heart does not pursue goals; it pursues meaning. There is a certain degree of madness in love, as it leaves us without concrete answers to "why?," "what for?," and "to what end?" The heart is brave. It does not pursue safety, comfort, or convenience; love causes us to expand ourselves before the experience of our soul in the clear sky of our interior. To love is to experience the expansive movement that erases differences and borders, unites hearts, and fuses souls. The embrace of love evaporates our exclusive attitude and expands the boundaries of our love for those we hold dear. Besides our family, we start to love our neighborhood, city, nation, world, and the entire universe. Love is humans' most wonderful potential. It is stored in our chests; it is a seed ready to bloom and release its nectarous and intoxicating scent.

People who purify this center discover their capacity to love. They cease to be "beggars of love" and become channels that pour out love; they reveal *anāhata-cakra* as the center of love in its highest expression. They harmonically draw in everyone who is close to their aura and inspire them to love. This center is the soil where the seed of devotion is planted and cultivated until it grows and reaches the heights of divine love as *prema* and *parā-bhakti*. The scriptures affirm that by focusing our attention on this center, it is possible to realize the very essence of our existence. *Anāhata-cakra* is considered the seat of the divine Self or Ātman. Patañjali Maharṣi says:

hṛdaye citta-saṁvit

> Focusing attention on the heart leads to knowledge of the nature of consciousness.
>
> (*Yoga Sūtras*, 3.34)

Within the limits of the first three chakras, we are waves that are born, hold on for a while, and meet our end when we weaken and arrive at the shore. To awaken *anāhata* is to discover our oceanic nature. This center is a gateway that provides direct access to our universal aspect, the Self.

List of the properties of *anāhata-cakra*

Meaning of the name: The word *anāhata* means "without striking or without beating." All sounds are created by the collision or friction of two bodies. Besides our own hearts, the heart of the universe beats in our chest. We can all hear physical heartbeats with our senses, but only those who are connected to the universal heart can perceive its beating. *Anāhata-nāda*, or "the primordial sound," is not created by any physical phenomenon; it is the eternal sound that has no beginning and no end.

Other names of the chakra: Another name of this center is *hṛt-padma* (the lotus of the heart). In Tantric terminology, this center is also known by the following names: *anāhata-purī* (the invincible city), *dvadaśa* (the twelfth one), *hṛt-paṅkeruha* (the lotus of the heart), *dvadaśa-dala* (the twelfth leaf), *hṛdayāmbhoja* (the lotus of the heart), *hṛd-abja* (the lotus of the heart), *hṛd-āmbhoja* (the lotus of the heart), *hṛdaya* (the heart, the essence), *hṛdaya-kamala* (the lotus of the heart), *hṛdayābja* (the lotus of the heart), *hṛdayāmbuja* (the lotus of the heart), *hṛd-ambuja* (the lotus of the heart), *hṛdaya-sarasija* (the lotus of the heart), *hṛt-padma* (the lotus of the heart), *hṛt-paṅkaja* (the lotus of the heart), *hṛt-saro-ruha* (the lotus of the heart), *padma-sundara* (beautiful lotus), *hṛt-patra* (the leaf of the heart), and *sūrya-saṅkhya-dala* (the leaf with the essence of the sun). The Vedas refer to *anāhata-cakra* as *hṛdaya-cakra* (the chakra of the heart) and *dvādaśāra-cakra* (the twelve-spoked chakra).

Location: It is found in the center of the chest, at the height of the heart, within *suṣumnā-nāḍī*. It is directly connected to the cardiac plexus. Fifteen *nāḍīs* originate from this center.

***Kṣetram*:** In the heart.

Presiding deity or deva: The presiding deity of the fourth chakra is Īśāna-rudra. He is the purifier and the embodiment of air. He is the ruler of the northwest, dressed in a tiger skin, and is effulgent like the sun. His nature is very peaceful and highly benevolent. He is associated with internal wisdom and cosmic power. His son is Mano-java, or "the quick witted." Snakes are entwined around his neck and the sacred Ganges flow from his braids. Inside *anāhata* there is a lingam with *Sadā-śiva*, or "the eternal God." He carries a trident in his right hand and a *ḍamaru* drum in his left hand.

Goddess or devi: The goddess or shakti of this chakra is Kākinī. In many scriptures, it is said that the shakti in this energy center is especially strong. She is the benefactor of all. She has three eyes, four heads, wears a beautiful sky-blue sari and her skin is golden yellow. In her four hands she carries a sword, a shield, a skull, and a trident. Kākinī-śakti is associated with spiritual art, which can help us transcend the idea of time. Swami Pūrṇānanda refers to her in the following way:

atrāste khalu kākinī nava-taḍit-pītā tri-ṇetrā śubhā
sarvālaṅkaraṇānvitā hita-karī samyag-janānāṁ mudā
hastaiḥ pāśa-kapāla-śobhana-varān saṁbibhratī cābhayaṁ
mattā pūrṇa-sudhā-rasārdra-hṛdayā kaṅkāla-mālā-dharā

> Here dwells Kākinī, who is yellow like a new lightning bolt, exhilarated and auspicious. She has three eyes and is the benefactress of all. She wears all kinds of ornaments, and her four hands carry a noose, carry a skull, make the sign of blessing, and make the sign that dispels fear. Her heart is softened by drinking nectar, and she wears a garland of skeletons.
>
> (*Ṣaṭ-cakra-nirūpaṇa* by Swami Pūrṇānanda, 24)

Element or *tattva*: Its element is air, or *vāyu*, which lies in the chest and serves as the vehicle of vital energy. Its main qualities are pressure, lightness, coolness, and dryness. This element is expressed in the muscles, heartbeats, the expansion and contraction of the lungs, nervous system activity, and movements of the stomach and the intestines. Air is also related to all types of movements in the universe of planets and stars. The different types of vital energies or pranas that sustain our body are also considered a form of air. The mind is activity, which is a product of prana, therefore, the relationship between the fourth center and the mind is obvious. Air represents the idea of expansion because in this center, consciousness can expand infinitely.

Power associated with this center: Control of vital energy and the senses. The power to heal sick people.

Color of the chakra: Green.

Color of the *tattva*: Smoke.

Esoteric symbolism of the chakra:

Number of petals: Twelve.

Mantras of the petals: *Kaṁ*, *Khaṁ*, *Gaṁ*, *Ghaṁ*, *Ṅaṁ*, *Caṁ*, *Chaṁ*, *Jaṁ*, *Jhaṁ*, *Ñaṁ*, *Taṁ*, and *Thaṁ*.

Mantra of the chakra: *Yaṁ*.

Shape of the mandala: Hexagon.

Animal of the chakra: The energetic movement in this center is symbolized by the antelope, whose traits are attentiveness and alertness. The antelope is fast, like air.

Plane or *loka*: *Mahar-loka*, or "the plane of equilibrium," the highest astral plane.

Subtle element or *tanmātra*: *Sparśa*, or "touch."

Air is associated with touch, its sensory organ is the skin, and its organs of action are the hands. The chakra of the heart and the hands are connected because they express giving and receiving. Since the sense of this chakra is touch, hugging is one of its activities. Receptivity to being touched comes from a sensitive heart chakra.

Gland: Supracardiac paraganglion or thymus.

Cognitive organ or *jñānendriya*: Skin (*tvak*) for touching (*sparsanendriya*).

Organ of action or *karmendriya*: Hands (*pāṇi*) for handling (*hastendriya*). According to Kashmir Shaivism: Genitals (*upastha*) for reproduction (*upasthendriya*).

Energetic channel or *nāḍī*: Varuṇa.

Bioelement or *doṣa*: *Vāta*, or "airy element."

Vital air or *vāyu*: Prana.

Sheath or *kośa*: *Mano-maya*, or "mental sheath."

Gemstones: Azabache, barite, calcopyrite, celestine, tiger's eye, sodalite, sapphire, emerald, malachite, green tourmaline, watermelon tourmaline, rose quartz, peridot, chrysoprase, jasper, and turquoise.

Fragrance: Rose.

Aromatherapy oils: Essence of roses, bergamot, lemon balm, geranium, and clary sage.

Planet or *graha*: Śukra, or "Venus."

Recommended postures or asanas: The spinal twist (*ardha-matsyendrāsana*), the cobra posture (*bhujaṅgāsana*), and the fish posture (*matsyāsana*).

Secondary chakras related to *anāhata-cakra*: *Agni-jvālā*, *anuchāyā*, and *bhairavī*: These three secondary centers work together with all the minor chakras and the *nāḍīs* connected to *maṇipūra-cakra*. They are responsible for the adequate flow of energy through the *nāḍīs*, which is controlled by *iḍa*.

Other chakras: *Nitya-cakrā, padminī, kuṇḍalinī, nityā, kurukuḷḷā, kūṣmāṇḍī, paramā, priyaṅkarī, caṇḍa-nāyikā, vāsinī, aparṇā, gaurī, ghaṇṭā, ghora-rūpā, bhadrā, rakta-dantikā, bhadra-kālī, bhagavatī, bhāskarī, rañjanī, vāñchanī, vandī, brāhmaṇa-priyā, brahmarī, arundhatī, ratī, raudrī, retilālasā, revatī, ripuhā, rohiṇī, vāma-ratā, vana-devatā, aśapurā, bala-pramāthanī, bala-vikariṇī, vana-devī, cāmuṇḍā, bhāva-gamayā, caṇḍī, diti, bhayaṅ-karī, kṣātra-mālinī, lajjā, nir-añjanā, niṣ-kalā, lākinī, lamboṣṭhī, lohitā, mādhavī, nārāyaṇī, aindrī, ambikā, aṅgā, brāhmaṇī, caṇḍā, durgā, garuḍī, gopalī, grahṇā, gṛhāśayā, hākinī, caṇḍa-ghaṇṭa, caṇḍāvatī, hara-siddhi, kalā, kāla-rātri, hariṇī, kubjā, kulajā, lalitā, hema-kāṇṭi, heṅgulā, purāṇānvīkṣikī, lambā, kumārī, parṇā, and kuṭāri-bhagavatī.*

***Sūrya-cakra*:** This is a secondary center that has six petals, and it is located just below *anāhata-cakra*. *Sūrya-cakra* is less active at night. As it heats the body, it allows for the activity of *agni-tattva*, or "fire element," in *maṇipūra-cakra*. In Sanskrit, *sūrya* means "the great light" and it refers to the Sun god, who crosses paradise in his carriage pulled by seven horses, which represent the seven chakras. His beautiful body is brilliant and luminous. He has three eyes and four arms. He sustains life on the planet with energy and light, provides day and night, and maintains the cycles of the seasons.

The centers related to the *sūrya-cakra* are *soma-cakra*, *maṅgala-cakra*, *budha-cakra*, *guru-cakra*, *śukra-cakra*, *śani-cakra*, *rāhu-cakra*, and *ketu-cakra*.

Balanced functioning of the chakra: When this center is open, it brings security in relationships, sensitivity, sympathy, confidence, love for oneself and others, kindness, helpfulness, flexibility, health, balance, liveliness, optimism, enthusiasm, warmth, inner peace, and harmony. When this center interacts harmoniously with the other centers, we are transformed into a welcoming nexus that harmonizes people around us. We radiate amiability and bestow natural joy and warmth that can open the hearts of those around us.

Imbalanced functioning of the chakra: A deficient functioning of this chakra is manifested as a lack of sensitivity toward others and their feelings, great vulnerability and excessive dependence on the affections, caring, and sympathy of others, emotional blocks, difficulty in creating new ties and relationships, nostalgia for prior relationships, difficulty in receiving love and care, negative feelings and thoughts, pessimism, lack of harmony and coherence between the emotional and the mental, lack of interest in life, lack of enthusiasm and motivation, and excessive sensitivity to rejection. In general, people with a closed fourth center seem dry and disinterested in their relationships with others. The physiological symptoms of an imbalanced *anāhata* are fallen shoulders, a flat chest, the sensation of having a metal band around the chest, respiratory problems, and diseases of the lungs, skin, and heart. Tension in the heart chakra can be expressed as difficulties breathing or complications with respiratory organs.

Yantra: Twelve *nāḍīs* originate from this center and are represented by twelve petals. They symbolize the twelve qualities of the heart: bliss, peace, harmony, love, understanding, sympathy, clarity, purity, unity, compassion, kindness, and forgiveness. According to tantra yoga, the downward-pointing triangle represents femininity and the upward-facing triangle represents masculinity. The message behind this star is balance and harmony between two halves: man and woman, inhalation and exhalation, night and day, life and death. These opposites are in fact complementary. We perceive conflict everywhere because we think we are made of parts and perceive only parts and not the Whole.

अनाहत चक्र

Anāhata-cakra yantra

Fifth Chakra

Viśuddha-cakra or "Throat Chakra"

The throat chakra is located in the neck. Unlike the other chakras, it is located in a very narrow space. *Viśuddha-cakra* is the first of the upper chakras and is intimately tied to our ability to communicate. The *Śiva Saṁhitā* speaks about the fifth energy center:

kaṇṭha-sthāna-sthitaṁ padmaṁ
viśuddhaṁ nāma pañcamam
suhemābhaṁ svaropetaṁ
ṣoḍaśa-svara-saṁyutam
chagalāṇḍo 'sti siddho 'tra
śākinī cādhidevatā

> This lotus, situated in the throat, is the fifth chakra. It is called *viśuddha*. Its color is brilliant gold, it is adorned with sixteen petals and is the seat of the vowel sounds (i.e., its sixteen petals are designated by the sixteen vowels: *A*, *Ā*, *I*, *Ī*, *Ū*, *Ṛ*, *Ṝ*, *Ḷ*, *Ḹ*, *E*, *Ai*, *O*, *Au*, *Aṁ*, and *Aḥ*).
>
> (*Śiva Saṁhitā*, 5.90)

dhyānaṁ karoti yo nityaṁ
sa yogīśvara-paṇḍitaḥ
kintvasya yogino 'nyatra
viśuddhākhye saro-ruhe
catur-vedā vibhāsante
sa rahasyā nidher iva

> One who always meditates on it (*viśuddha-cakra*) is truly the lord of yogis and deserves to be called wise. By meditating on the *viśuddha* lotus, a yogi at once understands the four Vedas and their mysteries.
>
> (*Śiva Saṁhitā*, 5.91)

This center gives rise to the need to share our experiences and communicate our ideas and feelings with other people, in other words, our need for expression and perception. Hence this center is connected to all aspects of art. Both *svādhiṣṭhāna* and *viśuddha* are related to art: the former through its ties to sex and the latter through its influence on communication. Creativity and sexuality are the same energy. The same power capable of creating a child can create a painting, a poem, or a symphony. Physically, the fifth center is closely tied to the throat, thyroid and parathyroid, lymph system, vocal cords, ears, voice, shoulders, mouth, and in general, our faculty of speech.

Wherever an exchange or transmission between two or more entities occurs, the fifth chakra plays a central role. Every communication requires a sender (who transmits a message), a receiver (who receives the message), a message (the information conveyed), and a channel (the element that allows the message to be conveyed). If there is any interference, that is to say, if any of these components fail, communication is impossible.

To communicate properly, we must be both a sender and a receiver. We need to develop our capacity to be receptive and expressive and give equal importance to both. If we wish to cultivate receptivity, we need to awaken our sincere interest in others, because only then we will develop an authentic will to meet them and learn about them. Listening to other points of view contributes greatly to our enrichment because it allows us to appreciate life from a different perspective. It is said that we were given two ears and one mouth because we should listen twice as much as we speak. It is a fact that we learn more by listening than by speaking.

In most conversations, practically everyone is more concerned with speaking than listening. Many people prefer the role of senders, but only few accept the place of the receiver. Rather than listening, most people prefer to be listened to. They are more interested in what they are saying than in paying attention to others. What we generally call a conversation is more like a monologue. It is impossible to hear clearly if there is a lot of noise around us. Similarly, in order to perceive clearly what is said to us, inner silence is essential. Our mental noise, which is the product of a mind agitated by desires, does not allow us to listen to the message attentively. Meditation is not a technique or method, but pure receptivity.

People quarrel, argue, and feel offended, and this is often due to communication problems. We live our lives from the known. Our past filters our reactions and attitudes. It is impossible for us to understand each other and avoid misunderstandings if we communicate from our past. Someone mentions something, and immediately we connect it to our past. Before the other person has finished expressing his or her point of view, we have reached a conclusion and we are prepared to answer. We really do not understand what is being said to us, but we interpret it according to our past experiences.

In our efforts to communicate, there is interference from the mind and the past. The mind interprets and compares to what it has stored in the great storehouse of the known. It does not know how to listen, because in order to listen it must be transformed into silence. The quality of communication will improve to the extent that we identify less with the mind. Perfect communication, without the risk of misunderstandings, occurs only without the mind. It only occurs between people who do not act with the mind—those who move in the now, without interpretations or comparisons. A dialogue can even be established without words; a glance or silence can be tremendously communicative. Only the enlightened being, one who does not act through the instrument of the mind, can have a dialogue with the trees, flowers, stars, life, existence, or God. For this reason, communication finds its highest expression in meditation.

List of the properties of *viśuddha-cakra*

Meaning of the name: The word *śuddhi* means "purification." This is the center of communication. It purifies us in the sense that we ultimately communicate with ourselves, with what we are, with our reality. Purity is not something that we can create, practice, cultivate, or acquire from the external world—it is our natural state and condition, it is what we really are.

Other names of the chakra: The fifth center is also called the larynx or throat chakra. In Tantric terminology it is called *ākāśa* (ether), *kaṇṭha* (the throat), *kaṇṭha-deśa* (the throat region), *kaṇṭhāmbhoja* (the lotus of the throat), *dvy-aṣṭa-patrāmbuja* (the lotus with sixteen petals), *kaṇṭhāmbuja* (the lotus of the throat), *kaṇṭha-padma* (the lotus of the throat), *kaṇṭha-paṅkaja* (the lotus of the throat), *nirmala-padma* (the spotless, pure lotus), *ṣoḍaśa* (the one of sixteen), *ṣoḍaśa-dala* (the one of sixteen petals), *ṣoḍaśa-patra* (the one of sixteen petals), *ṣoḍaśāra* (the one of sixteen), *ṣoḍaśollasa-dala* (the one of sixteen shining petals), *viśuddha* (the pure one), and *viśuddhi* (purification). In the Vedas and the Upanishads it is also called *kaṇṭha-cakra* (the chakra of the throat), *viśuddha* (the pure one), and *viśuddhi* (the purifier). In Puranic terminology it is called *viśuddha* (the pure one) or *viśuddhi* (purification).

Location: It is located in the neck at the height of the throat, within *suṣumṇā-nāḍī*. It is located where the spinal column and the medulla oblongata meet.

***Kṣetram*:** In the front of the neck, at the pit of the throat near the thyroid gland.

Presiding deity or deva: The fifth energy center is ruled by the deity called *Pañca-vaktra-śiva*. This name means "the Shiva of the five faces." His five heads or faces have different names that are each associated with one of the five elements (*pañca-bhūtas*): Aghora with ether (*ākāśa*), Īśāna of water (*ap* or *jala*), Mahā-deva of earth (*bhūmi* or *pṛthvī*), *Sadā-śiva* of air (*vāyu*), and Rudra of fire (*tejas* or *agni*). Similarly, *Pañca-vaktra-śiva* has four hands: his right hands hold a rosary (*mālā)* and make the sign *abhaya-mudrā* that banishes all fear and apprehension. His left hands hold the sacred trident and the *ḍamaru* drum.

Goddess or devi: The goddess and shakti of this chakra is Śākinī, or "the powerful one." The following verse describes her:

sudhā-sindhoḥ śuddhā nivasati kamale śākinī pīta-vastrā
śaraṁ cāpaṁ pāśaṁ sṛṇim api dadhatī hasta-padmaiś caturbhiḥ
sudhāṁśoḥ saṁpūrṇaṁ śaśa-pari rahitaṁ maṇḍalaṁ karṇikāyāṁ
mahā-mokṣa-dvāraṁ śriyam abhimata-śīlasya śuddhendriyasya

> Purer than the Ocean of Nectar is the shakti Śākinī who dwells in this lotus. Her dress is yellow, and in her four lotus-hands she carries a bow, an arrow, a noose, and a goad. The whole region of the moon without the mark of the hare is in the periphery of this lotus. This is the gateway of great liberation for one who desires the wealth of yoga and whose senses are pure and controlled.
> (*Ṣaṭ-cakra-nirūpaṇa* by Swami Pūrṇānanda, 30)

Element or *tattva*: Ether, or *ākāśa*. This element is the most subtle of all. Its main qualities are to transmit sound, cold, subtlety, and transparency. Ether is found in the cavities of our body: the nose, mouth, digestive system, respiratory pathways, tissues, the network of veins and capillaries, and cells. When ether is expressed negatively, our inclination is to feel bewildered when faced with problems or dangerous situations. When it is expressed properly, one enjoys a sensation of expansion. This element is the space that makes communication possible. It allows us to express and share information with others and describe what occurs in our inner world, our emotions, and our experiences. Similarly, it allows us to hear what others want to share with us, which is very important because it gives us the opportunity to get to know different perspectives on life.

Color of the chakra: Light blue.

Color of the *tattva*: Blue.

Power associated with this center: Knowledge of the sacred scriptures. The power to read the thoughts of others and to live without consuming food.

Esoteric symbolism of the chakra:

Number of petals: Sixteen.

Mantras of the petals: *Aṁ*, *Āṁ*, *Iṁ*, *Īṁ*, *Uṁ*, *Ūṁ*, *Ṛṁ*, *Ṝṁ*, *Ḷṛṁ*, *Ḹṝṁ*, *Eṁ*, *Aiṁ*, *Oṁ*, *Auṁ*, *Aṁ*, and *Aḥ*.

Mantra of the chakra: *Haṁ*.

Shape of the mandala: Circle.

Animal of the chakra: A white elephant is the symbol of this chakra. The white color represents purity.

By its majestic movement, the elephant also represents stability and determination.

Plane or *loka*: *Jana* or *Janar-loka*. According to the scriptures, this is the plane of the devas.

Subtle element or *tanmātra*: *Śabda*, or "sound." Few of us stop to appreciate the incredible miracle of the sense of hearing, which makes it possible to communicate. We usually think the basis for communication is speech, the ability to emit sounds and language, and the ability to understand and appropriately utilize these sounds. However, hearing is essential for proper communication. Without it, it is impossible to hear the sounds of nature or music. If we understand that the origin of the cosmic manifestation is sound, we can better comprehend the deep significance of hearing when developed at its subtlest levels.

What happens on the surface can be applied to our inner reality. In the same way that noise does not allow us to listen to what is said to us, mental noise prevents us from perceiving our inner silence. The noise of our ideas, concepts, conclusions, and thoughts does not allow us to listen to the silence of our interior space.

Gland: Thyroid or parathyroid.

Cognitive organ or *jñanendriya*: Ears (*śrotra*), or the auditory system.

Organ of action or *karmendriya*: Mouth (*vāk*) for speech (*vāgindriya*), which is the same in Kashmir Shaivism.

Energetic channel or *nāḍī*: Sarasvatī.

Bioelement or *doṣa*: *Vāta*, or "airy element."

Vital air or *vāyu*: *Udāna*.

Sheath or *kośa*: *Vijñāna-maya*, or "intellectual sheath."

Gemstones: Amazonite, amber, celestine, white quartz, citrine quartz, red jasper, aquamarine, ruby, blue agate, moss agate, turquoise, and lapis lazuli.

Fragrance: Eucalyptus.

Aromatherapy oils: Sage, eucalyptus, lavender, sandalwood, neroli, myrrh, and chamomile.

Planet or *graha*: Budha, or "Mercury."

Recommended postures or asanas: Shoulder stand (*sarvāṅgāsana*), fish posture (*matsyāsana*), plough posture (*halāsana*), and spinal twist (*ardha-matsyendrāsana*).

Secondary chakras related to *viśuddha-cakra*: *śaṅkya, śānti, śānti-karī, śiva-dhūti, śiva-rūpiṇī, śobhanā, śruti, śubhadā, siddhi, śivā, śiva-dhūti, skanda-mātā, smṛti, śreṣṭinī, śrī, śrī-bhīṣani, śrī-dhara-dhuri, śrī-ja, śrī-lampaṭā, śrī-nandinī, śucaṇḍā, śuddhā, sudharmiṇī, śūlakarā, sumaṅgalā, sunandā, suprabhā, surekhā, surūpā, sūrya-putrī, sumanā, suśītalā, sutārā, svāhā, śvetā, tapasvinī, tārā, totilā, tri-daśeśvarī, tri-purā, tṛpti, tuṣṭi, tvaritā, tgra-caṇḍā, ullotā, ullukā, umā, vaiṣṇavī, vāmanī, vārāhī, vāyavyā, vedārtha-jananī, vidyā, vijayā, vikaralī, vimalā, vināyakī,* and *virajā*.

Balanced functioning of the chakra: When it is functioning well, this chakra manifests great responsibility, creativity, a wealth of ideas, a developed capacity for communication, expression, and attention, enjoyment in giving and sharing, independence, flowing with life, a developed personality, and a strong immune system.

Imbalanced functioning of the chakra: Among the characteristic symptoms of a closed *viśuddha-cakra*, we find problems with the voice, difficulties in communication, stuttering, or a fear of appearing ridiculous by speaking. We may also see the excessive need to speak constantly, to speak very softly or very loudly, a lack of creativity, insecurity about creating, avoiding responsibility, childishness, nostalgia for stability and security, depression, stubbornness, isolation, self-hatred, or disgust with life. When this energy center is blocked, there is difficulty in self-expression, including expressing feelings, emotions, and experiences. The voice and the gestures are used in a superficial and timid way, without much meaning. Physiological problems include weakness, digestive problems, vocal problems, unstable weight, frequent colds, throat disorders, irritations and infections of the vocal cords, tension in the shoulders, neck, and nape, and stiffness in the arms and hands.

Yantra: Sixteen *nāḍīs* represented by sixteen petals originate from this center. Because this is the center of sound, the petals represent the sixteen vowels in the Sanskrit alphabet. The Sanskrit vowels (*bījākṣaras*) are *Aṁ, Āṁ, Iṁ, Īṁ, Uṁ, Ūṁ, Ṛṁ, Ṝṁ, Ḷṛṁ, Ḷṝṁ, Eṁ, Aiṁ, Oṁ, Auṁ, Aṁ*, and *Aḥ*.

The vibration of the heart of the center has its own letter, *Haṁ*. In the center of the circle lies a white triangle and in its center, there is another circle that represents ether.

विशुद्ध चक्र

Viśuddha-cakra yantra

Sixth Chakra

Ājñā-cakra or "Third Eye Chakra"

jvalad dīpākāraṁ tadanu ca navīnārka-bahula-
prakāśaṁ jyotir vā gagana-dharaṇī-madhya-militam
iha sthāne sākṣād bhavati bhagavān pūrṇa-vibhavo
'vyayaḥ sākṣī-vahneḥ śaśi-mihirayor maṇḍala iva

One then also sees the light in the form of a flaming lamp. It is lustrous and clear like the bright morning sun and glows between the sky and the earth. It is here that Bhagavān manifests himself in the fullness of his might. He knows no decay and he is the witness of fire. He is here, just as he is in the region of the moon and sun.
(*Ṣaṭ-cakra-nirūpaṇa* by Swami Pūrṇānanda, 37)

bhruvor madhye śiva-sthānaṁ
manas tatra vilīyate
jñātavyaṁ tat-padaṁ turyaṁ
tatra kālo na vidyate

> In between the eyebrows is the place of Shiva; there the mind is absorbed. This place, named *turīya*, should be sought after. There, death does not exist.
>
> (*Haṭha-yoga-pradīpika*, 4.48)

ājñā-padmaṁ bhruvor madhye
hakṣopetam dvi-patrakam
śuklābhaṁ tan mahā-kālaḥ
siddho devy atra hākinī

> The two-petalled chakra is called *ājñā* and is situated between the eyebrows. Its letters are *Ha* and *Kṣa*. It is lustrous white and its presiding deity is Mahā-kāla (great time). Its presiding goddess is Hākinī.
>
> (*Śiva Saṁhitā*, 5.96)

The sixth chakra is the seat of cognitive faculties such as *buddhi*, *citta*, *ahaṅkāra*, *manas*, and the senses (*indriyas*). *Ājnā-cakra* is closely associated with vision, the frontal lobe of the cerebrum, involuntary functions, and the ability to imagine and create fantasies. By focusing our attention, we directly engage this chakra, which is affected in proportion to the intensity of our concentration. When this center awakens, we experience more mental clarity and can observe our situation in life through new eyes.

Just as our physical eyes allow us to see the worldly, the third eye makes it possible to see hidden, transcendental dimensions. With the awakening of this center, extrasensory powers, clairvoyance, and intuitive faculties develop. This center makes it possible to perceive auras and the superior intelligence through which we gain access to visions of the future or past.

This is where the *rudra-granthi*, or "knot of Rudra," is found. It is the valve that blocks the ascent of *kuṇḍalinī-śakti* toward *sahasrāra-cakra* if the idea of a separate "I" has not been transcended. *Ājñā-cakra* marks the beginning of our own awakening, which is *savikalpa-samādhi*, or "*samādhi* with diversity."

When *ājñā-cakra* opens, observation sharpens considerably and intuition emerges that ends any mental, emotional, or spiritual nearsightedness. Only a few souls have awakened this center and transcended all attachment and selfishness. They are called *mahātmas*, or "great souls." When the *kuṇḍalinī-śakti* reaches this point, consciousness expands and yogis can perceive divinity while still perceiving themselves as different from consciousness.

List of the properties of *ājñā-cakra*

Meaning of the name: The word *ājñā* means "order, command, or authority." An alternative meaning is "unlimited power."

Other names of the chakra: This chakra is also known as *ātma-netra* (the eye of the soul), *tṛtīya-netra* (the third eye), *śiva-netra* (the eye of Shiva), *divya-cakṣu* (the divine eye), and *jñāna-cakṣu* or *jñāna-netra* (the eye of knowledge). It is also called *guru-cakra* (the chakra of the guru) because according to astrology, the planet Jupiter (*guru*) influences this chakra. Through this center, disciples receive some of the guidance and teachings of their spiritual masters. In Tantric terminology, this chakra is called *ājñā-patra* (the invincible leaf), *ājñā* (the authority or the unlimited power), *ājñā-pura* or *ājñā-purī* (the powerful city), *ājñā-paṅkaja* (the powerful lotus), *bhrū-mādhya* (the one who is between the eyebrows), *bhrū-mādhya-cakra* (the chakra between the eyebrows), *ājñāmbhoja* (the mighty lotus), *bhrū-mādhya-ga-padma* (the lotus that is located between the eyebrows), *bhrū-mūla* (the root of the eyebrows), *bhrū-saro-ruha* (the eyebrow lotus), *bhrū-maṇḍala* (the eyebrow circle), *dvi-dala* (the two-petalled one), *dvi-dala-kamala* (the lotus with two petals), *dvi-dalāmbuja* (the two-petalled lotus), *dvi-patra* (the two-petalled one), *jñāna-padma* (the lotus of wisdom), *netra-padma* (the eyes lotus), *netra-patra* (the leaf of the eyes), *Śiva-padma* (Shiva's lotus), and *tri-veṇi-kamala* (the lotus of the tri-fold confluence). In the Vedas and in the Upanishads, this center is referred to as *ājñā*, *baindava-sthāna* (the place of the all-powerful one), *bhrū-yuga-mādhya-bila* (the pit which is situated at the joint of the eyebrows), *bhrū-cakra* (the eyebrow chakra), and *dvi-dala* (two-petalled one). In Puranic terminology, we see it as *ājñā*, *dvi-dala*, and *tri-rasna* (the threefold one).

Location: The physical location of the sixth center is the pituitary gland below the base of the brain.

***Kṣetram*:** At *Bhrū-madhya*, the center point between the eyebrows.

Presiding deity: The deity of the sixth center is Ardha-nārīśvara, who is the union or fusion of Shiva and Shakti. This deity consists of two halves: the right is Shiva, masculine and camphor blue, while the left is Pārvatī, feminine and pink. Ardha-nārīśvara teaches us that God cannot remain separated from his shakti, or "creative energy." This deity represents the perfect combination of opposites: the fusion of masculine and feminine, the disappearance of all duality, and the revelation of the Whole. This characteristic is the same as the union of the linga and yoni. In the right hand, he holds the sacred trident, which represents the three modalities of nature (sattva, *rajas*, and tamas): the past, present, and future; the trinity (*tri-puṭī*) of knowledge, knower, and the known; and the material, astral, and causal planes. The feminine half is dressed in a beautiful red sari and holds a lotus flower that symbolizes purity.

Goddess: The goddess who presides over this center is Hākinī, who has six heads and four arms. The mantra of Hākinī-śakti is *Oṁ śrī-hākinyai namaḥ* (Om, respectful reverences to Śrī Hākinī). The goddess is seated on a lotus flower. Her skin is a beautiful pink color and she is very beautifully adorned with golden jewelry and precious gemstones. In her four hands, she holds a book as a sign of knowledge, the drum of Lord Shiva called *ḍamaru*, a skull, and a rosary (*mālā*). With her other two hands she makes the mudras that offer blessings and banish fear.

ājñānām āmbujaṁ tadd hima-kara-sadṛśaṁ
dhyāna-dhāma-prakāśaṁ
ha-kṣābhyāṁ vai kalābhyāṁ
parilasita-vapur-netra-patraṁ-suśubhram
tan madhye hākinī sā śaśi-sama-dhavalā vaktra-ṣaṭkaṁ dadhānā
vidyāṁ mudrāṁ kapālaṁ ḍamaru-japa-vaṭīṁ bibhratī śuddha-cittā

> The lotus named *ājñā* is like the moon [beautifully white]. On its two petals are the letters *ha* and *kṣa*, which are also white and enhance its beauty. It shines with the glory of *dhyāna* (meditation). Inside the lotus is the shakti Hākinī, whose six faces are like so many moons. In her hands she holds a book, a skull, a small drum, and a rosary. Her mind is pure (*śuddha-citta*).
>
> (*Ṣaṭ-cakra-nirūpaṇa* by Swami Pūrṇānanda, 32)

Element or *tattva*: Mind, or *manas*. The element of this chakra is the mind, which is the center of knowledge when it is focused on the relative and the material. It becomes the source of wisdom when it becomes introspective and melts.

Color of the chakra: Indigo.

Color of the *tattva*: It does not have a color.

Power associated with this center: The ability to enter another body and acquire mystical powers.

Esoteric symbolism of the chakra:

Number of petals: Two.

Mantras of the petals: *Kṣaṁ* and *Haṁ*.

Mantra of the chakra: Om.

Shape of the mandala: Circle.

Animal of the chakra: Black gazelle.

Plane or *loka*: *Tapa* or *Tapo-loka*, or "the plane of austerity."

Subtle element or *tanmātra*: None.

Gland: Pituitary, also known as the hypophysis.

Cognitive organ or *jñanendriya*: None.

Organ of action or *karmendriya*: None.

Energetic channel or *nāḍī*: *Iḍā* and *piṅgalā*.

Bioelement or *doṣa*: None.

Vital air or *vāyu*: *Prāṇa*, *apāna*, *vyāna*, *samāna*, and *udāna*.

Sheath or *kośa*: *Vijñāna-maya*, or "the intellectual sheath."

Gemstones: Aquamarine, amazonite, chalcedony, pyrite, siderite, topaz, turquoise, amethyst, jade, lapis lazuli, carnelian, blue sapphire, and moonstone.

Fragrance: Jasmine.

Aromatherapy oils: Peppermint, hyacinth, violet, geranium, jasmine, vetiver, basil, patchouli, and rosemary.

Planet or *graha*: Śani, or "Saturn."

Recommended postures or asanas: Cobra posture (*bhujaṅgāsana*) and seated forward fold (*paścimottānāsana*).

Secondary chakras related to *ājñā-cakra*: *Lalāṭā*, *agni-kuṇḍā*, *viśālākṣi*, *viṣṇu-māyā*, *visma-locanā*, *vriddhi*, *yama-bhaganī*, *yama-ghaṇṭā*, *yaśā*, *manotigā*, *mati*, *mātrikā*, *māyāvī*, *mayūrī*, *medhā*, *megha-vāsinī*, *mohinī*, and *mukta-keśī*.

Balanced functioning of the chakra: The harmonious functioning of this chakra is expressed as balance between the paired organs of the body, concentration, balance between the poles of the personality, consciousness of the soul, wisdom, intuition, spiritual experiences, thinking power, and markedly strong willpower.

Imbalanced functioning of the chakra: A hyperactive sixth center is expressed as excessive materialism, authoritarianism, and stubbornness. Someone with a weak sixth center is very easily influenced and lacks determination. Physiologically, a malfunctioning third-eye chakra is expressed as a lack of balance in the paired organs such as eyes and ears, headaches, and vision problems. Those with an *ājñā*-cakra that is not functioning in harmony with the rest of the chakras live only through the intellect; their lives occur only in their heads. They only accept what they are able to rationalize as real, and similarly, they completely reject everything they cannot understand. They suffer from problems with concentration and identity, accepting criticism, excessive repression, forgetfulness, an unstable personality, excessive egocentrism, irritability, lack of sensitivity toward others, a desire to escape from reality, and an inclination toward isolation. Generally, the malfunctioning of *ājñā*-cakra manifests as mental hyperactivity and excessive and continuous mental chatter.

Yantra: The diagram of *ājñā-cakra* has two petals, which represent the two eyes that we perceive physical reality with. Between them there is a circle that represents the third eye and the eye of the soul. Here, all duality fuses and is converted into integrated consciousness. The two petals of this center are also said to represent ātma and *param-ātma*. The letters of these two petals are *Kṣaṁ* and *Haṁ*. These two letters are the *bīja-mantras* of Shakti and Shiva. The two petals represent the *iḍā* and *piṅgalā nāḍīs*, which merge with the principal *nāḍī* or *suṣumṇā-nāḍī*, in this exact place, before ascending to *sahasrāra-cakra*. In *ājñā-cakra*, the experience of the fourth state of consciousness (*turīya*) takes place above the lower states of *jāgrat* (vigilance), *svapna* (sleep with dreams), and *suṣupti* (deep sleep). The vibration of this center's core has its own mantra, Om.

आज्ञा चक्र

Ājñā-cakra yantra

Seventh chakra

Sahasrāra-cakra or "Crown Chakra"

Brahma-randhra

Brahma-randhra means "hollow of Brahman" and is also known as *daśama-dvāra,* or "the tenth door." *Kuṇḍalinī-śakti* passes through *brahma-randhra* to reach *sahasrāra-cakra. Brahma-randhra* is the place on the crown of the head called the anterior or bregmatic fontanelle. Rectangular in shape, it is one of the soft spots on babies' skulls that does not grow together until they are twelve to eighteen months old. It is located between the division of the frontal and parietal bones. As the baby grows, sutures are formed and close to form a solid bony area throughout adult life. The nectar produced by the fusion of kundalini and Shiva flows from *brahma-randhra.* At the time of death, *brahma-randhra* is broken and life energy leaves through it.

tad-ūrdhve śaṅkhinyā nivasati śikhare śūnya-deśe prakāśaṁ
visargādhaḥ padmaṁ daśa-śata-dalaṁ pūrṇa-candrāti śubhram
adho vaktraṁ kāntaṁ taruṇa-ravi-kalā-kānti-kiñjalka-puñjaṁ
a-kārādyair varṇaiḥ pravilasita-vapuḥ kevalānanda-rūpam

> Above that (*ājñā-cakra*) is the lotus of a thousand petals, in the vacant space where *śānkhinī-nādī* is and below *Visarga*. This lotus, lustrous and whiter than the full moon, faces downward. It is enchanting. Its clustered filaments are tinged with the color of the young sun. Its body is luminous with all the letters beginning with the vowel *a*, and it is the personification of absolute bliss.
>
> (*Ṣaṭ-cakra-nirūpaṇa* by Swami Pūrṇānanda, 40)

Although each chakra is independent, they are all intimately linked, and all remain constantly connected to *sahasrāra-cakra*. The six lower centers find union and integration in the seventh chakra.

It is no coincidence that the crown center occupies the seventh position. Seven is a number of tremendous esoteric significance. In many cultures, the number seven is related to creation or the process through which consciousness expresses itself from the subtle to the gross. The chakra structure is a microcosm of creation. That is to say, it is a reflection of a universal process that begins from the subtle and then expresses itself at more and more gross levels. Kundalini yoga points in the opposite direction, toward an involutionary movement of consciousness from the gross to the subtle.

Sahasrāra-cakra represents the culmination of the ascension process of *kuṇḍalinī-śakti*, in which one experiences both the ecstasy of absolute bliss and an expansion of consciousness. It is the pinnacle of a movement that rises from *ājñā-cakra* as *savikalpa-samādhi*

(*samādhi* with seed or diversity) in order to express itself here, in the seventh center, as *nirvikalpa-samādhi* (*samādhi* without seed). When kundalini reaches and perforates the third eye chakra, the awakening begins, although there are still residues of sleep, or seeds. Only in the seventh center can the awakening be completed.

It is also called *sahasrāra-dala*, or "the lotus of a thousand petals," and is represented by a mandala with a moon and thousand petals. The number of petals seems to be symbolic, as it has been represented with one hundred, one hundred thousand, and one million petals. It symbolizes an infinite number of petals, because this center represents the infinite blossoming of the soul and the infinite expansion of consciousness. In the relative plane, we perceive flowering as a process that is always followed by decay. Everything is born, develops, and reaches maturity, only to finally die and decay. Every birth is the beginning of a death. In the entrails of every beginning, resides the end. *Sahasrāra* symbolizes the eternal blossoming in consciousness, which is enlightenment, an infinite expansion. It is the only chakra that opens upward toward the heights. Five open to the front and *mūlādhāra* opens downward. *Sahasrāra* opens upward toward the transcendental reality of the mind.

It is not an easy task to describe the transcendental or to define the mystery. It is difficult to verbalize what transcends the limits of language and explain what lies beyond words. To say something about *sahasrāra-cakra* is an authentic challenge because its existence precedes words and language. It is not a center to speak about because it is transcendental consciousness.

Only an authentic realized master can give us some information about the chakra of a thousand petals. Only one who moves in the transcendental and knows its meadows of silence can make the impossible possible and verbalize something of the mystery or explain something of the Absolute. Only from the lips of a realized guru can we hear authoritative words about the dwelling place of God at the crown of the head. Perhaps it is called the crown chakra because it is the only one located outside the physical body. The crown is something separate from the king, but when placed on his head it indicates his position as monarch.

atrāste śiśu-sūrya-sodara-kalā candrasya sā ṣoḍaśī
śuddhā nīraja-sūkṣma-tantu-śatadhā-bhāgaika-rūpā parā
vidyut-koṭi-samāna-komala-tanūr-vidyotitādho mukhī
nityānanda-paraṁparātivigalat-pīyūṣa-dhārādharā

Here is the excellent [supreme] sixteenth part of the moon, or *kalā*. She is pure and resembles [in color] the young sun. She is as thin as one one-hundredth of a fiber of a lotus stalk. She is lustrous and soft like ten million lightning bolts, and faces downward. From her, whose source is Brahman, the continuous stream of nectar flows copiously. She is the receptacle of the stream of excellent nectar which comes from the blissful union of *para* and *parā*, (Shiva and Shakti).

(*Ṣaṭ-cakra-nirūpaṇa* by Swami Pūrṇānanda, 46)

śiva-sthānaṁ śaivāḥ parama-puruṣaṁ vaiṣṇava-gaṇā
lapantīti prāyo hari-hara-padaṁ kecid apare
padaṁ devyā devī-caraṇa-yugalāṁbhoja-rasikā
munīndrāpy ante prakṛti-puruṣa-sthānam amalam

> The Shaivas call it the abode of Shiva; the Vaishnavas call it the dwelling place of *Parama-puruṣa* (the supreme). Others still call it the place of Hari-Hara. Those who are filled with a passion for the lotus feet of the Devi call it the excellent abode of the Devi. Other great sages (*munis*) call it the pure place of *Prakṛti-puruṣa.*
> (*Ṣaṭ-cakra-nirūpaṇa* by Swami Pūrṇānanda, 44)

It is here that the yogi completely sheds the personal plane and awakens to universal reality. It is the end of a very long path that spans many lives from here to here. It is the place of the great divine reunion, the true religion, where the individual is reabsorbed into the totality. It is the place of reintegration, which is the final step in the great cosmic process of consciousness. It is the door from the mundane to the transcendental, from the relative to the Absolute, from slavery to freedom. When the serpentine power arrives at the crown center, the boundary between human and divine is crossed.

This center corresponds to absolute Truth because it represents the transcendence of all relativity, in other words, the reintegration of duality into unity, the source and origin. The fusion of Shiva and Shakti means the evaporation of all duality. Shakti disappears only to reemerge with Shiva as the sole, absolute reality. When kundalini is absorbed there, there is a fusion of the knower, the knowledge, and the known. The cognitive platform of subject-object is dismantled. When the divine fire reaches the crown chakra, the sense of separation disappears, along with concepts such as space, time, and causation. The yogi transcends the "I" and its baggage of desires and ambitions, even the desire for enlightenment. The individual, emotions, longings, and desires are taken and reabsorbed into their source and origin: pure consciousness.

When we reach *sahasrāra*, the evolutionary process is complete. The individual emerges within the totality; the personal dissolves into the universal. Only beginning with this chakra can we speak of enlightenment, since it is a state of the complete absence of mental activity. The realization of the seventh chakra comes from the purity of the yogi, the grace of the spiritual master, and divine mercy.

List of the properties of *sahasrāra-cakra*

Meaning of the name: "The thousand-spoked wheel" also called *śūñya* (empty) and *cakra-nirālamba-purī* (the chakra of the independent city).

Other names of the chakra: In the Vedas, Upanishads, and Puranas, we find many names for this energy center. Tantric terminology calls *sahasrāra-cakra* by the following names: *adho-mukha-mahā-padma* (the great lotus which is facing downward), *amlāna-padma* (the bright lotus), *daśa-śata-dala-padma* or *sahasra-cchada-paṅkaja* (the thousand-petalled lotus), *sahasra-dala* (thousand-petalled), *paṅkaja* (lotus), *sahasrābja* (the lotus of thousand [petals]), *sahasra-dala* (thousand petalled), *adho-mukha-padma* (the lotus which is facing downward), *sahasra-dala-padma* (the thousand-petalled lotus), *sahasra-patra* (thousand petals), *sahasrāra* (thousand-spoked one), *sahasrārāmbuja* (thousand-spoked lotus), *sahasrāra-mahā-padma* (thousand-spoked great lotus), *sahasrāra-padma* (thousand-spoked lotus), *sahasrāra-saro-ruha* or *śiras-padma* (the lotus of the head), *śuddha-padma* (the pure lotus), *vyoman* (heaven), and *vyomāmbhoja* (the heavenly lotus). In Vedic terminology, up until the last Upanishads, we find the following names: *akāśa-cakra* (ether chakra), *kapāla-samputa* (the space between the two cavities situated in the head), *sahasra-dala/sahasrāra/sahasrāra-kamala/paṅkaja/padma* (all of these terms mean the thousand-spoked lotus), *sthāna* (the place), *vyoma* (heaven), and *vyomāmbuja* (the heavenly lotus). In the Puranas, the seventh chakra is referred to as *parama* (supreme), *sahasra-dala* (thousand-petalled), *sahasra-patra* (thousand-leaved), *sahasrāra-kamala/parikaja/padma* (all of these terms mean the thousand-spoked lotus), *samjñātita* (above our perception), *sahasrāra* (the thousand-spoked), and *samjñātita-pada* (the place above our perception, or the very clearly understood place).

Location: The upper part of the skull.

***Kṣetram*:** At the crown of the head.

Presiding deity: Shiva.

Goddess or devi: Mahā-śakti.

Element or *tattva*: Unlike the lower energy centers

which have specific elements and animals, the crown center does not have them because it is the transcendental center. That is to say, it is the divine union of Shiva and Shakti.

Color of the chakra: Violet.

Color of the *tattva*: It does not have a color; it is pure light.

Power associated with this center: Enlightenment.

Esoteric symbolism of the chakra:

Number of petals: One thousand.

Mantras of the petals: All the letters are found in an ordered way on each and every one of the petals.

Mantra of the chakra: *Aḥ*.

Shape of the mandala: None.

Animal of the chakra: None.

Plane or *loka*: *Satya-loka*, or "the plane of reality, of the Truth."

Subtle element or *tanmātra*: None.

Gland: The hypophysis or pituitary gland.

Cognitive organ or *jñanendriya*: None.

Organ of action or *karmendriya*: None.

Element or *tattva*: None.

Energetic channel or *nāḍī*: *Suṣumṇā*.

Bioelement or *doṣa*: *Kapha*, or "watery element."

Vital air or *vāyu*: None.

Sheath or *kośa*: *Ānanda-maya*, or "the bliss sheath."

Gemstones: Amazonite, amber, barite, zircon, white quartz, amethyst quartz, rose quartz, emerald, hematite, red jasper, lapis lazuli, magnetite, diamond, and zircon.

Fragrance: Lotus.

Aromatherapy oils: Frankincense, lavender, and sandalwood.

Planet: Ketu, or "the southern descending node of the moon."

Recommended postures or asanas: Headstand (*śīrṣāsana*).

Secondary chakras related to *sahasrāra-chakra*: *Mahā-devī, mahā-gaurī, mahā-kālī, mahā-lakṣmī, mahā-māyā, mahā-nidrā, mahā-tapā, mahā-vidyā, śaila-putrī, sākṣī, śakti, śāmbhavī, sarva-gatā, sarva-maṅgalā, saumyā, rudra-mukhī, rudrāṇī, sahajā, śākambarī, śākinī, samudra-tāriṇī, sandhyā, śaṅkarī, śāntā, śaraṇyā, mahodarī, mahā-bālā, mahā-bhadrā, sarvā, candra-maṇḍalā, candrāvalī, cāndrāyaṇī, chāyā, citrāṇī, dākinī, kāśikī, kātyāyanī, kāśikī, karṇā, karṇikā, kāpālinī, kanakānandā, kāmākhyā, īśānī, īśvarī, dīkṣā, dhṛvā, dīptā,* and *auṅ-kārātma.*

Balanced functioning of the chakra: When this center is functioning in a balanced way, human beings experience the most elevated level of development in all aspects, plenitude, and a pure and fresh mind. Interest in religion and spiritual topics as well as an attraction to divine consciousness, or the call of God, are closely associated with balance in this center.

Imbalanced functioning of the chakra: This chakra is related to the functions of the mind and the nervous system. An imbalance can be expressed as different types of mental disorders. Physiologically, malfunctioning can manifest as problems in the sexual organs, disease in the pineal gland, and general muscular weakness.

Yantra: None. The following illustration represents the one thousand petals of the *sahasrāra-cakra.*

सहस्रार चक्र

The one thousand petals of *sahasrāra-cakra*

The *Bindu-cakra*

Because the *bindu* is close to the seventh chakra, it is a very difficult chakra to describe and understand. It has sixteen petals and is located between *ājñā* and *sahasrāra-cakra*. Traditionally, when a brahman shaves his head, he leaves a tuft of hair called a *śikha* that marks the exact location of this chakra. This energy center is unknown to many and has been barely mentioned in the scriptures. The relationship between *bindu* and *viśuddha-cakra* is very close. They are connected through the network of nerves that pass from inside the nostrils and through *lalanā-cakra*, which is found in the small fleshy mass hanging from the soft palate, called the tonsils. One of the most interesting points is that from this center, nectar (*amṛta*) emanates, flowing from three *nāḍīs*: *ambikā*, *lambikā*, and *tālikā*. Many great masters have completely renounced food for years by consuming only the nectar that emanates from *bindu-cakra*. This *bindu* has three different levels of existence. At its highest level it is nectar, or *amṛta*; at the intermediate level, it is the vital energy that drives digestion; and at the lowest level, it is expressed as the fluid released by an orgasm. Energetically, *bindu* refers to vital energy and physiologically, to semen.

The *Yoga-cūḍāmaṇi Upaniṣad* notes the following:

khecary-āmudritaṁ yena
vivaraṁ laṁbikordhvataḥ
na tasya kṣīyate binduḥ
kāminy āliṅgitasya ca

yāvad binduḥ sthito dehe
tāvan mṛtyu-bhayaṁ kutaḥ
yāvad baddhā nabho mudrā
tāvad bindur na gacchati

One who closes the cavity of the palate from above with *khecari-mudrā* will not lose *bindu* even in the embrace of a woman. As long as *bindu* is retained in the body, whence will arise the fear of death? *Bindu* is not wasted as long as it is bound by *nabho-mudrā.*

(*Yoga-cūḍāmani Upaniṣad,* 57–58)

Yogis know how to keep this nectar in *viśuddha-cakra* so that it feeds, nourishes, and energizes the body. The nectar is transformed and stored in *lalanā-cakra*, also called *tālu-mūla-cakra* or *śīrṣāgara-cakra*, which is a center that lies behind the tongue. If the techniques to trap it are not known, the nectar of immortality falls and is burned by the fire of *maṇipūra-cakra* or it descends even lower, where it is transformed into semen. This is described in the *Yoga-cūḍāmaṇi Upaniṣad*:

jvalito 'pi yathā binduḥ
samprāptāś ca hutāśanaṁ

vrajaty ūrdhvaṁ gataḥ śaktyā
niruddho yoni mudrayā

> If *bindu* falls down and merges in the fire of *maṇipūra-cakra*, even while burning, after being prevented from dissipating further, it can be lifted upward with *yoni-mudrā* because of this practice's power.
>
> (*Yoga-cūḍāmaṇi Upaniṣad*, 59)

It is very common for people to be confused when the *bindu* is mentioned, because this word has different meanings in different scriptures.

bindu-mūla śarīrāṇi
śirā yatra pratiṣṭhitāḥ
bhāvayanti śarīrāṇi
āpāda-tala mastakaṁ

> The *bindu* is viewed as the original cause of the whole body. It is situated in the nerves and blood vessels and sustains the entire physical structure from head to toe.
>
> (*Yoga-cūḍāmaṇi Upaniṣad*, 56)

Tantric literature refers to *parā-bindu* as the mysterious point in which the entire universe dwells in its potential state, ready and able to be manifested. As such, it is also included in the symbol of Om, as a point on the crescent moon.

Some properties of *bindu-cakra*

Meaning of the name: The name of this chakra means "point or drop."

Other names of the chakra: *Bindu-cakra* is also known as *indu* (moon), *amṛta* (immortal or nectar), and *candra-cakra* (the moon chakra).

Location: It is located above *ājñā-cakra*.

***Kṣetra*:** On the forehead, between *ājñā* and *sahasrāra-cakra*.

Presiding deity or deva: *Śiva-kāmeśvara*, which refers to the aspect of Lord Shiva as the god of desire.

Goddess or devi: Kāmeśvarī. The *Lalitā-sahasra-nāma* refers to the devi as Śiva-kāmeśvarāṅka-sthā.

śivaś casau kāmeś casau īśvaraś ca iti śiva-kāmeśvaraḥ
tasya aṅke tiṣṭhati sā

She who takes a seat on the left thigh of Lord Śiva-kāmeśvara.

(*Lalitā-sahasra-nāma*, 21)

Color of the chakra: Transparent.

Esoteric symbolism of the chakra:

Number of petals: Sixteen.

Figure of the mandala: Inside the triangle ā, *kā*, *thā* formed by the *nāḍīs vāma*, *jyeṣṭha*, and *raudrī*, the place where Śiva-kāmeśvara and Kāmeśvarī reside.

Energetic channels or *nāḍīs*: *Vāma*, *jyeṣṭha*, and *raudrī*.

List of the principal minor chakras in alphabetical order

Abhokta, acala, adṛśya, advaita, agandha, agni, aiśvarya, aitareya, akarta, akhanda, akhira-sena, akṣara, amala, amana, amṛta, ānanda, ānanda-maya, ananta, aṅkuśa, anna-maya, aprāṇa, aruṇa-giri-nātha, arūpa, aśabda, aśakta, asaṅga, asparśa, asti, asura, atibala, atīndriya, ātman, āvāṅg-mano-gocara, avyakta, avyaya, bala, balavān, basti, bhadra, bhaviṣya, bhudha, bhūta, brahmā, brahma-svarūpa, brahma-vaivarta, brahmāṇḍa, bṛhad-āranyaka, bṛhan-nāradīya, caitanya, caitanya-puruṣa, candra, cetana, chandas, cid-ākāśa, cid-aṁbareśa, cid-agna, cin-maya, cid-ambara, dakṣa, dākṣyanī, dhadīci, dīpaka, draṣṭa, gaja, gala-baddha, garga, garuḍa, gau, gaiha, gulaha, guru, halasya-sundara, haṁsa, hrīṁ-kāra, īśa, jambukeśvara, jñāna, jñānam, jyotiṣa, kaivalya, kāla-bhairava, kāla-bheda, kāla-dahada, kāla-dvāra, kāla-hastīśvara, kalpa, kañci-nātha, kānta, kāpālīśvara, karagaka, kāraṇa, karma, karṇa-mūla, katha, kauśitaki, kena, ketu, kevala, kīrti, kubera, kuhu, kula-dīpa, kumara-guru-para, kumbheśvara-cakra-kuṇḍali, kūrma, kūṭastha, lalitā, liṅga, mahā-bhairava, maheśa, mahotsāha, maitrāyaṇi, makara, manas, māṇḍūkya, maṅgala, mano-maya, matsya, māyā-mayi, meṣa, mucu-kunda, mukteśvara, mukunda, muṇḍaka, nāgeśvara, nandi, nārada, nara-siṁha, naukula, nīla-lohita, nir-ādhara, nir-ākāra, nir-anjana, nir-atiśayānanda, nir-bala, nir-doṣa, nir-guṇa, nir-lipta, nir-mala, nir-ukta, nir-upādhika, nir-vikalpa, niś-cala, nitya, oṁ-kāra, oṁ-kāreśvara, padmā, pāpa-vimocaka, para-brahmā, parameśvara, parāśara, paśupati, prajñānānanda, prāṇa, prāṇa-maya, praśna, praśṛta-sthani, pratyakṣa, pūrṇa, rāhu, rameśvara, raudra, rohini, rudra, sākṣi, sāmba, sampūrṇa, sanat-kumāra, san-mantra, śāntam, sarpa, sarvā-nabhava, sarveśa, satyam, śani, śukra, siddha, śikṣa, siṁha, siṁha-mukha, śiva, śivācārī, śiva-kavi, śivam, śiva-rahasya, soma, śrī, sthūla, śubham, śuddha, sukha, sūkṣma, sundaram, sundareśa, sura, surasai, sūrya, svayaṁ-jyoti-prakāśa, śvetāśvatara, taittirīya, tan-maya, tāra, tārakeśvara, tejas, tejo-maya, tri-veṇi, tryambakeśvara, turīa, tyāgeśa, ūrdhva-randhra, umā-maheśvara, upāsana, urvasī, vāhana, vaidyanātha, vikkatappa, vairāgya, vajra, vāmana, vāñchitārtha-pradarśana, varāha, vijñāna-maya, vimala, vīra-bhadra, viṣṇu, viśveśa, and *vyākaraṇa.*

The senses and the animals that die because of them

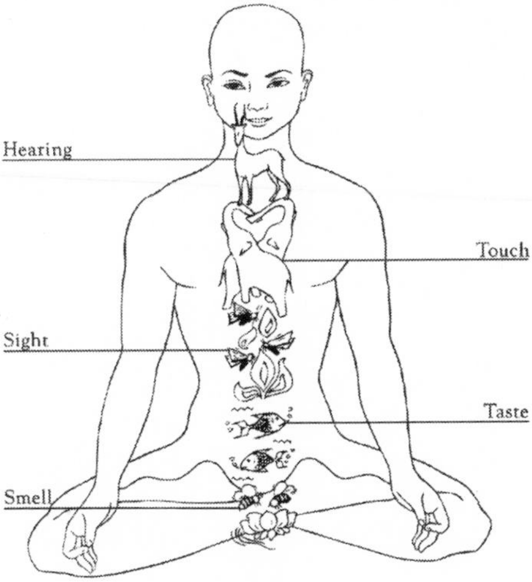

śabdādibhiḥ pañcabhir eva pañca
pañcatvam āpuḥ sva-guṇena baddhāḥ
kuraṅga-mātaṅga-pataṅga-mīna-
bhṛṅgā naraḥ pañcabhir añcitaḥ kim

Any of the five senses is more than sufficient to cause death, as seen with the moth, the deer, the elephant, the fish, and the bee. What then is the condition of one who has all five! It is the desire to see the color of the flame that kills the moth; the desire to hear kills the deer; the desire to touch kills the elephant; to taste, the fish; to smell, the black bee. Imagine what awaits one who is attached to all five senses! (*Viveka-cūḍāmaṇi* by Śrī Śaṅkarācārya, verse 76)

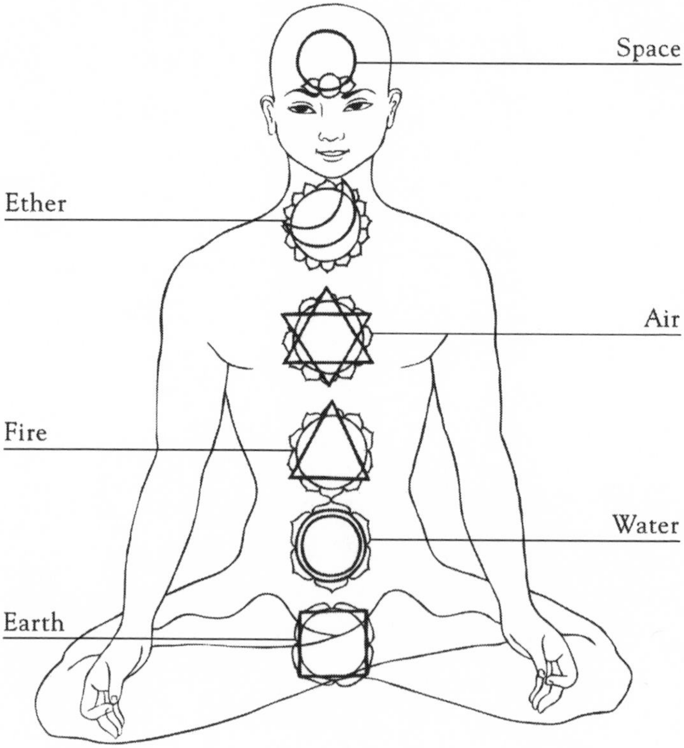

Chakras and their elements

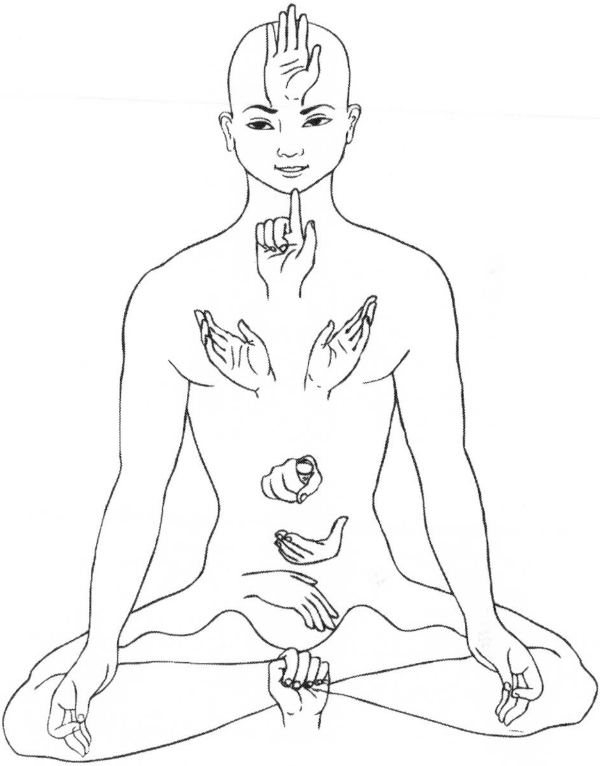

The chakras and their mudras

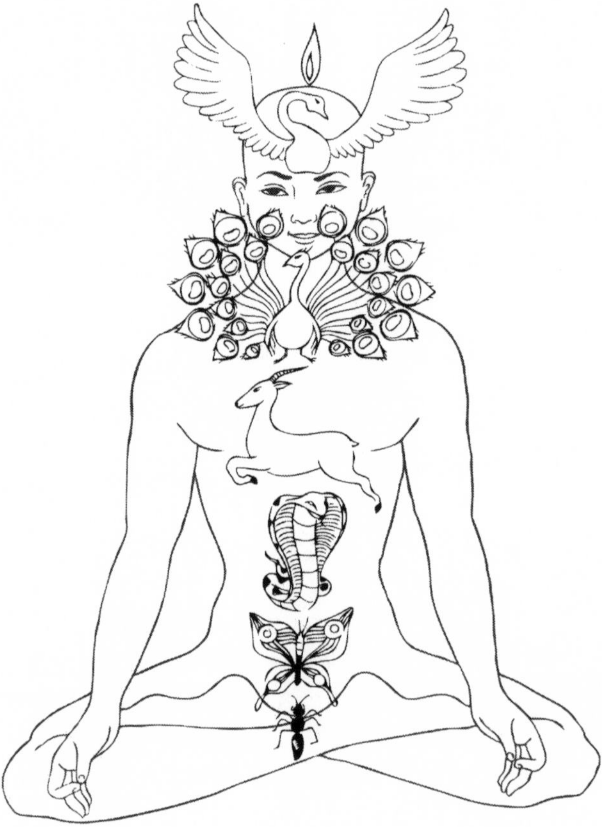

The chakras and their behaviors
In ascending order: ant, butterfly, cobra, deer,
peacock, swan, and enlightenment

Śrī Rāmakṛṣṇa Paramahaṁsa (1836–1886) described the experience of *kuṇḍalinī-śakti* like this:

> As she [the *kuṇḍalinī-śakti*] awakens, I sometimes experience a feeling as if ants are walking from my feet to my head. As long as it does not reach the brain, I maintain my consciousness, but when it arrives at the brain, I die to the external world. The functions of seeing and hearing are stopped. And who can talk then? The differences between "I" and "you" vanish. Sometimes I try to tell all of you what I see and feel when this mysterious power ascends to here (points at his heart) or to here (points to his throat). From that state you can still talk, which I do, but when kundalini goes higher than here (points to his throat) it is as if someone is blocking my mouth. Then, to put it in other words, I drop all ties. More than once, I have tried to tell you what I feel when kundalini ascends beyond the throat, but when I even think about it, the mind jumps up, and the whole thing is over.

In any case, even if in the beginning you do not experience what Rāmakṛṣṇa Paramahaṁsa speaks about, you can be assured that if you dedicate time for practice every day, you will immediately start feeling greater vitality, clarity, internal peace, and a considerably more balanced mood. Progressively, your personal charm will shine brighter and your possibilities of transformation will be unlimited, due to the awakening and elevation of your consciousness.

Section III
The sadhana of kundalini yoga

Padmāsana, or "lotus posture"

Sukhāsana, or "comfortable posture"

Siddhāsana, or "the accomplished pose"

Anyone who decides to begin the path of the serpentine power must take into account that it is not a path for the mildly interested. It is not advisable to take it up as a hobby, like an after-work activity. The practice of kundalini yoga involves a very moderate way of life. This path in particular should not be undertaken without the expert guidance and direction of an authentic spiritual master.

Before explaining the practices of this path, I would like to mention that although the techniques are important, they are only part of the basic levels. Practices are beneficial at the beginning of spiritual life, but they are not an end in themselves. They are essential in the beginning, but they can become a serious obstacle if we do not let them go at the right time. Although there are many techniques to visualize chakras, observe breathing, or repeat mantras, we must remember that religion's aim is to realize our divine nature, not to turn us into skillful visualizers of chakras, observers of breathing, or repeaters of mantras.

1. Purification

Kundalini yoga is a sophisticated system that prepares us to develop our energetic nature. It includes four levels of sadhana: awakening of the serpentine power, its elevation, piercing the chakras, and meeting Shiva. These practices are intended to create the necessary conditions for reaching the highest level.

Aspirants (*sādhakas*) who want to study kundalini yoga should comply with the essential requirements demanded by the scriptures: be properly initiated by an authentic spiritual master and loyally follow the master's guidance and teachings.

As egos, we are immersed in a noisy world saturated with ideas, concepts, and conclusions. Thus, we lack the necessary internal space to allow the Divine to manifest within us. Through sadhana, we silence the noise and expand our inner space.

This path demands a high degree of physical and astral purity. Strict vegetarianism, for example, is indispensable if we aspire to advance significantly on this path.

Kundalini yoga considers cleansing and purification of all aspects of the *sādhaka* to be essential. The sadhana of this type of yoga includes *kāya-śuddhi* (cleaning of the physical body), *nāḍī-śuddhi* (purification of the *nāḍīs*), and *citta-śuddhi* (purification of the mind).

1. *Kāya-śuddhi*: Physical hygiene is one of the fundamental requirements for all spiritual practices. The basic method is *snāna* (washing of the body). However, within the *kāya-śuddhi*, we also find practices such as *vinyāsas* (sequences of breath-synchronized movements) and asanas (postures) of hatha yoga, which tone the nervous system and give it the ability to withstand the intensity of the awakening and ascent of kundalini.
2. *Nāḍī-śuddhi*: There are several methods to purify the *nāḍīs*. Some are *samanu* (by repeating *bīja-mantras*), and others are *nirmanu* (without mantras). In *nāḍī-śuddhi*, there are various techniques that help regulate the flow of vital energy: mudras (energetic seals), *bandhas* (locks), *kriyās* (bodily actions), and *prāṇāyāma* (breathing exercises).
3. *Citta-śuddhi*: For mental cleansing, *japa* is used, which is the systematic repetition of mantras. *Citta-śuddhi* occurs as a natural consequence of *dhāraṇā* (concentration).

In order to begin our journey on the kundalini path, it is important to become stronger, clean ourselves, and purify our intentions. As long as we strive for personal benefit, the divine power will not awake, no matter how much we practice. Developing in yoga involves renouncing our attitude of exploitation and all selfish desires to attain mystical powers, fame, health, and so forth.

Since the practice of techniques is not enough to purify ourselves, it is necessary to develop the spirit of karma yoga (selfless service). In this way, it is possible to practice kundalini yoga by offering water to the thirsty, helping those in need, or feeding the hungry. Without opening the heart and adopting selfless service as an integral part of our lives, we will not know purity. This is essential to create a situation conducive to something greater happening.

Nāḍī-śuddhi or "purification of the *nāḍīs*"

Before trying to awaken the energy centers, it is essential to purify the *nāḍīs*. One classic technique for purification and cleaning the *nāḍīs* is described in the *Gheraṇḍa Saṁhitā* (5.33–45):

kuśāsane mṛgājine
vyāghrājine ca kambale
sthalāsane samāsīnaḥ
prāṅ-mukho vāpy udaṅ-mukhaḥ
nāḍī-śuddhiṁ samāsādya
prāṇāyāmaṁ samabhyaset

One should sit on a seat of *kuśa* grass, an antelope hide, tiger hide, a blanket, or on the earth, calmly and quietly, facing East or North. Having purified the *nāḍīs*, one should begin *prāṇāyāma*.

caṇḍa-kāpālir uvāca:
nāḍī-śuddhiṁ kathaṁ kuryān
nāḍī-śuddhis tu kīdṛśī

tat sarvaṁ śrotum icchāmi
tad vadasva dayā-nidhe
Caṇḍa-kāpāli said:

O ocean of mercy! How are the *nāḍīs* purified? What does the purification of the *nāḍīs* involve? I want to hear all of this, please tell me.

gheraṇḍa uvāca:

malākulāsu nāḍīṣu
māruto naiva gacchati
prāṇāyāmaḥ kathaṁ sidhyet
tattva-jñānaṁ kathaṁ bhavet
tasmād ādau nāḍī-śuddhiṁ
prāṇāyāmaṁ tato 'bhyaset
Gheraṇḍa said:

The *vāyu* [cannot] enter the *nāḍīs* as long as they are full of impurities. How then can *prāṇāyāma* be done? How can knowledge of the *tattvas* be acquired? Therefore, the *nāḍīs* should be first purified, and then *prāṇāyāma* should be practiced.

nāḍī-śuddhir dvidhā proktā
samanur nirmanus tathā
bījena samanuṁ kuryān
nirmanuṁ dhauti-karmaṇā

There are two ways to purify the *nāḍīs*: *samanu* and *nirmanu*. *Samanu* is done mentally with *bīja-mantras*. *Nirmanu* is done through physical cleanings.

dhauta-karma purā proktaṁ
ṣaṭ-karma-sādhane yathā
śṛṇuṣva samanuṁ caṇḍa
nāḍī-śuddhir yathā bhavet

The physical cleanings or *dhautis* have already been taught. They consist of the six sadhanas. Now, O Caṇḍa, listen to the *samanu* process of purifying the *nāḍīs*.

upaviśyāsane yogī
padmāsanaṁ samācaret
gurvādi nyāsanaṁ kuryād
yathaiva guru-bhāṣitam
nāḍī-śuddhiṁ prakurvīta
prāṇāyāma-viśuddhaye

Sitting in *padmāsana*, and performing the adoration of the guru, as taught by the teacher, one should purify the *nāḍīs* for success in *prāṇāyāma*.

vāyu-bījaṁ tato dhyātvā
dhūmra-varṇaṁ satejasam
candreṇa pūrayed vāyuṁ
bījaṁ ṣoḍaśakaiḥ sudhīḥ

catuḥ-ṣaṣṭyā mātrayā ca
kumbhakenaiva dhārayet
dvā-triṁśan mātrayā vāyuṁ
sūrya-nāḍyā ca recayet

Concentrating on *vāyu-bīja* (i.e., *Yaṁ*), full of energy and the color of smoke, inhaling through the left nostril, and repeating the *bīja* sixteen times is *pūraka*. Holding the breath for a period of sixty-four repetitions of the mantra is *kumbhaka*. Then, one should expel the air through the right nostril slowly, as long as it takes to repeat the mantra thirty-two times.

nābhi-mūlād vahnim utthāpya
dhyāyet tejo 'vanī-yutam
vahni-bīja-ṣoḍaśena
sūrya-nāḍyā ca pūrayet

catuḥ-ṣaṣṭyā mātrayā ca
kumbhakenaiva dhārayet
dvā-triṁśan mātrayā vāyuṁ
śaśi-nāḍyā ca recayet

The root of the navel is the seat of *agni-tattva*. Lifting the fire up from this root, join it with *pṛthivī-tattva*. Then, concentrate on this mixed light. Repeating *agni-bīja* (*Raṁ*) sixteen times, inhale through the right nostril, hold it for the period of sixty-four repetitions of the mantra, and then exhale through the left nostril for a period of thirty-two repetitions of the mantra.

nāsāgre śaśadhṛg-bimbaṁ
dhyātvā jyotsnā-samanvitam
ṭhaṁ bīja-ṣoḍaśenaiva
iḍyā pūrayen marut

catuḥ-ṣaṣṭyā mātrayā ca
vaṁ bījenaiva dhārayet
amṛtaṁ plāvitaṁ dhyātvā
nāḍī-dhautiṁ vibhāvayet
la-kāreṇa dvā-triṁśena
dṛḍhaṁ bhāvyaṁ virecayet

Fixing the gaze on the tip of the nose and contemplating the luminous reflection of the moon, inhale through the left nostril while repeating *bīja Ṭhaṁ* sixteen times and hold your breath while repeating the *bīja* sixty-four times. Meanwhile, imagine [or contemplate] that the nectar flowing from the moon at the tip of your nose is running through all the *nāḍīs* of the body, purifying them. Thus contemplating, exhale while repeating *pṛthivī-bīja Laṁ* thirty-two times.

evaṁ vidhāṁ nāḍī-śuddhiṁ
kṛtvā nāḍīṁ viśodhayet
dṛḍho bhūtvāsanaṁ kṛtvā
prāṇāyāmaṁ samācaret

Through these three *prāṇāyāmas*, the *nāḍīs* are purified. Then, sitting firmly with good posture, begin regular *prāṇāyāma*.

Practical instructions for performing *nāḍī-śuddhi*: Sit in *siddhāsana* or *padmāsana* with a straight back. Offer sincere and respectful obeisance to your spiritual master and devotedly repeat the master's *praṇati* mantra. Mentally repeat *vāyu-bīja* (*Yaṁ*) sixteen times while inhaling through the left nostril and blocking the right one with your thumb. Then block both nostrils and hold your breath while mentally repeating *Yaṁ* sixty-four times. Keeping the left nostril closed, exhale out through the right nostril while repeating *Yaṁ* thirty-two times. Then, with the left nostril still blocked, inhale through the right nostril, silently repeating *agni-bīja* (*Raṁ*) sixteen times. Close both nostrils and hold your breath while silently repeating *Raṁ* sixty-four times. Then close the right nostril and exhale through the left nostril while silently repeating *Raṁ* thirty-two times. Meditate on the glow of the moon while gazing steadily at the end of your nose. Inhale through the left nostril, close the right one with the thumb, and silently repeat *bīja Ṭhaṁ* sixteen times. Hold your breath (*kumbhaka*) while performing silent *japa* with *Ṭhaṁ* sixty-four times. Finally, exhale out through the right nostril, close the left one, and repeat the *bīja* of *pṛthivī* (*Laṁ*) thirty-two times.

2. Practice to Open the Chakras

The first center: *mūlādhāra-cakra*

Sit in *siddhāsana* with your back straight. Keep your eyes closed and breathe deeply. Press your heel against your perineum and direct your attention to the area between your anus and genitals. With an inhalation, feel how the air flows to the area around the perineum and heats the first center as it arrives. With an exhalation, allow the air to leave your body through *mūlādhāra*. With each inhalation and exhalation mentally repeat the mantra *Laṁ*. Practice at the hour of *Brahma-muhūrta* for twenty minutes.

The second center: *svādhiṣṭhāna-cakra*

Sit in *siddhāsana* with a straight back. Keep your eyes closed and breathe deeply. Direct your attention to the base of the genitals. When you inhale, feel how the air circulates at the base of the genitals and heats the second center as it arrives. When you exhale, allow the air to leave the body through *svādhiṣṭhāna-cakra*. With each inhalation and exhalation mentally repeat the mantra *Vaṁ*. Practice daily at the hour of *Brahma-muhūrta* for about twenty minutes.

The third center: *maṇipūra-cakra*

Sit in *siddhāsana* with your back straight. Keep your eyes closed and breathe deeply. Direct your attention toward your navel. When you inhale, perceive the air circulating through the navel and heating *maṇipūra-cakra* as it reaches *suṣumṇā*. When you exhale, allow the air to leave the body from the third center. With each inhalation and exhalation mentally repeat the mantra *Raṁ*. Practice daily at the hour of *Brahma-muhūrta* for about twenty minutes.

The fourth center: *anāhata-cakra*

Sit in *padmāsana*, *siddhāsana*, or *sukhāsana*. Relax the body while keeping your back straight. Inhale and exhale deeply. Close your eyes and direct your attention to the center of your chest. With each inhalation and exhalation, perceive how the area around *anāhata* expands and contracts. Become aware of the breath in the chest area. With each inhalation, feel the air circulating toward the center of the thorax and from there to *anāhata-cakra*. When you exhale, feel how the air flows from the chakra and passes through the center of the thorax and then is expelled from the body. With each inhalation and exhalation mentally repeat the mantra *Yaṁ*. Practice daily at the hour of *Brahma-muhūrta* for about twenty minutes.

The fifth center: *viśuddha-cakra*

Sit in *padmāsana*, *siddhāsana*, or *sukhāsana*. Relax the body and keep your back straight. Breathe deeply. Close your eyes and direct your attention to your throat. When you inhale, perceive the air circulating through the throat and heating *viśuddha-cakra* when it reaches *suṣumṇā*. When you exhale, the air leaves the body through the fifth center. Along with each inhalation and exhalation, mentally repeat the mantra *Haṁ*. Practice daily at the hour of *Brahma-muhūrta* for about twenty minutes.

The sixth center: *ājñā-cakra*

Sit in *padmāsana*, *siddhāsana*, or *sukhāsana*. Relax while keeping your back straight. Inhale and exhale deeply. Close your eyes and direct your attention to the space between your eyebrows. When you inhale, perceive the air circulating through the third eye and heating *ajñā-cakra* as it reaches *suṣumṇā*. When you exhale, the air leaves the body through the sixth center. With each inhalation and exhalation, mentally repeat the mantra Om. Practice daily at the hour of *Brahma-muhūrta* for about 20 minutes.

General technique to open the chakras

Sit comfortably in *padmāsana*, *siddhāsana*, or *sukhāsana*. Keep your back straight but not tense. Proceed to focus your attention on each chakra, one after another, for approximately five minutes each, mentally repeating the following mantras:

1. *Mūlādhāra-cakra*, at the base of the spinal column: *Laṁ*.
2. *Svādhiṣṭhāna-cakra*, at the base of the genitals: *Vaṁ*.
3. *Maṇipūra-cakra*, in the navel: *Raṁ*.
4. *Anāhata-cakra*, in the center of the chest: *Yaṁ*.

5. *Viśuddha-cakra*, in the throat: *Haṁ*.
6. *Ājñā-cakra*, between the eyebrows: Om.

When you finish, direct your attention to *sahasrāra-cakra* at the crown of your head, and stay silent for no longer than ten minutes.

3. Techniques to Awaken the Kundalini Energy

Just as vapor and ice share a common essence, which is water, it is important to understand that *kuṇḍalinī-śakti* and *prāṇa-śakti* are two different forms of the same energy. The former is its universal form, while the latter is its vital form. Our body, just like the universe, is nothing more than shakti in constant movement, which in its evolutionary process manifests the universe of names and forms. Shakti is the main energy responsible for a process that starts in the mineral, vegetal, and animal kingdoms, until it reaches the human. The human being is the highest expression of the planet's evolution. Shakti is to Shiva as wetness is to water or heat to fire. Shakti is the glare of the sun: although it is part of the sun, it hides it from view. Shakti is not different from Shiva.

A master level of prana is a fundamental and indispensable condition for awakening kundalini. Through *prāṇāyāma*, the first energy center is stimulated, awakening *kuṇḍalinī-śakti*. On this path of liberation, it is recommended to begin with *prāṇāyāma*. Many *prāṇāyāma* exercises and practices are performed by the physical body, or *sthūla-śarīra*, but they influence the astral body, or *liṅga-śarīra*.

I learned this technique directly from His Holiness Swami Vinodānanda, disciple of His Holiness Swami Śivānanda of Rishikesh: Sit in a meditative posture with your back straight but not tense. With your right thumb, close your right nostril. Inhale deeply through your left nostril and count three seconds. Then, close your left nostril with the pinky and ring finger of the right hand. Hold your breath for twelve seconds while making your prana descend through the spinal column until it collides with *mūlādhāra-cakra* and awakens *kuṇḍalinī-śakti*. Next, exhale through your right nostril for six seconds. Then, repeat the technique from the other side: starting by inhaling through the right nostril and closing the left nostril. Use the same counting sequence: 3–12–6. It is advisable to perform three rounds of this *prāṇāyāma* in the morning and three in the evening.

4. The mudras or "seals"

The Sanskrit term mudra means "seal or mark." From the practice of asanas and *prāṇāyāma*, prana accumulates in specific areas. Mudras are postures that aim to block or seal this vital energy in order to channel it toward the opening of *suṣumṇā* and awaken kundalini. Since every point of the hand corresponds to a different area of the body and brain, mudras influence our emotions and help us have the required attitude. Since *bandhas* (locks) and mudras (seals) are interconnected, they are often practiced together. The most relevant mudras are *mahā-mudrā*, *mahā-vedha-mudrā*, *khecarī-mudrā*, *vajroli-mudrā*, *śāmbhavī-mudrā*, *agocarī-mudrā*, *śakti-cālanī-mudrā*, *nāsikāgra-mudrā*, *aśvinī-mudrā*, and *viparīta-karaṇī-mudrā*.

Mahā-mudrā

This mudra is described in the *Haṭha-yoga-pradīpikā* (3.10–14):

pāda-mūlena vāmena
yoniṁ saṁpīḍya dakṣiṇam
prasāritaṁ padaṁ kṛtvā
karābhyāṁ dhārayed dṛḍham

Pressing the yoni (perineum) against the heel of the left foot, the right foot should be stretched forward and grasped strongly with both hands.

kaṇṭhe bandhaṁ samāropya
dhārayed vāyum ūrdhvataḥ
yathā daṇḍa-hataḥ sarpo
daṇḍā-kāraḥ prajāyate

ṛjvībhūtā tathā śaktiḥ
kuṇḍalī sahasā bhavet
tadā sā maraṇāvasthā
jāyate dvi-puṭāśrayā

By locking the throat (with *jālandhara-bandha*), air is drawn in from the outside and carried down. Just as a snake struck with a stick becomes straight like a stick, shakti (*suṣumṇā*) becomes immediately straight. Then, kundalini leaves both *iḍā* and *piṅgalā* and enters *suṣumṇā*.

tataḥ śanaiḥ śanair eva
recayen naiva vegataḥ
mahā-mudrāṁ ca tenaiva
vadanti vibudhottamāḥ
iyaṁ khalu mahā-mudrā
mahā-siddhaiḥ pradarśitā
mahā-kleśādayo doṣāḥ
kṣīyante maraṇādayaḥ
mahā-mudrāṁ ca tenaiva
vadanti vibudhottamāḥ

> Next, the air should be expelled slowly and not violently. For this very reason, the best of the wise men call it *mahā-mudrā*. This *mahā-mudrā* has been propounded by great masters. As it destroys great evils and pains such as death, wise men call it *mahā-mudrā*.

Technique: Sit on the floor with your back straight and your legs stretched out and together. Bend your left leg and bring your heel against your perineum. Looking at your extended right leg, inhale deeply and elongate the spine. Exhaling, bend forward until your forehead rests on your right knee. Grasp your right big toe with the index fingers of both hands. While holding this posture, inhale deeply and proceed to practice *jālandhara-bandha* by pressing your chin against your chest. Next, practice *mūla-bandha* by contracting the perineal area. Practice *uḍḍīyāna-bandha* by performing abdominal contractions and practice *śāmbhavī-mudrā* by fixing the gaze between your eyebrows. Hold your breath for as long as comfortable. To release *mahā-mudrā*, first release *mūla-bandha*, then *jālandhara-bandha*, and finally breathe gently. Afterward, repeat the process with the other leg.

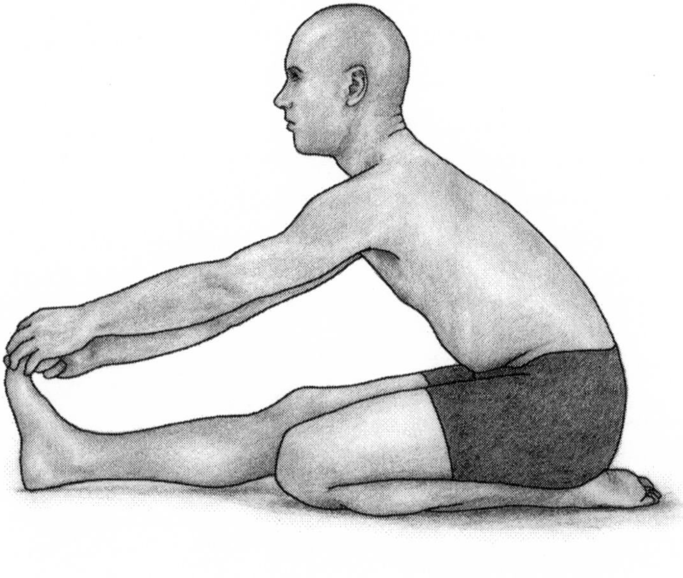

Mahā-mudrā

Mahā-vedha-mudrā

The *Śiva Saṁhitā* (4.23 and 4.26-27) refers to this technique in the following way:

apāna-prāṇayor aikyaṁ
kṛtvā tri-bhuvaneśvari
mahā-vedha-sthito yogi
kukṣim āpūrya vāyunā
sphicau santāḍayed dhīmān
vedho 'yaṁ kīrtito mayā

O goddess of the three worlds, when the yogi, while performing *mahā-vedha*, unifies prana and *apāna vāyus*, fills the viscera with air, and drives [the united *prāṇa* and *apāna*] slowly toward the bottom, it is called *mahā-vedha*.

cakra-madhye sthitā devāḥ
kampanti vāyu-tāḍanāt
kuṇḍaly api mahā-māyā
kailāse sā vilīyate

The gods residing in the chakras tremble at the gentle inflow and outflow of air in *prāṇāyāma*; the great goddess, Kuṇḍlī-mahā-māyā, is also absorbed in mount Kailāsa (i.e., with Lord Shiva).

mahā-mudrā-mahā-bandhau
niṣphalau vedha-varjitau
tasmād yogī prayatnena
karoti trityaṁ kramāt

> *Mahā-mudrā* and *mahā-bandha* are fruitless if they are not followed by *mahā-vedha*; therefore, yogis should practice all three in order with great care.

Technique: Sit with your perineum against your left heel and place your right foot on your left thigh. Slowly inhale, filling the lungs and holding your breath. Stretch your neck, move your head slightly backward, and then place your chin against your chest. Place both palms on the floor and let them support your weight. Without releasing the posture, slowly raise your bottom off the floor and then place it gently back down.

Mahā-vedha-mudrā

Viparīta-karaṇī-mudrā

The *Śiva Saṁhitā* refers to the *viparīta-karaṇī* in the following verse:

bhū-tale svaśiro dattvā
khe nayec caraṇa-dvayam
viparīta-kṛtiś caiṣā
sarva-tantreṣu gopitā

> Placing your head on the ground, stretch your legs upward, moving them around and around. This is *viparīta-karaṇī*, a secret kept in all the Tantras.
> (*Śiva Saṁhitā*, 4.45)

Technique: Lie on the floor face up with your legs together and extended, your arms at your sides, and your palms face down. As you inhale, support yourself with your hands and bring your knees to your chest. Elevate your hips and support your back with both hands while most of your weight rests on your elbows. Extend both legs upward above you. In this posture, practice *khecarī-mudrā*.

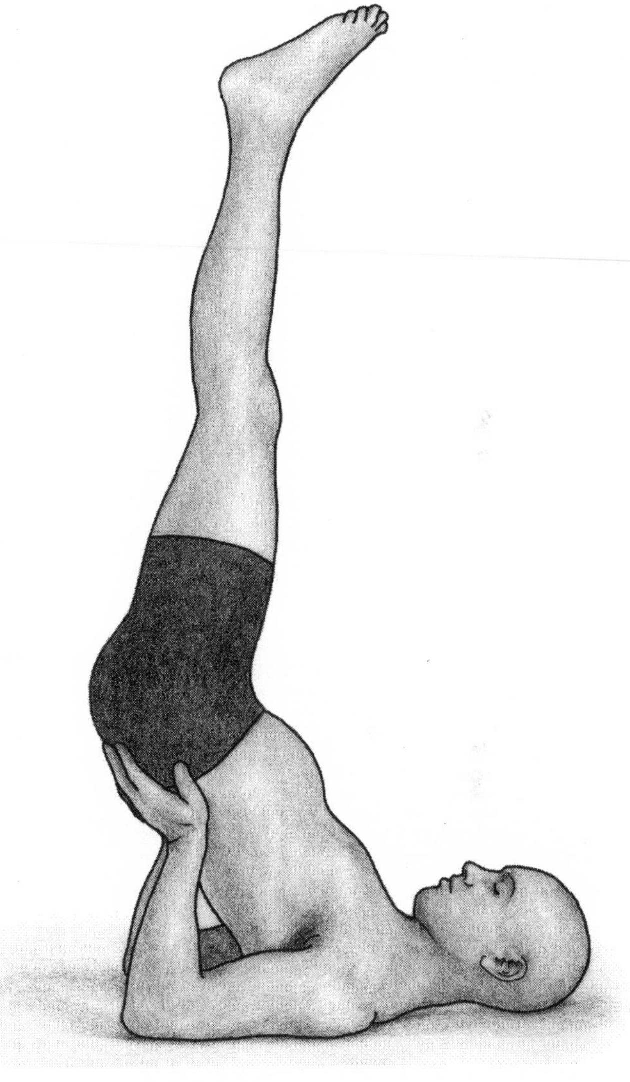

Viparīta-karaṇī-mudrā

Khecarī-mudrā

The *Haṭha-yoga-pradīpikā* refers to this technique in the following way:

kapāla-kuhare jihvā
praviṣṭā viparītagā
bhruvor antargatā dṛṣṭir
mudrā bhavati khecarī

Khecarī-mudrā is done by thrusting the tongue into the gullet, by turning it over itself, and keeping the gaze in the middle of the eyebrows.

(*Haṭha-yoga-pradīpikā* , 3.32)

The Gheraṇḍa Saṁhitā also mentions it:
rasanāṁ tālu-madhye tu
śanaiḥ śanaiḥ praveśayet
kapāla-kuhare jihvā
praviṣṭā viparītagā
bhruvor madhye gatā dṛṣṭir
mudrā bhavati khecarī

Next, slowly move the tongue [lengthened and turned upward and backward] inward so it touches the palate and reaches the holes of the nostrils in the mouth. Covering these holes with the tongue (thus stopping the breathing), fix your gaze on the space between the eyebrows. This is called *khecarī*.

(*Gheraṇḍa Saṁhitā*, 3.27)

The *Śiva Saṁhitā* says the following about this mudra:

mudraiṣā khecarī yas tu
śvāsa-citto hy atandritaḥ
śata-brahma-gatenāpi
kṣaṇārdhaṁ manyate hi saḥ

To whomever practices this *khecarī-mudrā* calmly and without laziness, the time it takes to count one hundred *brahmās* seems like half a second.

gurūpadeśato mudrāṁ
yo vetti khecarīm imām
nānā-pāpa-rato dhīmān
sa yāti paramāṁ gatim

One who follows this *khecarī-mudrā* according to the instructions of the guru obtains the highest goal, even immersed in great sins.

(*Śiva Saṁhitā*, 4.35–36)

Technique: Sit in *padmāsana* or *siddhāsana* with your back straight. Slowly fold your tongue and lift it upward and back as far as possible. With the lower surface of your tongue, touch and lightly press against the soft palate. Move the tip of the tongue as close as possible to the nasopharynx. Without tilting your head back, direct your eyeballs upward, consciously and slowly. Focus your gaze on the space between the eyebrows for as long as possible, without blinking and without tensing the muscles of the neck. At the end of the exercise, close your eyes and relax. Do not practice this mudra beyond your limitations.

Vajroli-mudrā

In the *Haṭha-yoga-pradīpikā* there is an interesting statement about this mudra:

svecchayā vartamāno 'pi
yogoktair niyamair vinā
vajrolīṁ yo vijānāti
sa yogī siddhi-bhājanam

> Even one who lives a wayward life without observing any rules of yoga, but performs *vajrolī*, deserves success and is a yogi.
>
> (*Haṭha-yoga-pradīpikā*, 3.82)

Technique: Sit comfortably in *siddhāsana*. Place your attention on the urethral sphincter and at the base of the genitals. Try to draw it upward as if stopping the urge to urinate. Contract this muscle for fifteen seconds while repeating the mantra *Vaṁ* and then relax for ten seconds. Repeat this exercise for ten to fifteen minutes.

Śāmbhavī-mudrā

The *Haṭha-yoga-pradīpikā* refers to the *śāmbhavī-mudrā* in the following way:

veda-śāstra-purāṇāni
sāmānya-gaṇikā iva
ekaiva śāṁbhavī mudrā
guptā kula-vadhūr iva

> While Vedas, shastras, and Puranas are like ordinary public women, *śāṁbhavī-mudrā* is like a wife of respectable family not exposed to everyone's gaze.

antar lakṣyaṁ bahir dṛṣṭir
nimeṣonmeṣa-varjitā
eṣā sā śāmbhavī mudra
veda-śāstreṣu gopitā

> Focusing inward, while keeping the gaze on external objects, without blinking the eyes. This is called *śāṁbhavī-mudrā*, preserved secretly in the Vedas and shastras.

antar lakṣya-vilīna-citta-pavano yogī yadā vartate
dṛṣṭyā niścala tārayā bahir adhaḥ paśyann apaśyann api
mudreyaṁ khalu śāmbhavī bhavati sā labdhā prasādāt guroḥ
śūnyāśūnya-vilakṣaṇam sphurati tat tattvaṁ paraṁ śāmbhavam

> When a yogi remains inwardly attentive, keeping the mind and prana absorbed and the gaze steady, as if seeing everything while in reality seeing nothing outside, below, or above, then it is truly called *śāmbhavī-mudrā*, which is learned by the favor of a guru. Whatever wonderful *śūnya* (existence) or *asūnya* (non-existence) is perceived, it is to be regarded as the manifestation of the supreme Śambhu (Shiva).
>
> (*Haṭha-yoga-pradīpikā*, 4.34–36)

Technique: Sit in *siddhāsana* or *padmāsana* with your back straight, your hands in *cin-mudrā*, and the facial muscles very relaxed. Close your eyes for several minutes before beginning, then open them and focus your gaze on a distant point. Without tilting your head, direct your eyeballs slowly and consciously upward. Focus your eyes on the central point located between your eyes. Keep your gaze focused on the third eye without blinking, for as long as possible and without tensing your neck muscles. At the end, close your eyes and relax. Try to increase the length of this exercise as you advance in your practice.

Agocarī-mudrā

Technique: Sit in *siddhāsana* or *padmāsana* with a straight and elongated spine. Plug your ears with cotton. Remain in a state of deep and attentive observation. With time, you will begin to hear the sounds of *anāhata* (divine inner sounds). At an advanced level, these sounds can be heard even with the ears unplugged.

Śakti-cālanī-mudrā

The *Gheraṇḍa Saṁhitā* refers to this mudra in the following way:

mūlādhāre ātma-śaktiḥ
kuṇḍalī para-devatā
śayitā bhujagākārā
sārdha-tri-valayānvitā

The great goddess Kundalini, the energy of the Self, *ātma-śakti* (spiritual force), sleeps in *mūlādhāra*. She has the form of a serpent with three and a half coils.

yāvat sā nidritā dehe
tāvaj jīvaḥ paśur yathā
jñānaṁ na jāyate tāvat
koṭi-yogaṁ samabhyaset

As long as she is asleep in the body, jiva is a mere animal. True knowledge will not arise even if ten million types of yoga are practiced.

udghāṭayet kavāṭaṁ ca
yathā kuñcikayā haṭhāt
kuṇḍalinyāḥ prabodhena
brahma-dvāraṁ prabhedayet

Like a key opens a door, hatha yoga awakens kundalini by unlocking the door of Brahman.

nābhiṁ saṁveṣṭya vastreṇa
na ca nagno bahiḥ sthitaḥ
gopanīya-gṛhe sthitvā
śakti-cālanam abhyaset

Covering the [loins up to the] navel with a piece of cloth, seated in a secret room, not naked in an outer room, one should practice *śakti-cālana.*

vitasti-pramitaṁ dīrghaṁ
vistāre catur-aṅgulam
mṛdulaṁ dhavalaṁ sūkṣmaṁ
veṣṭanāmbara-lakṣaṇam
evam ambara-yuktaṁ ca
kaṭi-sūtreṇa yojayet

The covering cloth should be one cubit long and four fingers wide (three inches), soft, white, and of fine texture. Tie this cloth with a *kaṭi-sūtra* (a string worn around the loins).

bhāsmanā gātraṁ saṁlipya
siddhāsanaṁ samācaret
nāsābhyāṁ prāṇam ākṛṣya
apāne yojayed balāt

tāvad ākuñcayed guhyam
aśvinī-mudrayā śanaiḥ
yāvad gacchet suṣumṇāyāṁ
vāyuḥ prakāśayed dhaṭhāt

Rub the body with ashes, sit in *siddhāsana*, draw in *prāṇa-vāyu* through the nostrils, and force it to unite with *apāna*. Contract the rectum slowly with *aśvinī-mudrā* until *vāyu* enters *suṣumṇā* and manifests its presence.

tadā vāyu-prabhandhena
kumbhikā ca bhujaṅginī
baddha-śvāsas tato bhūtvā
ca ūrdhva-mātraṁ prapadyate

By holding the breath through *kumbhaka* in this way, the serpent kundalini, feeling suffocated, awakes and rises upward [to the *brahma-randhra*].
(*Gheraṇḍa Saṁhitā*, 3.49–56)

The *Śiva Saṁhitā* also refers to *śakti-cālana-mudrā* in the following manner:

ādhāra-kamale suptāṁ
cālayet kuṇḍalīṁ dṛḍhām
apāna-vāyum āruhya
balād ākṛṣya buddhimnā
śakti-cālana-mudreyaṁ
sarva-śakti-pradāyinī

Let the wise yogi forcibly and firmly draw up the goddess Kuṇḍalī, who is sleeping in the *ādhāra* lotus, by means of *apāna-vāyu*. This *śakti-cālana-mudrā* is the giver of all powers.

śakti-cālanam evaṁ hi
praty ahaṁ yaḥ samācaret
āyur-vṛddhir bhavet tasya
rogāṇāṁ ca vināśanam

In this way, one who practices *śakti-cālana* daily has a longer life and destroys ailments.

vihāya nidrāṁ bhujagī
svayam ūrdhve bhavet khalu
tasmād abhyāsanaṁ kāryaṁ
yoginā siddhim icchatā

Leaving its slumber, the serpent (i.e., Kuṇḍalī) goes up. Therefore, let yogis who want power practice this. (*Śiva Saṁhitā*, 4.53–55)

Technique: Begin this practice in *vajrāsana* (the thunderbolt posture), relaxed and with your back straight. Hold your heels with your hands. Lift your bottom and strike it gently against your hands. Next, perform *bhastrikā-prāṇāyāma*, followed by one *kumbhaka*, for as long as possible.

5. The bandhas or "locks"

The word *bandha* means "to tie up, to moor, to trap, or to close." The *bandhas* carry out a very important function in the process of purification and awakening of *kuṇḍalinī-śakti*. These practices allow us to isolate specific areas of the body where vital energy does not flow freely, due to accumulated waste. *Bandhas* help us to control the body's *agni* (fire) and use it to burn this waste. In general, the instructions that govern the practice of *bandhas* and mudras are the same as for asanas: they must be performed on an empty stomach and in solitude. According to the *Yoga-śikha Upaniṣad*, the most important *bandhas* are *jālandhara-bandha*, *uddīyana-bandha*, and *mūla-bandha*. The *Śiva Saṁhitā* emphasizes the importance of *bandhas* and mudras for awakening the serpentine energy.

adhunā kathayiṣyāmi
yoga-siddhi-karaṁ param
gopanīyaṁ susiddhānāṁ
yogaṁ parama-durlabham

Now I shall tell you the best means of attaining success in yoga. Practitioners should keep it secret. It is the most inaccessible yoga.

suptā guru-prasādena
yadā jāgarti kuṇḍalī
tadā sarvāṇi padmāni
bhidyante granthayo 'pi ca

When the sleeping goddess Kundalini is awakened through the grace of the guru, then all the lotuses and the knots are readily pierced, through and through.

tasmāt sarva-prayatnena
prabodhayitum īśvarīm
brahma-randhra-mukhe suptāṁ
mudrābhyāsaṁ samācaret

Therefore, in order to awaken the goddess, who is asleep at the mouth of *brahma-randra* (the innermost hollow of *suṣumṇā*), the mudras should be practiced with greatest care.

mahā-mudrā mahā-bandho
mahā-vedhaś ca khecarī
jālandharo mūla-bandho
viparītākṛtis tathā

uḍḍīyānaṁ caiva vajrolī

daśame śakti-cālanam
idaṁ hi mudrā-daśakaṁ
mudrāṇām uttamottamam

Of the many mudras, the following ten are the best: *mahā-mudrā, mahā-bandha, mahā-vedha, khecarī, jālandhara, mūla-bandha, viparīta-karaṇī, uḍḍīyāna, vajrolī*, and *śakti-cālana.*

(*Śiva* Saṁhitā, 4.12–15)

Mūla-bandha

The Sanskrit word *mūla* means "root, origin, or source" and refers to the area around *mūlādhāra-cakra*, while *bandha* means "lock." This is one of the basic techniques for awakening *kuṇḍalinī-śakti* because it directly stimulates the first center, which is the home of Kundalini. The book *Haṭha-yoga-pradīpikā* (3.61–69) refers to it in detail:

pārṣṇi-bhāgena saṁpīḍya
yonim ākuñcayed gudam
apānam ūrdhvam ākṛṣya
mūla-bandho 'bhidhīyate

Pressing the yoni (perineum) against the heel, contract the anus. By drawing the *apāna* up like this, *mūla-bandha* is performed.

adho-gatim apānaṁ vā
ūrdhva-gaṁ kurute balāt

ākuñcanena taṁ prāhur
mūla-bandhaṁ hi yoginaḥ

Apāna, which naturally flows downward, is forced up. Yogis refer to *mūla-bandha* as a contraction of the anus.

gudaṁ pārṣṇyā tu saṁpīḍya
vāyum ākuñcayed balāt
vāraṁ vāraṁ yathā cordhvaṁ
samāyāti samīraṇaḥ

Pressing the heel well against the anus, draw the air up by force, again and again, until [the air] goes up.

prāṇāpānau nāda-bindū
mūla-bandhena caikatām
gatvā yogasya saṁsiddhim
gaccato nātra sāṁśayaḥ

Prana, *apāna*, *nāda*, and *bindu*, united in one through *mūla-bandha*, will lead to success in yoga, undoubtedly.

apāna-prāṇayor aikyaṁ
kṣayo mūtra-purīṣayoḥ
yuvā bhavati vṛddho 'pi
satataṁ mūla-bandhanāt

By purifying prana and *apāna*, urine and excrement decrease. An old man also becomes young by constantly practicing *mūla-bandha*.

apāne ūrdhvage jāte
prayāte vahni-maṇḍalam
tadānala-śikhā dīrghā
jāyate vāyunā hatā

Going up, *apāna* enters the region of fire, the stomach. Struck by the [*apāna*] air, the flame of the fire grows larger.

tato yāto vahny apānau
prāṇam uṣṇa-svarūpakam
tenātyanta-pradīptas tu
jvalano dehajas tathā

These, fire and *apāna*, go to the naturally hot prana, which, becoming inflamed, causes a burning sensation in the body.

tena kuṇḍalinī suptā
santaptā samprabudhyate
daṇḍā-hatā bhujaṅgīva
niśvasya ṛjutāṁ vrajet

In this way, the sleeping Kundalini, which is very hot, awakens completely. It becomes straight like a serpent struck dead with a stick.

bilaṁ praviṣṭeva tato
brahma-nāḍy antaraṁ vrajet
tasmān nityaṁ mūla-bandhaḥ
kartavyo yogibhiḥ sadā

It enters the *brahma-nāḍī*, just as a serpent enters its hole. Therefore, yogis should always practice *mūla-bandha*.

Technique: Sit in *siddhāsana* and place your hands on your knees. Press the perineum against your left heel and press your right heel against the space above the genitals. Exhale all the air from your lungs and inhale deeply. Hold your breath and practice *jālandhara-bandha* (see below). Next, contract the muscles of the perineum, the area situated between the anus and the genitals, lifting it vertically toward the navel. In women, this is where the vagina and uterus come together. Simultaneously, the abdomen contracts inward and upward in the direction of the spine. While holding your breath, maintain the muscular contraction around the first energy center. Then, release *mūla-bandha* and *jālandhara-bandha*. Finally, breathe normally.

Mūla-bandha involves a simultaneous physical contraction of the perineum and an energetic contraction of the first center. With practice, the physical contraction disappears and only the energetic contraction of *mūlādhāra-cakra* remains. It is capable of awakening *kuṇḍalinī-śakti* and placing it in *suṣumṇā-nāḍī*. *Mūla-bandha* reverses the descent of *apāna-vāyu*, making it move upward to unite with *prāṇa-vāyu*, which is in the chest area, where it unites *nāda* and *bindu*. Most human beings lack a clear awareness and control over muscles such as anal sphincters. Only through systematic training and regular practice is it possible to increase the strength of these muscles. In the beginning, one should not practice this more than five times daily.

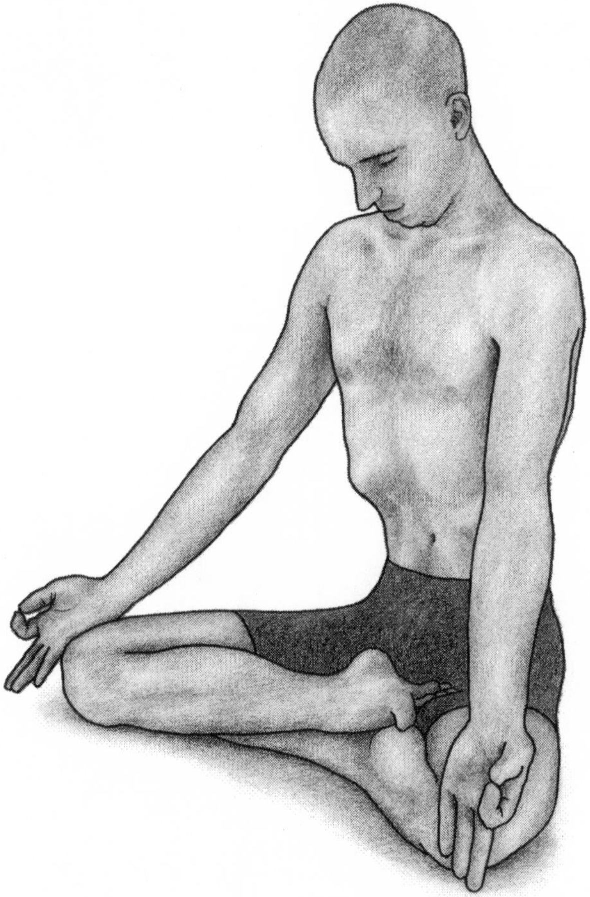

Mūla-bandha

Jālandhara-bandha

This technique is described in the *Gheraṇḍa Saṁhitā* in the following way:

atha jālandhara-bandha-kathanam:

kaṇṭha-saṁkocanaṁ kṛtvā
cibukaṁ hṛdaye nyaset
jālandhare kṛte bandhe
ṣoḍaśādhāra-bandhanam
jālandhara-mahā-mudrā
mṛtyoś ca kṣaya-kāriṇī

Contracting the throat, place the chin against the chest. This is called *jālandhara*. With this *bandha*, the sixteen *ādhāras* (points of vital support) are closed. This *mahā-mudrā* destroys death.

siddhaṁ jālandharaṁ bandhaṁ
yogināṁ siddhi-dāyakam
ṣaṇ-māsam abhyased yo hi
sa siddho nātra saṁśayaḥ

One who attains perfection in the practice of *jālandhara-bandha*, the giver of success to yogis, and practices it for six months continuously, undoubtedly will become an adept.

(*Gheraṇḍa Saṁhitā*, 3.12–13)

Technique: In order to practice this *bandha*, your back must be straight and erect. Inhaling, stretch your neck, move your head backward slightly, and hold your breath. Tilt your head forward and tuck your chin against the top of your sternum toward the jugular notch. Press your chin against your thorax.

Uḍḍīyāna-bandha

The *Gheraṇḍa Saṁhitā* refers to this *bandha* in the following way:

udare paścimaṁ tānaṁ
nābher ūrdhvaṁ tu kārayet
uḍḍīnaṁ kurute yasmād
aviśrāntaṁ mahā-khagaḥ
uḍḍīyānaṁ tvasau bandho
mṛtyu-mātaṅga-kesarī

> Contract the bowels equally above and below the navel toward the back, so that the abdominal viscera touch the back. Whoever practices this *uḍḍīyāna* (flying-up) without ceasing conquers death. The Great Bird (breath), by this process, is instantly forced up into *suṣumṇā*, and flies (moves) constantly therein.
>
> (*Gheraṇḍa Saṁhitā*, 3.10)

Technique: First learn this technique standing. Once you have mastered it, you can begin to practice it seated in *padmāsana*, *siddhāsana*, or *sukhāsana*.

Stand with your feet about one foot apart. Flex your legs enough for them to support your palms. Place your palms on your thighs with the fingers pointing inward. Bending your torso forward, lightly curve your spine. Inhale, exhale, empty your lungs completely, and expel the air suddenly. Pressing your palms against your thighs, hold your breath and without inhaling, relax your abdomen and lift your diaphragm up, bringing your intestines upward. Bring the abdominal wall toward the spine as if bringing your navel close to your back. Focus on *maṇipūra-cakra* while holding your breath and keeping the abdomen pulled in. Next, relax the abdominal muscles so that they return to their original position. Breathe only after the abdomen has returned to its original position, never before. At first, practice no more than six times daily.

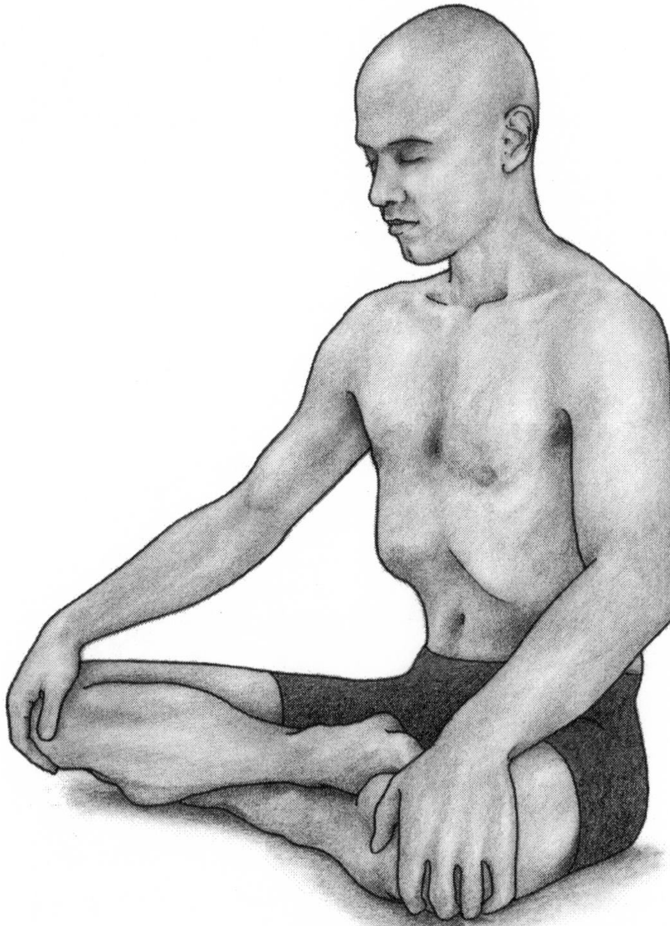

Uḍḍīyāna-bandha

Mahā-bandha

Mahā-bandha is the combined practice of all three *bandhas* described above. Therefore it is not recommended to practice this technique before having mastered the three *bandhas* separately.

Technique: Sit in *siddhāsana*, support yourself firmly on your knees, raise your shoulders, and extend your arms. Exhaling, practice the *bandhas* in this order: *jālandhara-bandha*, *uḍḍīyāna-bandha*, and *mūla-bandha*. After releasing *mahā-bandha*, the order is reversed: first *mūla-bandha*, then *uḍḍīyāna-bandha*, and finally *jālandhara-bandha*.

EPILOGUE

THE PATH OF KUNDALINI

This path lies in the foundation of every type of yoga. Every feeling of love and devotion that we experience is Kundalini herself yearning to be reunited with her Lord. One who approaches this path to attain power, strength, or energy will be disappointed; but not one who takes this path to grow, evolve, and develop.

The message of kundalini yoga speaks of the need to spread our wings and fly from this earth, or rather, to distance ourselves from the worldly. This yoga path gives us the means to escape the control of the gravitational field of our attachments.

Many human beings waste the greatest blessing and pass their days on the planet surviving, merely interested in satisfying their basic physical needs to make a living. It is a great tragedy to survive when you have the marvelous opportunity to live.

We refer to the spiritual process as an elevation, as if it were a physical direction, because in seeing ourselves from the heights, our life within society, with its worries, goals, and interests, seems so small.

As we overcome weaknesses and transcend addictions, pleasures offered by this world decrease and mundane enjoyment diminishes. When observing the worldly from the heights of the spirit, our consciousness grows, expands, and flourishes, even though our bodies remain in the same place. It is an experience in which nothing changes physically, but nothing will remain the same.

In terms of consciousness, to ascend is to pursue fusion, while to descend leads us to multiplicity. Upward is synonymous with interiorization, while downward is exteriorization. As we go within we elevate, as we go outward we descend into the relative world of names and forms, and our perception of life becomes superficial. To really grow is to know ourselves. The better we know ourselves, the greater the heights we will reach.

In this transformative return from earth to heaven, in this flourishing from what we have to what we are, it is very difficult to precisely mark where each stage begins and ends. The awakening of each center does not depend only on the method that we practice, but on the price we are willing to pay. Techniques are intended to create enough space within for something to occur, but God happens according to his own will, which is absolutely free. Techniques are not meant to manipulate heaven, since it cannot be controlled by humans. Rather, techniques are an invitation that does not obligate the guest to come.

Just like seeds buried in the soil, we remain in the basic chakras. This type of yoga suggests we elevate ourselves, mature, grow, and blossom in and from consciousness.

The distance between one chakra and the next will depend upon our thirst for freedom, our hunger for bliss, and our desire to love. We will move from the first center to the third only when we understand the true value of material objects and realize that to be is more important than to have.

The distance to reach and awaken the heart center is proportional to the time we delay in accepting our solitude. From *ajña* to *sahasrāra* there is only a step: from what we believe ourselves to be to our reality.

Kundalini yoga trusts in the human being; it teaches us that our divine potential will not be found in anything external because it lies within, and we only need to awaken it. Just as noise and commotion awaken the mind, silence and observation disturb the sleep of consciousness. We must fill ourselves with silence and observe attentively in order to awaken it.

Water in its liquid or solid form is attracted by the force of gravity. To awaken kundalini is to ignite the divine fire that evaporates water; it is the only way water can go up and reach the heights. Our attraction to the light implies an unconditional acceptance of the fire and its heat. Only people worthy of the grace to accept this heat and their own evaporation will emerge in totality.

Kundalini yoga is a path that begins when we become aware that we are buried in the earthly. The master will say that there is nothing wrong with that, as long as we do not make the mundane our hearth and home. Kundalini yoga leads us to responsibility, maturity, freedom, and the heights. It teaches us that we are a seed of light with infinite potential, which, from the depths of the earthly and mundane, is capable of growing, elevating, and transcending, until it manifests as the most fascinating lotus of creation, as the most marvelous flower in the garden of the Lord.

Appendix

Summary of the Main Chakras Characteristics

Name	***Mūlādhāra***	***Svādhiṣṭhāna***	***Maṇipūra***	***Anāhata***	***Viśuddha***	***Ājñā***	***Sahasrāra***
Name explana-tion	Root chakra	Sacral chakra	Solar plexus chakra	Heart chakra	Throat chakra	Third eye chakra	Crown chakra
Kṣetram	At the base of the spinal cord	At the level of pubic bone, just above the genitals	At the navel	In the heart	In the front of the neck, at the pit of the throat	At *Bhrū-mad-*hya, the center point between the eyebrows	The upper part of the skull
Deity or devas	Brahmā and Gaṇeśa	Viṣṇu	Bradhna-rudra	Īśāna-rudra	Pañca-vak-tra-śiva	Ardha-nārīś-vara	Shiva
Goddess or devi	Ḍākinī	Rākiṇī	Lākinī	Kākinī	Śākinī	Hākinī	Mahā-śakti
Element or *tattva*	Earth, or *tattva-pṛthvī*	Water, *āpa-tat-tva or āpas*	Fire, or *agni*	Air, or *vāyu*	Ether, or *ākāśa*	Mind, or *manas*	None
Color of chakra	Red	Orange	Yellow	Green	Light blue	Indigo	Violet
Color of *tattva*	Yellow	White	Red	Smoke	Blue	None	None

Power	Knowledge of kundalini	The power of communicating with the astral plane and astral beings	Perfect knowledge of one's own body	Control of vital energy and the senses. The power to heal sick people	Knowl-edge of the sacred scriptures. The power to read the thoughts of others and to live without consuming food.	The ability to enter another body and acquire mystic powers	Enlightenment
Number of petals	Four	Six	Ten	Twelve	Sixteen	Two	One thousand
Mantras of the petals	*Vaṁ*, *Śaṁ*, *Ṣaṁ*, and *Saṁ*	*Baṁ*, *Bhaṁ*, *Maṁ*, *Yaṁ*, *Raṁ*, and *Laṁ*	*Ḍaṁ*, *Ḍhaṁ*, *Ṇaṁ*, *Taṁ*, *Thaṁ*, *Daṁ*, *Dhaṁ*, *Naṁ*, *Paṁ*, and *Phaṁ*	*Kaṁ*, *Khaṁ*, *Gaṁ*, *Ghaṁ*, *Ṅaṁ*, *Caṁ*, *Chaṁ*, *Jaṁ*, *Jhaṁ*, *Ñaṁ*, *Ṭaṁ*, and *Ṭhaṁ*	*Aṁ*, *Āṁ*, *Iṁ*, *Īṁ*, *Uṁ*, *Ūṁ*, *Ṛṁ*, *Ṝṁ*, *Ḷṁ*, *Ḹṁ*, *Eṁ*, *Aiṁ*, *Oṁ*, *Auṁ*, *Aṁ*, and *Aḥ*	*Kṣaṁ* and *Haṁ*	All the letters are found in an ordered way on each and every one of the petals
Mantra of the chakra	*Laṁ*	*Vaṁ*	*Raṁ*	*Yaṁ*	*Haṁ*	Om	*Aḥ*

Name	***Mūlādhāra***	***Svādhiṣṭhāna***	***Maṇipūra***	***Anāhata***	***Viśuddha***	***Ājñā***	***Sahasrāra***
Figure of the mandala	Square	Half-moon	Triangle	Hexagon	Circle	Circle	None
Animal	Elephant Airāvata	Crocodile	Ram	Antelope	White ele-phant	Black gazelle	None
Plane or *loka*	*Bhūr-loka*, or "earthly physical plane"	*Bhuvar-loka*, or "astral plane"	*Svarga*, *svar-loka*, or "the celes-tial plane"	*Mahar-loka*, or "the plane of equilibrium"	*Janar-loka*, or "the plane of the devas"	*Tapo-loka*, or "the plane of austerity"	*Satya-loka*, or "the plane of reality, of the Truth"
Subtle element or *tan-mātra*	*Gandha*, or "smell"	*Rasa*, or "taste"	*Rūpa*, or "form or color"	*Sparśa*, or "touch"	*Śabda*, or "sound"	None	None
Gland	Suprarenal glands	The gonads or the sexual glands	The pan-creas	Supra-cardiac paragan-glion or thymus	Thyroid or parathyroid	Pituitary gland, also known as the hypophysis	The hypophysis or pituitary gland

Cognitive organ or *jñanen-driya*	Nose (*ghrāṇa*) for smelling (*ghranendriya*)	Tongue (*rasanā*) for tasting (*rasanen-driya*)	Eyes (*cakṣu*) for seeing (*cakṣur-indriya*)	Skin (*tvak*) for touching (*sparsanen-driya*)	Ears (*śrotra*) the auditory system	None	None
Organ of action or *karmen-driya*	Anus (*pāyu*) for excretion (*pāyvindriya*)	Genitals (*upastha*) for reproduction (*upasthendriya*)	Feet (*pāda*) for walking (*pādendriya*)	Hands (*pāṇi*) for handling (*hastendriya*)	Mouth (*vāk*) for speech (*vāgindriya*)	None	None
Energy channel or *nāḍī*	*Alambusā*	*Kuhu*	*Viśvodarā*	*Varuṇa*	*Sarasvatī*	*Iḍā* and *piṅgalā*	*Suṣumṇā*
Bioele-ment or *doṣa*	*Kapha*	*Kapha*	*Pitta*	*Vāta*	*Vāta*	None	*Kapha*
Vital air or *vāyu*	*Apāna*	*Vyāna*	*Samāna*	*Prana*	*Udāna*	*Prāṇa*, *apāna*, *vyāna*, *samāna*, and *udāna*	None

Name	*Mūlādhāra*	*Svādhiṣṭhāna*	*Maṇipūra*	*Anāhata*	*Viśuddha*	*Ājñā*	*Sahasrāra*
Sheath or *kośa*	*Anna-maya*, or "physical gross body"	*Prāṇa-maya*, or "energetic body"	*Prāṇa-maya*, or "vital body"	*Mano-maya*, or "mental sheath"	*Vijñā-na-maya*, or "intellectual sheath"	*Vijñāna-ma-ya*, or "the intellectual sheath"	*Ānanda-maya*, or "the bliss sheath"
Aroma	Sandalwood	Vanilla	Lavender	Rose	Eucalyptus	Jasmine	Lotus
Planet or *graha*	Maṅgala, or "Mars"	Bṛhaspati, or "Jupiter"	Sūrya, or "Sun"	Śukra, or "Venus"	Budha, or "Mercury"	Śani, or "Saturn"	Ketu, or "the southern descending node of the moon"
Postures or asanas	Triangle posture (*trikoṇāsana*) and forward fold posture (*pāda-hastā-sana*)	Crow posture (*kakāsana*), the peacock posture (*mayūrāsana*), and the pin-cers posture (*paścimottānāsana*)	Bow posture (*dhanur-āsana*), spinal stretch (*ardha-mat-syendrāsana*), and the locust posture (*śalabhāsana*)	Spinal twist (*ardha-mat-syendrāsana*), the cobra posture (*bhujaṅgāsa-na*), and the fish posture (*matsyāsana*)	Shoulder stand (*sarvāṅgāsa-na*), fish posture (*matsyāsana*), plough posture (*halāsana*), and spi-nal twist (*ardha-matsy-endrāsana*)	Cobra posture (*bhujaṅgāsana*) and seated forward fold (*paścimottān-āsana*)	Headstand (*śīrṣāsana*)

Glossary of Sanskrit Terms

A

Abhinava Gupta: An important spiritual master. He lived in India between A.D. 950 and 1016. He was the exponent of the *pratyabhijñā*, a philosophical system of Kashmir monistic Shaivism. He wrote numerous works about Shaivism, tantra, bhakti, drama, poetics, dance, and aesthetics.

***Ahaṇkāra* (or *ahaṁ-kāra*):** Ego. "I am the doer."

***Ājñā-cakra*:** Third eye energy center.

***Anāhata-cakra*:** Heart energy center.

***Apāna*:** One of the five types of vital energy that flows in the body.

***Asana*:** Seat, a place to sit, a posture in hatha yoga. Also, the third stage of *aṣṭāṅga-yoga*.

***Ashram*:** Hermitage or spiritual community.

***Atharva Veda*:** One of the four sacred Vedas.

***Airāvata*:** Unspotted white elephant. He is the Lord of elephants and has eight tusks and five trunks.

B

Bhagavad Gita: Literally, 'the song of God.' The most essential and widely accepted text by all philosophies and paths of *Sanātana-dharma*. Lord Krishna explains the essence of sadhana and spiritual knowledge in the form of a conversation to his disciple Arjuna in the battlefield of Kurukṣetra.

***Bhagavān*:** The personal aspect of the Divine.

***Bhastrikā-prāṇāyāma*:** An important technique of *prāṇāyāma*. It includes rapid and forceful inhalation and exhalation powered by the movement of the diaphragm.

***Bījākṣara*:** Letter that represents a *bīja-mantra*.

***Bīja-mantra*:** Seed or one-syllable mantra. The most concentrated and powerful form of sound vibration. The *bīja-mantra* spectrum comprises all the Sanskrit letters, ending with *anusvāra*, the pure nasal sound.

***Bindu*:** Literally, "dot or spot." A condensed drop of light that contains both the static and dynamic aspects of the Absolute. When the pure and infinite consciousness desires to emanate forth, it condenses itself into *bindu*. It is represented in the *anusvāra* dot from Sanskrit, which denotes a pure nasal sound.

Brahmā: The creator god. One of the three gods of the Vedic trimurti (triad): Brahmā, Vishnu, and Shiva.

***Brahmacarya*:** Brahma is the Absolute or Supreme Self, *carya* means "behavior or conduct." Hence, *brahmacarya* means "behavior of God." In general, it is associated with celibacy.

***Brahma-muhūrta*:** The hour of Brahmā, which begins 96 minutes before the sunrise. It is a lapse of time highly auspicious for practicing yoga and meditating.

Brahman: Supreme and absolute consciousness.

***Brāhmaṇa*:** A member of the highest class (*varṇa*) of traditional Vedic society. The members of this class are engaged in learning, teaching, and practicing yoga.

***Brahma-randhra*:** The cave of Brahman. It is a hole in the crown of the head through which the soul leaves at the time of death.

***Brahmachari* or *brahmacārin*:** A person in the state of *brahmacarya* or celibate student.

***Buddhi*:** Intellect.

C

***Chāndogya Upaniṣad*:** One of the oldest, largest, and most important Upanishads. It is part of the *Chāndogya-brahmaṇa* section of the *Sāma Veda.*

D

***Deva*:** Deity, god, divine being.

***Devi*:** Divine Mother, goddess.

***Devī Sūktam*:** A famous poem glorifying the Divine Mother. It appears in the *Mārkaṇḍeya Purana*. It is also called *Devī-māhātmyam*, *Durgā-sapta-śatī*, and *Caṇḍī-pāṭha.*

***Durgā-sapta-śatī*:** See *Devī Sūktam.*

***Devī-gītā*:** "The song of the goddess." A poem in the *Devī-bhāgavatam*, presented as a conversation between the Himalaya mountains (Himavan) and the Devi. It contains philosophical and practical guidance for the worship of Devi.

***Devī-bhāgavatam* or *Devī-bhāgavata Purāṇa*:** One of the central scriptures of Shaktism. It reveres the feminine aspect of the Divine as the origin of existence, the creator, the preserver, and the destroyer, as well as the one who bestows spiritual liberation.

Dharma: Literally, "that which is established." Law, religion, duty, or morals.

***Doṣas*:** Biological elements. Humors of the body. According to the Ayurveda, there are three *doṣas*: *vāta* (airy element), *pitta* (fiery element), and *kapha* (watery element). When their balance is disturbed, there are diseases.

G

***Garuḍa*:** Divine eagle, the vehicle of Lord Vishnu.

***Gheraṇḍa Saṁhitā*:** Literally, "the collection of Gheraṇḍa." It is the yoga manual that Gheraṇḍa used to instruct Caṇḍa Kāpālī. One of the three classic texts of hatha yoga.

***Granthis*:** Literally, "knots." Energetic valves that block the elevation of *kuṇḍalīṇī-śakti* in order to protect us.

Guru: Master and spiritual guide in Hinduism.

H

Hatha yoga: Literally, "forced yoga." An ancient yoga system disseminated throughout the world. It consists of physical postures (asanas), relaxation, and *prāṇāyāma*, which aim to prepare the body for meditation.

***Haṭha-yoga-pradīpikā*:** A classic Sanskrit text about hatha yoga and kundalini. It was compiled by Swami Svātmārāma in the fifteenth century AD.

***Hari*:** One of the names of Lord Vishnu.

I

***Iḍā*:** The left *nāḍī*.

***Indra*:** King of the gods, the lord of heaven, rain, and war.

J

***Jambū-dvīpa*:** The earthly island or continent. According to Vedic cosmology, it is the realm where ordinary human beings live.

Jiva: Soul, life.

***Jñānendriyas*:** The five cognitive organs: mouth, hands, feet, anus, and genitals.

K

***Kailāsa*:** A mountain in the Himalaya range, the abode of Lord Shiva where he lives united with Pārvatī.

***Kanda*:** A center in the astral body from which *nāḍīs* come out. Located between the anus and the base of the genitals, under *mūlādhāra-cakra*.

***Kapha*:** Waterly biological element (*doṣa*).

***Karmendriyas*:** The five organs of action. They perform the following actions: speech (mouth), handling (hands), locomotion (legs), excretion (anus), and reproduction (genitals).

Kashmir Shaivism: Nondualist Tantra Shaivism tradition that originated in Kashmir. Its philosophy is the *pratyabhijñā* (recognition) system expounded mainly by Abhinavagupta.

Kali: Goddess, a form of Durga Devi, the Divine Mother. She has dark complexion, red eyes, and long black hair. Often, she appears with a garland of skulls around her neck. She is worshipped by Shaktas as the ultimate reality or Brahman, as the divine protector, which bestows liberation.

***Kośas*:** Sheaths or casings that cover the soul.

***Kṣemarāja*:** See *Pratyabhijñā-hṛdayam.*

***Kṣetram* or *kṣetra*:** Area, field, or region. In kundalini, it is the reflection of the chakras on the front surface of the body.

Krishna: Incarnation of Lord Vishnu, also regarded as the personification of the Absolute.

***Kumbhaka*:** Retention of breath. It is one of the main components of *prāṇāyāma* practice.

M

***Maya*:** The power of illusion.

***Manas*:** Mind.

***Maheśvara*:** Literally, "the great Lord." One of the names of Shiva.

***Maheśvarī*:** Literally, "the great goddess." One of the names of Shakti.

***Maṇḍala*:** Literally, "circle." Spiritual and ritual diagram. Also, a division or book in the Rig Veda.

***Maṇipūra-cakra*:** Solar plexus energy center.

***Meḍhra*:** Area of the genitals. Another name for *svādhiṣṭhāna-cakra*.

***Mudrā*:** Literally, "seal." Postures to block or seal vital energy in order to channel it toward the opening of *suṣumṇā-nāḍī* and awake *kundalini*.

***Mūlādhāra-cakra*:** Root energy center.

***Mantra*:** Mystical sacred syllable.

N

***Nāda*:** Sound, often used to denote the divine sound or pulsation.

***Nāḍīs*:** Channels through which the vital energy (prana) flows in the subtle body.

O

Om: The original sound.

P

***Padmāsana*:** Literally, "the lotus pose." Recommended sitting posture for meditation.

***Parama-śiva*:** The formless (*nirguṇa*) aspect of Shiva. The transcendental reality, supreme consciousness, the absolute, timeless, infinite, indivisible Truth, which is beyond the senses and mind.

***Piṅgalā*:** Right *nāḍī*.

***Pitta*:** Fiery biological element (*doṣa*).

***Prakriti*:** Nature. The source of the three modes of nature: sattva, *rajas*, and tamas. It is the manifestation of Shakti, the divine feminine energy. It refers to superficial reality.

Prana: Life energy, vital air.

Pratyabhijñā-hṛdayam: Literally, "the secret of self-recognition." Digest of the *pratyābhijñā* system of Kashmir Shaivism. Written by the sage Kṣemarāja, the illustrious disciple of Abhinava Gupta who was the main exponent of this philosophy.

Puranas: Scriptures that reveal the Vedic values in a simple way, mainly through traditional stories about saints, kings, and great devotees.

Purusha: The supreme soul or being. The individual

manifestation of Shiva (or divinity). It refers to the subjective internal world.

R

***Rajas*:** Mode of passion, one of the three gunas (modes of nature).

***Rig Veda*:** One of the four Vedas.

Rishi: Seer, a self-realized sage.

S

***Sāma Veda*:** One of the four Vedas.

***Sādhaka*:** Spiritual aspirant.

Sadhana: Spiritual practice.

***Sadhu*:** A virtuous and holy person.

***Sahasrāra-cakra*:** Crown energy center.

Shakti: Power. The feminine, external, active, immanent, and creative aspect of Shiva, or the Absolute.

Samadhi: Complete union with the divine. The last of the eight stages of *aṣṭāṅga-yoga*.

***Sanātana-dharma*:** Literally, "eternal religion." Hinduism.

***Sāṅkhya*:** One of the six orthodox schools (*darśanas*) in *Sanātana-dharma*. It promotes metaphysical dualism and its classical formulation.

Śaṅkarācārya: The main exponent of the Advaita Vedanta school of philosophy.

***Sannyasi*:** Monk.

***Sattva*:** One of the three modes of nature (*guṇas*). Mode of goodness and clarity.

***Saundarya-laharī*:** Literally, "waves of beauty." Poem attributed to Śaṅkarācārya. Comprises 103 shlokas that glorify the beauty, grace, and kindness of Goddess Pārvatī, the consort of Shiva. It also mentions worship to the goddess, the principals of kundalini, and the union of Shiva and Shakti.

***Siddhāsana*:** Literally, "the accomplished pose." Sitting posture recommended for meditation. It is one of the most recommended asanas by the scriptures.

Shiva: Divinity. Supreme consciousness. God of destruction.

***Śiva-liṅgam*:** Abstract deity of Lord Shiva (the absolute) and his energy. Its shape comprises the male genital organ within the female genital organ.

***Śiva Saṁhitā*:** The most comprehensive classical scripture of hatha yoga, written by an unknown author. In the text, Lord Shiva addresses his consort Pārvatī.

***Suśruta Saṁhitā*:** One of the fundamental texts of Ayurveda, the ancient Vedic system of medicine and surgery.

Shloka: Verse in the Sanskrit scriptures.

Shruti: Literally, "what was heard." The literature that was revealed directly by God. It includes the four Vedas and the *Upanishads*.

***Sukhāsana*:** Literally, "the comfortable pose." Sitting posture recommended for meditation.

***Suṣumṇā*:** The central *nāḍī*, which connects *mūlādhāra-cakra* with *sahasrāra-cakra*. When kundalini energy is awakened, it flows through this *nāḍī*.

Sutra: An aphorism that expresses essential knowledge in a minimum of words or letters.

***Svādhiṣṭhāna-cakra*:** Sacral energy center.

***Svastika*:** A sacred and auspicious symbol. A shape of a cross with its lower lines bent ninety degrees to one side.

T

Tamas: One of the three modes of nature (gunas). The mode of darkness or ignorance.

Tantras: Scriptures that teach mystical formulas, usually in the form of dialogues between Shiva and Durga.

***Tantrāloka*:** Literally, "light on Tantra." It is a comprehensive text containing the synthesis of the monistic *āgamas* and all the schools of Kashmir Shaivism. This work contains both the rituals and philosophy of the path.

Tattva: Principle, element, or category of existence.

***Trimurti*:** Vedic triad of gods Brahmā, Vishnu, and Shiva, who are the creator, the preserver, and the destroyer, respectively.

U

Upanishads: Testimonies personally written by sages of antiquity. They include the final part of the Vedas called *Vedanta*. They present the final conclusion of the Vedas.

***Vāta*:** Airy biological element (*doṣa*).

***Vāyu*:** Wind. It is also the name of the wind god.

Vedas: The revealed scriptures received from God (shruti).

Vedanta: Literally, "the end of the Vedas." The final conclusion, the essence of the Vedas. Also one of the schools of philosophy within *Sanātana-dharma*.

Vishnu: One of the forms of God. The aspect of God that is responsible for maintenance. Regarded by vaishnavas as the Supreme God.

***Viśuddha-cakra*:** Energy center of the throat.

***Viveka-cūḍāmaṇi*:** Literally, "the jewel of wisdom." A famous book by Śrī Śaṅkarācārya introducing the Advaita Vedanta philosophy.

Varuṇa: Lord of the cosmic oceans.

Y

Yantra: Literally, "instrument." A mystical geometric diagram, used as a meditation aid in Tantric worship.

***Yoga-cūḍāmaṇi Upaniṣad*:** Literally, "the crown jewel of yoga." Minor Upanishad attached to the *Sāma Veda*. It is one of the twenty Upanishads about yoga, notable for its discussions of kundalini yoga.

Yoni: Perineum. Mostly refers to the female genitals. Depicted with the male organ of generation, *liṅga*, as the *Śiva-liṅga*, the abstract deity of Lord Shiva (the Absolute) and his energy.

***Yajur Veda*:** One of the four Vedas.

Sanskrit pronunciation guide

Sanskrit
PRONUNCIATION GUIDE

The Sanskrit Alphabet

Vowels

अ *a* आ *ā* इ *i* ई *ī* उ *u* ऊ *ū*
ऋ *ṛ* ॠ *ṝ* ऌ *ḷ* ए *e* ऐ *ai* ओ *o* औ *au* अं *aṁ* अः *aḥ*

Consonants

Gutturals	क *ka*	ख *kha*	ग *ga*	घ *gha*	ङ ṅa
Palatals	च *ca*	छ *cha*	ज *ja*	झ *jha*	ञ ña
Cerebrals	ट *ṭa*	ठ *ṭha*	ड *ḍa*	ढ *ḍha*	ण ṇa
Dentals	त *ta*	थ *tha*	द *da*	ध *dha*	न na
Labials	प *pa*	फ *pha*	ब *ba*	भ *bha*	म ma
Semivowels	य *ya*	र *ra*	ल *la*	व *va*	
Sibilants	श *śa*	ष *ṣa*	स *sa*		
Aspirates	ह *ha*				

Pronunciation

Vowels

Sanskrit letter	Transliteration	Sounds like
अ	*a*	but
आ	*ā*	father
इ	*i*	fit, if, lily
ई	*ī*	fee, police
उ	*u*	put
ऊ	*ū*	boot, rule, rude
ऋ	*ṛ*	(between ri and ru, as in the name Krishna)
ॠ	*ṝ*	(between ri and ru) crucial
ऌ	*ḷ*	(similar to lr)
ए	*e*	made
ऐ	*ai*	bite, aisle
ओ	*o*	oh
औ	*au*	found, house

Consonants

Gutturals

(back of the throat)

Sanskrit letter	Transliteration	Sounds like
क	*ka*	kill, seek, kite
ख	*kha*	Eckhart
ग	*ga*	get, dog, give
घ	*gha*	log-hut
ङ	*ṅa*	sing, king, sink

Palatals

(tip of the tongue touches the roof of the mouth)

Sanskrit letter	Transliteration	Sounds like
च	*ca*	chicken
छ	*cha*	catch him
ज	*ja*	joy, jump
झ	*jha*	hedgehog
ञ	*ña*	canyon

Cerebrals

(tip of the tongue against the front part of the roof of the mouth)

Sanskrit letter	Transliteration	Sounds like
ट	*ṭa*	true, tub
ठ	*ṭha*	anthill
ड	*ḍa*	dove, drum, doctor
ढ	*ḍha*	red-hot
ण	*ṇa*	under

Dentals

(tip of the tongue against the teeth)

Sanskrit letter	Transliteration	Sounds like
त	*ta*	(between t and th) water
थ	*tha*	lighthearted
द	*da*	(between d and th) dice, then
ध	*dha*	adhere
न	*na*	not, nut

Labials

(lips together, the tongue is not used)

Sanskrit letter	Transliteration	Sounds like
प	*pa*	pine, put, sip
फ	*pha*	uphill
ब	*ba*	bird, bear, rub
भ	*bha*	abhor
म	*ma*	mother, map

Semivowels

Sanskrit letter	Transliteration	Sounds like
य	*ya*	yet, loyal, yes
र	*ra*	red, year
ल	*la*	lull, lead
व	*va*	(between v and w) ivy, vine

Sibilants

Sanskrit letter	Transliteration	Sounds like
श	*śa*	sure
ष	*ṣa*	shrink, bush, show
स	*sa*	saint, sin, hiss

Aspirate

Sanskrit letter	Transliteration	Sounds like
ह	*ha*	hear, hit, home

Additional Sounds

Anusvāra

A nasal sound, written as a dot above and to the right of a Sanskrit letter.

Sanskrit letter	Transliteration	Sounds like
ं	*ṁ*	hum, tempt, pump

Visarga

A final aspirate sound, written as two dots after a Sanskrit letter.

Sanskrit letter	Transliteration	Sounds like
ः	*ḥ*	ha or hi
तः	*taḥ*	'ta-ha'
तीः	*tīḥ*	'tee-hi'

Prabhuji

H.H. Avadhūta Śrī Bhaktivedānta Yogācārya Ramakrishnananda Bābājī Mahārāja

Biography

Prabhuji is a writer, painter, Krishnaite devotee (*Kṛṣṇa-bhakta*), *avadhūta* mystic, the creator of Retroprogressive Yoga, and a realized spiritual master. In 2011, he chose to retire from society and lead the life of a hermit. Since then, his days have been spent in solitude, praying, writing, painting, and meditating in silence and contemplation.

Prabhuji is the sole disciple of H.D.G. Avadhūta Śrī Brahmānanda Bābājī Mahārāja, who in turn is one of the closest and most intimate disciples of H.D.G. Avadhūta Śrī Mastarāma Bābājī Mahārāja.

Prabhuji was appointed as the successor of the lineage by his master, who conferred upon him the responsibility of continuing the line of disciplic succession of *avadhūtas*, or the sacred *paramparā*, officially appointing him as guru and ordering him to serve as Ācārya successor under the name H.H. Avadhūta Śrī Bhaktivedānta Yogācārya Ramakrishnananda Bābājī Mahārāja.

Prabhuji's Hinduism is so broad, universal, and pluralistic that at times, while living up to his title of *avadhūta*, his lively and fresh teachings transcend the boundaries of all philosophies and religions, even his own. His teachings promote critical thinking and lead us to question statements that are usually accepted as true. They do not defend absolute truths but invite us to evaluate and question our own convictions. The essence of his syncretic vision, Retroprogressive Yoga, is self-awareness and the recognition of consciousness. For him, awakening at the level of consciousness, or the transcendence of the egoic phenomenon, is the next step in humanity's evolution.

Prabhuji was born on March 21, 1958, in Santiago, the capital of the Republic of Chile. When he was eight years old, he had a mystical experience that motivated his search for the Truth, or the Ultimate Reality. This transformed his life into an authentic inner and outer pilgrimage. He has completely devoted his life to deepening the early transformative experience that marked the beginning of his process of retroevolution. He has dedicated more than fifty years to the exploration and practice of different religions, philosophies, paths of liberation, and spiritual disciplines. He has absorbed the teachings of great yogis, pastors, rabbis, monks, gurus, philosophers, sages, and saints whom he personally visited during years of searching. He has lived in many places and traveled the world thirsting for Truth.

Prabhuji is a recognized authority on Eastern wisdom. He is known for his erudition in the *Vaidika* and *Tāntrika* aspects of Hinduism and all branches of yoga (*jñāna*, *karma*, *bhakti*, *haṭha*, *rāja*, *kuṇḍalinī*, tantra, mantra, and others). He has an inclusive attitude toward all religions and is intimately familiar with Judaism, Christianity, Buddhism, Sufism, Taoism, Sikhism, Jainism, Shintoism,

Bahaism, and the Mapuche religion, among others. He learned about the Druze religion directly from Salach Abbas and Kamil Shchadi.

His curiosity for Western thought led him to venture into the field of philosophy. He had the privilege of studying intensively for several years with his uncle Jorge Balazs, philosopher, researcher, writer, and author of The Golden Deer. He also studied philosophy very intensively with Dr. Jonathan Ramos, who is a renowned philosopher, historian, and professor at the Catholic University of Salta. Prabhuji also studied philosophy with Dr. Alejandro Cavallazzi Sánchez, who holds an undergraduate degree in philosophy from the Universidad Panamericana, a master's degree in philosophy from the Universidad Iberoamericana, and a doctorate in philosophy from the Universidad Nacional Autónoma de México (UNAM).

Prabhuji holds a doctorate in Vaishnava philosophy from the respected Jiva Institute in Vrindavan, India, and a doctorate in yogic philosophy from the Yoga Samskrutum University.

His profound studies, his masters' blessings, his research into the sacred scriptures, and his vast teaching experience have earned him international recognition in the field of religion and spirituality.

His spiritual search led him to study with masters of diverse traditions and travel far from his native Chile to places as distant as Israel, India, and the USA. Prabhuji studied Hebrew and Sanskrit to deepen his understanding of the holy scriptures. He also studied Pali at the Oxford Centre for Buddhist Studies. Furthermore, he learned ancient Latin and Greek from Javier Álvarez, who holds a degree in Classical Philology from Sevilla University.

His father, Yosef Har-Zion ZT"L, grew up under strict discipline because he was the son of a senior police sergeant. As a reaction to this upbringing, Yosef decided to raise his own children with complete freedom and unconditional love. Prabhuji grew up without any pressure. During his early years, his father showed his son the same love regardless of his successes or failures at school. When Prabhuji decided to drop out of school in the seventh grade to devote himself to his inner quest, his family accepted his decision with deep respect. From the time his son was ten years old, Yosef talked to him about Hebrew spirituality and Western philosophy. They engaged in conversations about philosophy and religion for days on end and late into the night. Yosef supported him in whatever he wanted to do in his life and his search for Truth. Prabhuji was the authentic project of freedom and unconditional love of his father.

At an early age and on his own initiative, Prabhuji began to practice karate and study philosophy and religion. During his adolescence, no one interfered with his decisions. At the age of 15, he established a deep, intimate, and long friendship with the famous Uruguayan writer and poet Blanca Luz Brum, who was his neighbor on Merced Street in Santiago de Chile. He traveled throughout Chile in search of wise and interesting people to learn from. In southern Chile, he met machis who taught him about the rich Mapuche spirituality and shamanism.

In Chile in 1976, Prabhuji met H.D.G Bhaktikavi Atulānanda Ācārya Swami, disciple of A.C. Bhaktivedanta Swami Prabhupāda, with whom he began the initial stage of his retroprogressive process. In those days, Atulānanda Swami was a young *brahmacārī* who held the position of president of the ISKCON temple at Eyzaguirre 2404, Puente Alto, Santiago, Chile. Years later, he gave Prabhuji first initiation and Brahminical initiation. Eventually, he initiated Prabhuji into the sacred order of renunciation called *sannyāsa* within the Brahma Gauḍīya Saṁpradāya line of disciplic succession. H.D.G Bhaktikavi Atulānanda Ācārya connected him to the devotion to Kṛṣṇa. He imparted to him the wisdom of bhakti yoga and instructed him in the practice of *māhā-mantra* and the study of the holy scriptures.

Prabhuji wanted to confirm his *sannyāsa* initiation in an Advaita Vedanta lineage. His *sannyāsa-dīkṣā* was confirmed by H.H. Swami Jyotirmayānanda Sarasvatī, founder of the Yoga Research Foundation and disciple of H.H. Swami Śivānanda Sarasvatī of Rishikesh.

In 1984, he learned and began to practice Maharishi Mahesh Yogi's Transcendental Meditation technique. In 1988, he took the *kriyā-yoga* course on Paramahaṁsa Yogananda. After two years, he was officially initiated into the technique of *kriyā-yoga* by the Self-Realization Fellowship.

In 1996, Prabhuji met his guru, H.D.G. Avadhūta Śrī Brahmānanda Bābājī Mahārāja, in Rishikesh, India. Guru Mahārāja, as Prabhuji called him, revealed that his own master, H.D.G. Avadhūta Śrī Mastarāma Bābājī

Mahārāja, had told him years before he died that a person would come from the West and request to be his disciple. He commanded him to accept only that particular seeker. When he asked how he would identify this person, Mastarāma Bābājī replied, "You will recognize him by his eyes. You must accept him because he will be the continuation of the lineage."

From the first moment Guru Mahārāja saw Prabhuji, he recognized him and officially initiated him into the *māhā-mantra* in Rishikesh, India. The initiation he received marked the end of a quest that began with his mystical experience at the age of eight. It also marked the beginning of the most intense and mature stage of Prabhuji's retroprogressive process. Under the guidance of Guru Mahārāja, he studied Advaita Vedanta and deepened his meditation.

The enlightened *bābājī* guided Prabhuji on his first steps toward the sacred level of *avadhūta*. In March 2011, H.D.G. Avadhūta Śrī Brahmānanda Bābājī Mahārāja ordered Prabhuji, on behalf of his own master, to accept the responsibility of continuing the line of disciplic succession of *avadhūtas*. With this title, Prabhuji is the official representative of the line of this disciplic succession for the present generation.

Besides his *dikṣā-guru*, Prabhuji studied with important spiritual and religious personalities, such as H.H. Swami Dayananda Sarasvatī, H.H. Swami Viṣṇu Devānanda Sarasvatī, H.H. Swami Jyotirmayānanda Sarasvatī, H.H. Swami Pratyagbodhānanda, H.H. Swami Swahananda of the Ramakrishna Mission, and H.H.

Swami Viditātmānanda of the Arsha Vidya Gurukulam. The wisdom of tantra was awakened in Prabhuji by H.G. Mātājī Rīnā Śarmā in India.

In Vrindavan, he did in-depth studies on the bhakti yoga path with H.H. Narahari Dāsa Bābājī Mahārāja, disciple of H.H. Nityananda Dāsa Bābājī Mahārāja of Vraja.

He also studied bhakti yoga with various disciples of His Divine Grace A.C. Bhaktivedānta Swami Prabhupāda: H.H. Kapīndra Swami, H.H. Paramadvaiti Mahārāja, H.H. Jagajīvana Dāsa, H.H. Tamāla Kṛṣṇa Gosvāmī, H.H. Bhagavān Dāsa Mahārāja, and H.H. Kīrtanānanda Swami, among others.

Prabhuji has been honored with various titles and diplomas by many leaders of prestigious religious and spiritual institutions in India. He was given the honorable title *Kṛṣṇa Bhakta* by H.H. Swami Viṣṇu Devānanda (the only title of Bhakti Yoga given by Swami Viṣṇu), disciple of H.H. Swami Śivānanda Sarasvatī and the founder of the Sivananda Organization. He was given the title *Bhaktivedānta* by H.H. B.A. Paramadvaiti Mahārāja, the founder of Vrinda. He was given the title *Yogācārya* by H.H. Swami Viṣṇu Devānanda, the Paramanand Institute of Yoga Sciences and Research of Indore, India, the International Yoga Federation, the Indian Association of Yoga, and the Shri Shankarananda Yogashram of Mysore, India. He received the respectable title *Śrī Śrī Rādhā Śyam Sunder Pāda-Padma Bhakta Śiromaṇi* directly from H.H. Satyanārāyaṇa Dāsa Bābājī Mahant of the Chatu Vaiṣṇava Saṁpradāya.

Prabhuji spent more than forty years studying hatha yoga with prestigious masters in classical and traditional yoga, such as H.H. Bapuji, H.H. Swami Viṣṇu Devānanda Sarasvatī, H.H. Swami Jyotirmayānanda Sarasvatī, H.H. Swami Satchidananda Sarasvatī, H.H. Swami Vignanananda Sarasvatī, and Śrī Madana-mohana.

He attended several systematic hatha yoga teacher training courses at prestigious institutions until he achieved the level of Master Ācārya. He has completed studies at the following institutions: the Sivananda Yoga Vedanta, the Ananda Ashram, the Yoga Research Foundation, the Integral Yoga Academy, the Patanjala Yoga Kendra, the Ma Yoga Shakti International Mission, the Prana Yoga Organization, the Rishikesh Yoga Peeth, the Swami Sivananda Yoga Research Center, and the Swami Sivananda Yogasana Research Center.

Prabhuji is a member of the Indian Association of Yoga, Yoga Alliance ERYT 500 and YACEP, the International Association of Yoga Therapists, and the International Yoga Federation. In 2014, the International Yoga Federation honored him with the position of Honorary Member of the World Yoga Council.

His interest in the complex anatomy of the human body led him to study chiropractic at the prestigious Institute of Health of the Back and Extremities in Tel Aviv, Israel. In 1993, he received a diploma from Dr. Sheinerman, the founder and director of the institute. Later, he earned a massage therapy diploma at the Academy of Western Galilee. The knowledge he acquired in this field deepened his understanding of hatha yoga and contributed to the creation of his own method.

Retroprogressive Hatha Yoga is the result of Prabhuji's efforts to improve his practice and teaching methods. It is a system based especially on the teachings of his gurus and the sacred scriptures. Prabhuji has systematized various traditional yoga techniques to create a methodology suitable for Western audiences. Retroprogressive Yoga aims to experience our true nature. It promotes balance, health, and flexibility through proper diet, cleansing techniques, preparations (*āyojanas*), sequences (*vinyāsas*), postures (*asanas*), breathing exercises (*prāṇayama*), relaxation (*śavāsana*), meditation (*dhyāna*), and exercises with locks (*bandhas*) and seals (*mudras*) to direct and empower *prāṇa*.

Since his childhood and throughout his life, Prabhuji has been an enthusiastic admirer, student, and practitioner of classic karate-do. From the age of 13, he studied different styles in Chile, such as kenpo and kung-fu, but specialized in the most traditional Japanese style of Shotokan. He received the rank of black belt (third dan) from Shihan Kenneth Funakoshi (ninth dan). He also learned from Sensei Takahashi (seventh dan) and practiced Shorin Ryu style with Sensei Enrique Daniel Welcher (seventh dan), who granted him the rank of black belt (second dan). Through karate-do, he delved into Buddhism and gained additional knowledge about the physics of motion. Prabhuji is a member of Funakoshi's Shotokan Karate Association.

Prabhuji grew up in an artistic environment and his love of painting began to develop in his childhood.

His father, the renowned Chilean painter Yosef Har-Zion ZT"L, motivated him to devote himself to art. He learned with the famous Chilean painter Marcelo Cuevas. Prabhuji's abstract paintings reflect the depths of the spirit.

Since he was a young boy, Prabhuji has been especially drawn to postal stamps, postcards, mailboxes, postal transportation systems, and all mail-related activities. He has taken every opportunity to visit post offices in different cities and countries. He has delved into the study of philately, the field of collecting, sorting, and studying postage stamps. This passion led him to become a professional philatelist, a stamp distributor authorized by the American Philatelic Society, and a member of the following societies: the Royal Philatelic Society London, the Royal Philatelic Society of Victoria, the United States Stamp Society, the Great Britain Philatelic Society, the American Philatelic Society, the Society of Israel Philatelists, the Society for Hungarian Philately, the National Philatelic Society UK, the Fort Orange Stamp Club, the American Stamp Dealers Association, the US Philatelic Classics Society, Filabras – Associação dos Filatelistas Brasileiros, and the Collectors Club of NYC.

Based on his extensive knowledge of philately, theology, and Eastern philosophy, Prabhuji created "Meditative Philately" or "Philatelic Yoga," a spiritual practice that uses philately as the basis for practicing attention, concentration, observation, and meditation. Meditative Philately is inspired by the ancient Hindu *maṇḍala* meditation and it can lead the practitioner to elevated states of consciousness, deep relaxation, and concentration that fosters the recognition of consciousness. Prabhuji wrote his thesis on this new type of yoga, "Meditative Philately," attracting the interest of the Indian academic community due to its innovative way of connecting meditation with different hobbies and activities. For this thesis, he was honored with a PhD in Yogic Philosophy from Yoga-Samskrutum University.

Prabhuji lived in Israel for many years, where he furthered his studies of Judaism. One of his main teachers and sources of inspiration was Rabbi Shalom Dov Lifshitz ZT"L, whom he met in 1997. This great saint guided him for several years on the intricate paths of the Torah and Chassidism. The two developed a very intimate relationship. Prabhuji studied the Talmud with Rabbi Raphael Rapaport Shlit"a (Ponovich), Chassidism with Rabbi Israel Lifshitz Shlit"a, and the Torah with Rabbi Daniel Sandler Shlit"a. Prabhuji is a great devotee of Rabbi Mordechai Eliyahu ZT"L, who personally blessed him.

Prabhuji visited the United States in 2000 and during his stay in New York, he realized that it was the most appropriate place to found a religious organization. He was particularly attracted by the pluralism and respectful attitude of American society toward freedom of religion. He was impressed by the deep respect of both the public and the government for religious minorities. After consulting his master and requesting his blessings, Prabhuji relocated to the United States in 2001. In 2003, the Prabhuji Mission was born, a Hindu church aimed at preserving Prabhuji's universal and pluralistic vision of Hinduism and his Retroprogressive Yoga.

Although he did not seek to attract followers, for 15 years (1995–2010), Prabhuji considered the requests of a few people who approached him asking to become his monastic disciples. Those who chose to see Prabhuji as their spiritual master voluntarily accepted vows of poverty and life-long dedication to spiritual practice (*sadhāna*), religious devotion (*bhakti*), and selfless service (*seva*). Although Prabhuji no longer accepts new disciples, he continues to guide the small group of monastic disciples of the Ramakrishnananda Monastic Order that he founded.

In 2011, Prabhuji founded the Avadhutashram (monastery) in the Catskills Mountains in upstate New York, USA. The Avadhutashram is the headquarters of the Prabhuji Mission, his hermitage, and the residence of the monastic disciples of the Ramakrishnananda Monastic Order. The ashram organizes humanitarian projects such as the Prabhuji Food Distribution Program and the Prabhuji Toy Distribution Program. Prabhuji operates various humanitarian projects, inspired in his experience that serving the part is serving the Whole.

In January 2012, Prabhuji's health forced him to officially renounce managing the mission. Since then, he has lived in solitude, completely away from the public, writing and absorbed in contemplation. He shares his experience and wisdom in books and filmed talks. His message does not promote collective spirituality, but individual inner search.

In 2022, Prabhuji founded the Institute of Retroprogressive Yoga. Here, his most senior disciples can systematically share Prabhuji's teachings and message through video conferences. The institute offers support and help for a deeper understanding of Prabhuji's teachings.

Prabhuji is a respected member of the American Philosophical Association, the American Association of Philosophy Teachers, the American Association of University Professors, the Southwestern Philosophical Society, the Authors Guild, the National Writers Union, PEN America, the International Writers Association, the National Association of Independent Writers and Editors, the National Writers Association, the Alliance Independent Authors, and the Independent Book Publishers Association.

Prabhuji's vast literary contribution includes books in Spanish, English, and Hebrew, for example, *Kundalini Yoga: The Power is in you*, *What is, as it is*, *Bhakti-Yoga: The Path of Love*, *Tantra: Liberation in the World*, *Experimenting with the Truth*, *Advaita Vedanta: Be the Self*, commentaries on the *Īśāvāsya Upanishad* and the *Diamond Sūtra*.

About the Prabhuji Mission

Prabhuji, H.H. Avadhūta Śrī Bhaktivedānta Yogācārya Ramakrishnananda Bābājī Mahārāja, founded the Prabhuji Mission in 2003, a Hindu church aimed at preserving Prabhuji's universal and pluralistic vision of Hinduism.

The main purpose of the mission is to preserve Prabhuji's teachings of Pūrvavyāpi-pragatiśīlaḥ Yoga, or Retroprogressive Yoga, which advocates for a global awakening of consciousness as the radical solution to humanity's problems.

The Prabhuji Mission operates a Hindu temple called Śrī Śrī Radha-Śyāmasundara Mandir, which offers worship and religious ceremonies to parishioners. An extensive library and virtual institute provides religious and spiritual education about many theologies and philosophies for those who want to study Prabhuji's message in depth. The Avadhutashram monastery educates monastic disciples on various aspects of Prabhuji's approach to Hinduism and offers them the opportunity to express devotion to God through devotional service by selflessly contributing their skills and training to the Mission's programs, such as the Prabhuji Food Distribution program, among others.

Service and glorification of the guru are fundamental spiritual principles in Hinduism. The Prabhuji Mission, as a traditional Hindu church, practices the millenary *guru-bhakti* tradition of reverence to the master. Some disciples and friends of the Prabhuji Mission, on their own initiative, help to preserve Prabhuji's legacy and his interfaith teachings for future generations by disseminating his books, videos of his internal talks, and websites.

About the Avadhutashram

The Avadhutashram (monastery) was founded by Prabhuji in the Catskills Mountains in upstate New York, USA. It is the headquarters of the Prabhuji Mission and the hermitage of H.H. Avadhūta Śrī Bhaktivedānta Yogācārya Ramakrishnananda Bābājī Mahārāja and his monastic disciples of the Ramakrishnananda Monastic Order.

The ideals of the Avadhutashram are love and selfless service, based on the universal vision that God is in everything and everyone. Its mission is to distribute spiritual books and organize humanitarian projects such as the Prabhuji Food Distribution Program and the Prabhuji Toy Distribution Program.

The Avadhutashram is not commercial and operates without soliciting donations. Its activities are funded by Prabhuji's Gifts, a non-profit company founded by Prabhuji, which sells esoteric items from different traditions that Prabhuji himself has used for spiritual practices during his evolutionary process. Its mission is to preserve and disseminate traditional religious, mystical, and ancestral crafts.

Avadhutashram
Round Top, NY, USA

The Retroprogressive Path

The Retroprogressive Path does not require you to be part of a group or a member of an organization, institution, society, congregation, club, or exclusive community. Living in a temple, monastery, or *āśram* is not mandatory, because it is not about a change of residence, but of consciousness. It does not urge you to believe, but to doubt. It does not demand you to accept something, but to explore, investigate, examine, inquire, and question everything. It does not suggest being what you should be but being what you really are.

The Retroprogressive Path supports freedom of expression but not proselytizing. This route does not promise answers to our questions but induces us to question our answers. It does not promise to be what we are not or to attain what we have not already achieved. It is a retro-evolutionary path of self-discovery that leads from what we think we are to what we really are. It is not the only way, nor the best, the simplest, or the most direct. It is an involutionary process par excellence that shows what is obvious and undeniable but usually goes unnoticed: that which is simple, innocent, and natural. It is a path that begins and ends in you.

The Retroprogressive Path is a continuous revelation that expands eternally. It delves into consciousness from an ontological perspective, transcending all religion and spiritual paths. It is the discovery of diversity as a unique and inclusive reality. It is the encounter of consciousness with itself, aware of itself and its own reality. In fact, this path is a simple invitation to dance in the now, to love the present moment, and to celebrate our authenticity. It is an unconditional proposal to stop living as a victim of circumstance and to live as a passionate adventurer. It is a call to return to the place we have never left, without offering us anything we do not already possess or teaching us anything we do not already know. It is a call for an inner revolution and to enter the fire of life that only consumes dreams, illusions, and fantasies but does not touch what we are. It does not help us reach our desired goal, but instead prepares us for the unexpected miracle.

This path was nurtured over a lifetime dedicated to the search for Truth. It is a grateful offering to existence for what I have received. But remember, do not look for me. Look for yourself. It is not me you need, because you are the only one who really matters. This life is just a wonderful parenthesis in eternity to know and love. What you long for lies in you, here and now, as what you really are.

Your unconditional well-wisher,
Prabhuji

Prabhuji today

Prabhuji is retired from public life

Prabhuji is the sole disciple of H.D.G. Avadhūta Śrī Brahmānanda Bābājī Mahārāja, who is himself one of the closest and most intimate disciples of H.D.G. Avadhūta Śrī Mastarāma Bābājī Mahārāja.

Prabhuji was appointed as the successor of the lineage by his master, who conferred upon him the responsibility of continuing the line of disciplic succession of *avadhūtas*, or the sacred *paramparā*, officially designating him as guru and commanding him to serve as the successor Ācārya under the name H.H. Avadhūta Śrī Bhaktivedānta Yogācārya Ramakrishnananda Bābājī Mahārāja.

In 2011, he chose to retire from society and lead the life of a hermit. Since then, his days have been spent in solitude, praying, writing, painting, and meditating in silence and contemplation. He no longer participates in *sat-saṅgs*, lectures, gatherings, meetings, retreats, seminars, study groups, or courses. We ask everyone to respect his privacy and do not try to contact him by any means for gatherings, meetings, interviews, blessings, *śaktipāta*, initiations, or personal visits.

Prabhuji's teachings

As a mystic, Hindu *avadhūta*, and realized Spiritual Master, Prabhuji has always appreciated and shared the essence and spiritual wisdom of a wide variety of religious practices from around the world. He does not consider himself a member or representative of any particular religion. Although many see him as an enlightened being, Prabhuji has no intention of presenting himself as a preacher, guide, coach, content creator, influencer, preceptor, mentor, counselor, consultant, monitor, tutor, teacher, instructor, educator, enlightener, pedagogue, evangelist, rabbi, *posek halacha*, healer, therapist, satsangist, psychic, leader, medium, savior, or guru. In fact, Prabhuji believes spirituality is an individual, solitary, personal, private, and intimate search. It is not a collective endeavor to be undertaken through social, organized, institutional, or community religiosity.

To that end, Prabhuji does not proselytize or preach, nor does he try to persuade, convince, or make anyone change their perspective, philosophy, or religion. Instead, he shares his personal view through books and lectures that are available online. Others may find his insights valuable and apply them wholly or in part to their own development, but Prabhuji's teachings are not meant to be seen as personal advice, counseling, guidance, self-help methods, or techniques for spiritual, physical, emotional, or psychological development. He only seeks to share what he has experienced on his own retroprogressive process. His experiences will not provide solutions to life's spiritual, material, financial, psychological, emotional, romantic, family, social, or physical problems. Prabhuji does not promise miracles, mystical experiences, astral journeys, healings, connections with spirits, supernatural powers, or spiritual salvation.

Although he did not seek to attract followers, for 15 years (1995–2010), Prabhuji considered the requests of a few people who approached him asking to become his monastic disciples.Those who chose to see Prabhuji as their spiritual master voluntarily accepted vows of poverty and life-long dedication to spiritual practice (*sādhanā*), religious devotion (*bhakti*), and selfless service (*seva*). Prabhuji no longer accepts new disciples, but he continues to guide the small group of veteran disciples of the Ramakrishnananda Monastic Order that he founded.

Public services

Even though the monastery does not accept new residents, volunteers, donations, collaborations, or sponsorships, the public is cordially invited to participate in daily religious services and attend devotional festivals at the Śrī Śrī Radha-Śyāmasundara Mandir temple.

Titles by Prabhuji

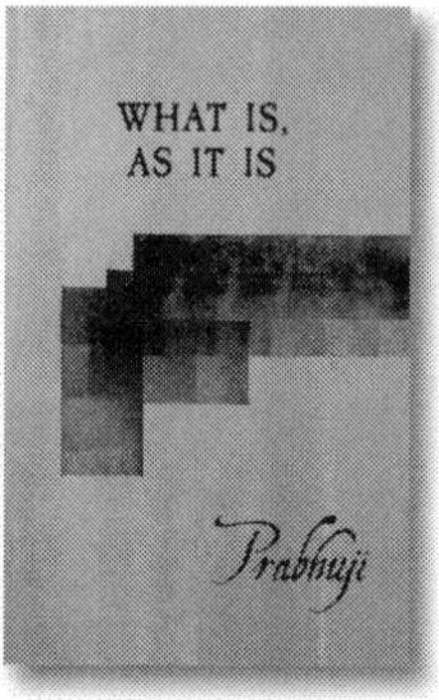

What is, as it is: Satsangs with Prabhuji (**English**)
ISBN-13:978-0-9815264-4-7
Lo que es, tal como es: Satsangs con Prabhuji (**Spanish**)
ISBN-13:978-0-9815264-5-4
Russian: ISBN-13: 978-1-945894-18-3

Kundalini yoga: The power is in you (**English**)
ISBN-13:978-1-945894-02-2
Kundalini yoga: El poder está en ti (**Spanish**)
ISBN-13:978-1-945894-01-5

Bhakti yoga: The path of love (**English**)
ISBN-13:978-1-945894-03-9
Bhakti-yoga: El sendero del amor (**Spanish**)
ISBN-13:978-1-945894-04-6

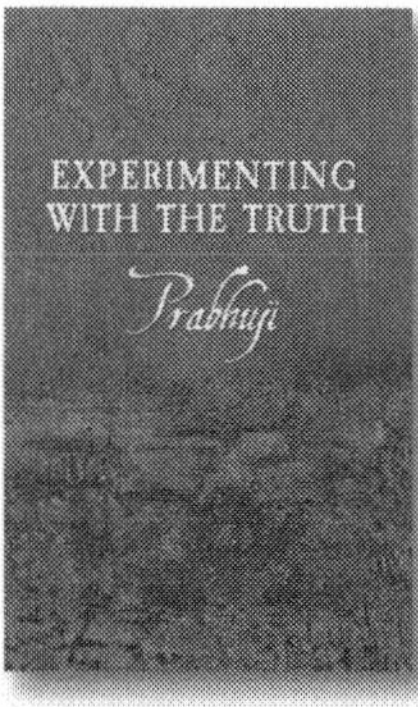

Experimenting with the Truth (English)
ISBN-13: 978-1-945894-08-4
Experimentando con la Verdad (Spanish)
ISBN-13: 978-1-945894-09-1

Tantra: Liberation in the world (English)
ISBN-13: 978-1-945894-21-3
Tantra: La liberación en el mundo (Spanish)
ISBN-13: 978-1-945894-23-7

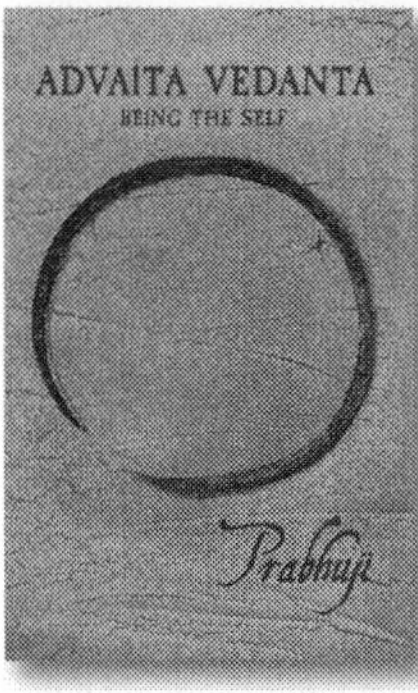

Advaita Vedanta: Being the Self (English)
ISBN-13: 978-1-945894-20-6
Advaita Vedanta: Ser el Ser (Spanish)
ISBN-13: 978-1-945894-16-9

Īśāvāsya Upanishad
commented by Prabhuji
(English)
ISBN-13: 978-1-945894-39-8
Īśāvāsya Upaniṣad
comentado por Prabhuji
(Spanish)
ISBN-13: 978-1-945894-41-1

The Diamond Sūtra
commented by Prabhuji
(English)
ISBN-13: 978-1-945894-46-6
El Sūtra del Diamante
comentado por de Prabhuji
(Spanish)
ISBN-13: 978-1-945894-49-7

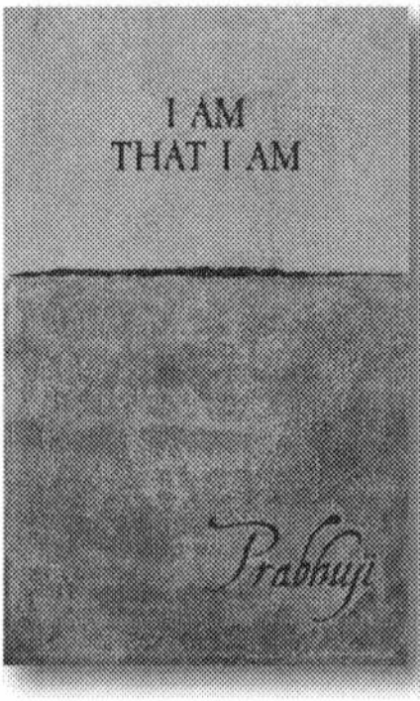

I am that I am
(English)
ISBN-13: 978-1-945894-46-6
Soy el que soy
(Spanish)
ISBN-13: 978-1-945894-49-7

Made in the USA
Middletown, DE
24 February 2023

25286395R00196